T0321993

AI–Enabled Agile Internet of Things for Sustainable FinTech Ecosystems

Sandeep Kautish
Lord Buddha Education Foundation, Nepal

Guneet Kaur
Independent Researcher, UK

A volume in the Advances
in Finance, Accounting, and
Economics (AFAE) Book Series

Published in the United States of America by
　　IGI Global
　　Engineering Science Reference (an imprint of IGI Global)
　　701 E. Chocolate Avenue
　　Hershey PA, USA 17033
　　Tel: 717-533-8845
　　Fax: 717-533-8661
　　E-mail: cust@igi-global.com
　　Web site: http://www.igi-global.com

Library of Congress Cataloging-in-Publication Data

Names: Kautish, Sandeep Kumar, 1981- editor. | Kaur, Guneet, 1994- editor.
Title: AI-enabled agile Internet of things for sustainable fintech
　　ecosystems / Sandeep Kautish, and Guneet Kaur, editors.
Description: Hershey PA : Engineering Science Reference, [2022] | Includes
　　bibliographical references and index. | Summary: "This book presents the
　　advances in AI-assisted agile IoT for fintech, helping readers to reveal
　　new applications, current issues, challenges and future directions in
　　the field of AI-assisted agile IoT for fintech applications and
　　ecosystems"-- Provided by publisher.
Identifiers: LCCN 2022012069 (print) | LCCN 2022012070 (ebook) | ISBN
　　9781668441763 (hardcover) | ISBN 9781668441770 (library binding) | ISBN
　　9781668441787 (ebook)
Subjects: LCSH: Finance--Data processing. | Financial services
　　industry--Technological innovations. | Artificial
　　intelligence--Financial applications. | Internet of Things. | Agile
　　software development.
Classification: LCC HG104 .A42 2022 (print) | LCC HG104 (ebook) | DDC
　　332.0285--dc23/eng/20220419
LC record available at https://lccn.loc.gov/2022012069
LC ebook record available at https://lccn.loc.gov/2022012070

This book is published in the IGI Global book series Advances in Finance, Accounting, and
Economics (AFAE) (ISSN: 2327-5677; eISSN: 2327-5685)

British Cataloguing in Publication Data
A Cataloguing in Publication record for this book is available from the British Library.

All work contributed to this book is new, previously-unpublished material.
The views expressed in this book are those of the authors, but not necessarily of the publisher.

For electronic access to this publication, please contact: eresources@igi-global.com.

Advances in Finance, Accounting, and Economics (AFAE) Book Series

ISSN:2327-5677
EISSN:2327-5685

Editor-in-Chief: Ahmed Driouchi, Al Akhawayn University, Morocco

MISSION

In our changing economic and business environment, it is important to consider the financial changes occurring internationally as well as within individual organizations and business environments. Understanding these changes as well as the factors that influence them is crucial in preparing for our financial future and ensuring economic sustainability and growth.

The **Advances in Finance, Accounting, and Economics (AFAE)** book series aims to publish comprehensive and informative titles in all areas of economics and economic theory, finance, and accounting to assist in advancing the available knowledge and providing for further research development in these dynamic fields.

COVERAGE

- Finance
- Theoretical Issues in Economics, Finance, and Accounting
- Interest Rates and Annuities
- Banking
- Economics of Innovation and Knowledge
- Risk Analysis and Management
- Economic Theory
- Microeconomics
- Auditing
- Accounting information systems

IGI Global is currently accepting manuscripts for publication within this series. To submit a proposal for a volume in this series, please contact our Acquisition Editors at Acquisitions@igi-global.com or visit: http://www.igi-global.com/publish/.

Titles in this Series

For a list of additional titles in this series, please visit:
http://www.igi-global.com/book-series/advances-finance-accounting-economics/73685

For an entire list of titles in this series, please visit:
http://www.igi-global.com/book-series/advances-finance-accounting-economics/73685

701 East Chocolate Avenue, Hershey, PA 17033, USA
Tel: 717-533-8845 x100 • Fax: 717-533-8661
E-Mail: cust@igi-global.com • www.igi-global.com

Table of Contents

Chapter 10

Detailed Table of Contents

Chapter 1
 Babita Jha, Christ University (Deemed), India
 Pratibha Giri, Christ University (Deemed), India
 Deepak Jha, Lingaya's Vidyapeeth, Faridabad, India
 Usha Badhera, Jaipuria Institute of Management, Jaipur, India

Meeting ESG (environmental, social, and governance) standards is becoming an essential goal for businesses, one that is supported by both investors and customers. FinTech can help companies evaluate and reduce their environmental effect, as well as investors channel their operations toward more sustainable assets. Embracing sustainability has become one of the priorities for many fintech companies today. Green fintech innovations have provided technologically enabled solutions for financial services that help in increasing the flow of financial resources for sustainable development. Recognizing the importance of green fintech in today's scenario, this chapter will initially focus on the components of the fintech ecosystem and IoT and AI-enabled fintech innovations in India, drivers of green fintech potentials of green fintech IoT, and AI-enabled green fintech from global perspective and has highlighted the green fintech solutions provided by the topmost companies.

Chapter 2
 Guneet Kaur, Cointelegraph, UK

The internet of things (IoT) is a global network that connects devices and people, yet it still confronts various challenges. This chapter explores the challenges banks face and how blockchain technology (integrated with IoT devices) can help address them. The chapter has also conducted a review of the different consensus mechanisms employed by the blockchain systems to find out which consensus method should be deployed by IoT-based banks. The underlying consensus method was first created for permissionless blockchain on a trustless network model using proof-of-work, which is a mathematical challenge that demands a lot of computing power. The findings of the study revealed that considering the regulatory requirements such as permissioned blockchains are best suitable for banks due to know your client (KYC) and anti-money laundering (AML) regulatory requirements. Additionally, for such a blockchain network, the practical byzantine fault tolerance (PBFT) and proof of authority (PoA) consensus methods ensure business resiliency.

Chapter 3

    Pawan Whig, Vivekananda Insitute of Professional Studies, India
    Arun Velu, Equifax, USA
    Rahul Reddy Nadikattu, University of the Cumberlands, USA

IoT provided a unified operating picture across a wide range of modern-day applications. The operating image is accomplished thanks to improvements in wireless sensor network devices that can interact over a network, exchanging data and executing various analyses. The only way to share information and authenticate data in the internet of things is through a central server, which raises security and privacy problems. Device spoofing, incorrect authentication, and a lack of data exchange dependability are all possibilities. A central server idea is abolished, and blockchain technology is used as part of IoT to solve such security and privacy problems. This chapter examines the potential security and privacy concerns associated with component interaction in the internet of things, as well as how the distributed ledger-based blockchain technology might help. Here, in this chapter, the authors discuss the application of BC to certain areas and categories. Various IoT and IoT with BC problems were also highlighted in order to better comprehend blockchain technology's role.

Chapter 4

    Farjana Nur Saima, Bangladesh University of Professionals,
        Bangladesh
    Md H Asibur Rahman, Bangladesh University of Professionals,
        Bangladesh
    Ratan Ghosh, Bangaladesh University of Professionals, Bangladesh

This study explores gender diversity in fintech usage for creating an equitable and sustainable fintech industry in Bangladesh. A closed-ended structured questionnaire was developed and distributed to fintech users by email and social media platforms. A total of 527 complete responses were documented. SPSS and SmartPLS have been used for analyzing data. Moreover, structural equation modeling (SEM) has been employed to test the study's hypotheses. Results reveal that perceived ease of use, perceived credibility, and perceived usefulness have a significant positive relationship with satisfaction. Furthermore, satisfaction has a positive and significant relationship with loyalty. While investigating the role of gender diversity on fintech, there is no moderating effect of gender on the effects of perceived ease of use, perceived credibility, and satisfaction on loyalty. However, the relationship between perceived usefulness and satisfaction is moderated by gender. Satisfaction is a significant predictor of ensuring fintech loyalty of both males and females.

S. B. Goyal, City University, Malaysia
Pradeep Bedi, Galgotias University, India
Anand Singh Rajawat, Shri Vaishnav Vidyapeeth Vishwavidyalaya,
India
Divya Prakash Shrivastava, Higher Colleges of Technology, Dubai,
UAE

A wireless sensor network (WSN) is capable of monitoring, fetching, and transmitting data from one place to another in any condition. The internet of things (IoT) network, a type of WSN, and its protection have always been a big problem. There are lots of risks related to security in this network. Authentication of node identity is an essential security concern. Conventional security algorithms for IoT rely on trustworthy third parties. They might fail at a single stage point. Therefore, in this chapter, the model is proposed as the solution to the security concerns by blockchain concepts. So, in this chapter, a trust model is introduced based on blockchain for WSN for communicating with several nodes without having any risks related to security.

Poshan Yu, Soochow University, China & Australian Studies Centre,
Shanghai University, China
Duo Chen, Independent Researcher, China
Aashrika Ahuja, Independent Researcher, India

Digital economy using internet, cloud computing, big data, as well as fintech in order to drive economic activities using digital information as a key factor for production has permeated all aspects of society as a result of unexpected onset of the COVID-19 pandemic. Recently, a white paper titled "The Development and Employment of China's Digital Economy in 2021" was released by The China

Academy of Information and Communications Technology (CAICT), analyzing the development pattern of China's digital economy since the onset of COVID-19. This chapter summarizes the development of digital economy, the employment situation in various regions and industries in China, thereby making an in-depth analysis of the digital transformation of traditional industries along with putting forward policy suggestions for promoting further development of China's digital economy. Since the onset of COVID-19, China's digital and smart economy has ushered in creating new opportunities for growth and development as well as simultaneously combatting challenges in the macro environment.

Chapter 7

Pranav Saraswat, Nirma University, Ahmedabad, India
Vineet Chouhan, Rajasthan Vidyut Utpadan Nigam Ltd., India

In India, 40 companies are currently providing the electronic wallet service for approximately 500 million mobile internet users, and this number is constantly growing. For the payment wallets, the key strategy for the success and survival of any business depends on the service quality it provides to its customers. Thus, with such a huge number of consumers using these services, it is essential to study how effective and consumer friendly these new age payment instruments are. The payment wallets being a new concept in the financial market may not be easily accepted by the consumers. Consumers above the age of 40 may not feel comfortable in using the electronic modes of payments, especially where the payment wallet market is majorly dominated by private players. The data collected from 1000 respondents has been interpreted with the help of the SERVQUAL model for the payment wallets. The Paired t test for all payment wallets revealed an expected and perception gap, and the level of satisfaction is measured with ANOVA analysis revealing that PayTm has better perception.

Chapter 8

Ratan Ghosh, Bangladesh University of Professionals, Bangladesh
Asia Khatun, University of Dhaka, Bangladesh

The internet of things (IoT) is changing the paradigm in every aspect of human life. IoT embedded with big data is sparking the adoption of artificial intelligence (AI) in the business field. Subsequently, this study investigates the role of technological readiness in adopting artificial intelligence (AI) in the accounting profession of Bangladesh. To analytically assess the impact of technological readiness on the adoption of AI, four dimensions of technological readiness (TR) have been measured: TR optimism,

TR innovativeness, TR discomfort, and TR insecurity. A self-administered closed-ended questionnaire is developed and distributed among the students studying accounting in various public universities in Bangladesh. Six hundred eight responses are recorded and used to test this study's hypothetical relationships. Findings reveal that TR optimism and TR innovativeness have a positive and significant relationship with AI adoption. TR insecurity and TR discomfort have a negative and significant relationship with AI adoption.

According to the 2020-2021 evaluation report on the development of human intelligence computing power in China released by the global market analysis agency IDC, the scale of China's artificial intelligence infrastructure market reached $3.93 billion, a year-on-year increase of 26.8%. For the traditional financial industry, artificial intelligence will be an important step in improving its business efficiency and innovation. AI is an essential technology for traditional risk management and financial supervision. China's FinTech ecosystem will gradually move towards a new ecosystem of "AI + Finance." This chapter aims to study how AI-enabled agile internet of things can enhance the business efficiency of China's FinTech ecosystem. This chapter will investigate the characteristics of China's AI-enabled agile internet of things. Case studies will be used for discussion. In addition, scientometrics analysis through CiteSpace will be conducted. Finally, this chapter will provide suggestions for policymakers to build a sustainable FinTech ecosystem for enterprises.

Chapter 10

The international aviation market was worth USD 4.95 billion in 2020 and is anticipated to increase at a compound annual growth rate (CAGR) of 21.4% between 2021 and 2028. The industry is projected to increase because of the exponential growth in air passenger volume and a significant emphasis on improving customer experience. Continuous advancements in wireless technology, as well as an increasing desire for smart airport construction, are driving market expansion. In recent years, the aviation sector has seen unparalleled growth in passenger volume. The major companies in the aviation sector, in particular, are using data-driven techniques to make business choices. The internet of things (IoT) plays an important role in data collection in the aviation sector by providing statistical summaries to aid airport management. These data summaries may be used by aviation firms to gain meaningful information while eliminating human intervention.

Preface

INTRODUCTION

The growing demand for digital and convenience in financial services and FinTechs necessitates significant investments in IT solutions to simplify and streamline procedures (Beerbaum, 2021). As a result, the need for FinTech to integrate new and innovative technologies into their legacy operations has grown due to increasing risk management requirements, regulatory changes, and channel variety. While FinTechs recognize the importance of adopting agile approaches to address such difficulties, adoption is hampered by existing processes, legacy technology, and organizational structures (Nguyen, 2021). But why is agility significant? When it comes to coping with risks and uncertain situations like the COVID-19 pandemic, traditional product development processes can be ineffective at times (Sharma et al., 2022). Moreover, client discontent and irritation are frequently the results of a lack of feedback loops in traditional product development processes. As a result of the inherited nature of projects, the agile methodology expects fluctuations in scope, cost, and duration. When executing projects utilizing an Agile strategy may allow FinTechs to better react to consumer needs as market conditions change. The idea behind agile IoT is to encourage FinTechs to manage any change in the project requirement effectively and efficiently (Chow & CAO, 2008). For example, in the banking world, there is always the possibility of a rapid change in regulatory compliance requirements. As a result, it becomes extremely difficult for IT teams to understand new requirements and make appropriate changes in such scenarios (Dewantari et al., 2021). The Agile approach solves this challenge by defining a high-level yet focused scope in the form of user stories, which are then scheduled to be released in accordance with the project's release plan.

In addition to the above, green and sustainable finance is gradually receiving attention in the post-COVID-19 world of financial services. It is now expanding into the mainstream through policy, market dynamics, legislation, and, most crucially, consumer demand - both corporate and retail. The role of finance in any economy puts it in a solid position to lead the transition to a more sustainable world.

Furthermore, in light of the recent IPCC (Intergovernmental Panel on Climate Change) report, which has been dubbed "a code red for humanity," it has become even more critical to assure the best possible allocation of capital (estimated at $6-$7 trillion per year) to this transition (Shing & Serret, 2021). That said, a sustainable FinTech firm, sometimes known as a "green business," has a low negative impact on the environment, community, society, or economy on a global or local scale. It is a company that strives for triple profits (Macchiavello & Siri, 2020). Sustainable FinTech companies frequently adopt progressive environmental and human rights principles. A company is considered green or sustainable if it meets all of the following criteria:

- It incorporates sustainability ideas into all of its business decisions.
- It is less harmful to the environment than the competition.
- It has demonstrated a strong dedication to environmental ideals in their commercial operations.

Therefore, the involvement of the financial sector in accomplishing the seventeen United Nations-defined "Sustainable Development Goals" (SDGs) is critical for FinTech companies' long-term viability. Moreover research studies like Alshehhi et al., (2018) identified and concluded that sustainability practises and business financial performance have a beneficial relationship. In the publications, 78% of 132 journals report a favourable relationship between company sustainability and financial performance, 7% show no influence, and 6% report a negative impact, according to this study. Similarly, the study by Bofondi & Gobbi (2017) highlighted that Fintech boosted flexibility and efficiency in financial services. Fintech's great promise is the ability to save costs by employing digital technologies; however, operational risk and insecurity may increase, necessitating a strong defence against threats.

Our book will be one of the first to compile recent research and developments in the field of FinTech enabled by artificial intelligence (AI) and internet of things (IoT) technologies. The COVID-19 epidemic has recently placed even more focus on lean and agile concepts. For example, amidst the global outbreak of COVID-19 financial firms worldwide were required to adopt collaboration tools and remote working, necessitating greater agility across business lines and a lean attitude, and not just in development. Similarly, in order to ensure the sustainability of FinTech ecosystems that includes FinTech start-ups and scale-ups, regulators, financial institutions, investors, governments, and talent institutions, blockchain, the IoT, and big data are examples of new financial technologies that have the potential to enable green finance innovations. This makes it an interesting topic to further evaluate the application of blockchain to resolve security issues in IoT And smart networks, review consensus algorithms that are best for IoT-based banking, assess the service quality of payment wallet services, and how AI-enabled agile IoT can enhance the efficiency of FinTech ecosystems of both developed and developing countries. Consequently, the book will help both academicians and industry professionals learn and understand the core concepts of agile FinTech ecosystems, their importance, application, implementation challenges, and novel solutions to address the issues. The book will serve the following purposes:

- To highlight new developments, trends, concerns, and practical obstacles and solutions encountered in the field of AI-enabled agile IoT for FinTech ecosystems.
- To provide outstanding reference material for academic scientists, researchers, and scholars working on agile FinTech ecosystems.
- The proposed book will strengthen thought processes on agile FinTech ecosystems, such as how banks integrate information, analyze data, and apply the consensus algorithms in networks with several faulty nodes to achieve reliability.
- The theoretical principles, framework, security aspects, system architecture implementation, analytical tools, and approaches to apply AI and IoT in FinTech ecosystems to achieve agility and thereby sustainability in the long run.

ORGANIZATION OF THE BOOK

The book is organized into 10 chapters. A brief description of each of the chapters follows:

Chapter 1 recognizes the importance of Green FinTech in today's scenario by focusing on IoT and AI-Enabled FinTech innovations, drivers of Green FinTech, IoT, and AI-enabled Green FinTech solutions from a global perspective, and potential of Green FinTech. The authors provided that FinTech can assist companies in evaluating and reducing their environmental effect, as well as investors in channeling their activities towards more sustainable assets, using technology such as advanced data analytics, blockchain, IoT, and artificial intelligence. FinTech is positioned to play a leadership role in the provision of green finance by combining big data analytics and artificial intelligence to encourage consumers and small and medium-sized businesses (SMEs) to make the green transition. In recent years, the term "green Fintech" has become popular. The authors define Green FinTech innovation as unique, technologically enabled financial services solutions developed by start-ups, existing technological organizations, or traditional financial service providers with the goal of enhancing the flow of financial resources for long-term sustainability.

They recommended that Green FinTech can help financial organizations better examine costs and efficiency while also improving data integrity in their green finance operations. Green FinTech can aid in the development of financial regulatory standards, accounting, and auditing services, as well as the prevention of greenwashing. New financial technologies such as blockchain, the Internet of Things, and big data, have the potential to unlock green finance innovations.

Chapter 2 establishes the need for permissioned blockchains (the type of blockchain network suitable for banks), which are best suited for banks due to know your customer (KYC) and anti-money laundering (AML) regulatory regulations. The author of this chapter contends that the Practical Byzantine Fault Tolerance (PBFT) and Proof of Authority (PoA) consensus mechanisms offer the best solution for banks to develop a blockchain network that ensures corporate robustness. The blockchain's PBFT mechanism has the potential to make the system more transparent, responsible, and free of corruption. Similarly, the PoA consensus mechanism allows a system of certified banks to achieve an agreement without giving up a lot of power, privacy, or authority by requiring a majority to acknowledge the blockchain's status.

Chapter 3 examines the potential security and privacy concerns associated with component interaction in the Internet of Things (IoT), as well as how the distributed ledger-based blockchain technology might help. Here, in this chapter, the authors discussed the application of blockchain technology to certain areas and categories. Various IoT and IoT with blockchain technology problems were also highlighted in order to better comprehend blockchain technology's role. Existing blockchain and IoT research articles were examined in terms of several aspects in order to demonstrate their strengths and limitations. Furthermore, the study provides a general overview of blockchain components as well as numerous industry standards.

Chapter 4 presents how the epoch-making innovations of the 21st century have made our life more convenient and brought socio-economic progress. Such a technological innovation, Fintech, has emerged with the potential to bring sustainable development by creating an inclusive financial service system, according to the authors of this chapter. This study explores gender diversity in Fintech to create an equitable and sustainable Fintech industry in Bangladesh. The authors found that Bangladesh is working towards achieving the Digital Bangladesh Vision 2021 aligned with Sustainable Development Goals (SDGs). However, Bangladesh has not yet implemented full-fledged Fintech systems except Mobile Financial System, operated by different financial institutions. But, the GSMA consumer survey 2020 and Global Findex Database 2017 revealed that there is a huge gender gap in mobile phone subscription, mobile internet, and mobile money usage rates. So, to create a gender-based sustainable Fintech solution, it is important to know whether the loyalty towards Fintech usage differs by gender. To test this, the authors collected data through a close-ended structured questionnaire and analyzed using Structural

Equation Modeling (SEM). The results disclose that gender does not influence post-adoption factors of Fintech usage.

Chapter 5 addresses the issue of external intrusion attackers intercepted by outside attackers who might be the source of these malicious nodes. The authors discovered that trust management technology might be used to construct a routing node that effectively selects the most dependable related routing links. However, because the trust values of nearby routing nodes may only be accessible by one routing node that does not follow the distributed multi-hop wireless sensor network (WSN) fully, its use is limited. In WSNs, the problem of a malicious node can be handled using either of the two types indicated; a) either WSN protocol or (b) propose a secure model. In the proposed study, the authors adopted and proposed a model of trust for WSNs based on blockchain notions. The Authors combine Long Range Wide Area Networks (LoRaWAN)with blockchain by considering the economy and crowdsensing. They built a LoRaWAN server to address trust issues caused by network coverage gaps and private network operators. This chapter proposes a technique for confirming data presence on a network at a certain moment. CMA (Confusion Mechanism Algorithm) is a system that protects the user's information by encrypting data acquired through sensors. Another application of blockchain is to safeguard user data and distribute rewards depending on involvement frequency. The results reveal that the mechanism presented increased user engagement from 20% in the traditional method to 80% in the suggested manner.

Chapter 6 narrates that innovation in the digital space has proved to be a great boon for humanity, contributing to sustainable use of limited resources and enabling access for a large number of people to places, civilizations, communities, cities, and countries which they probably cannot think of visiting in the ordinary course of life. The author explored opportunities and challenges faced by Chines companies while integrating digital strategies into their businesses. Case studies were used for discussion. The review disclosed that innovation in digital technology has the potential to become the core driving force for a sustainable and smart economy in China.

Chapter 7 analyzes service quality issues in the case of payment wallets in India. The authors provided that these services are provided by 40 (forty) companies in India, having 500 million mobile internet users. With such a large number of people utilizing these services, it's critical to investigate how successful and user-friendly these new payment instruments are. Payment wallets, being a novel idea in the financial industry, may be difficult for customers to embrace. As a result, the authors applied the SERVQUAL Model for payment wallets to analyze and display the data received from 1000 respondents. The Paired t-test for all payment wallets indicated an expected and perception gap, as well as a degree of satisfaction, which was examined using ANOVA analysis. The study finding revealed that PayTm has a superior perception.

Chapter 8 investigates the role of technological readiness in adopting artificial intelligence (AI) in the accounting profession in Bangladesh. To analytically assess the impact of technological readiness on the adoption of AI, four dimensions of technological readiness (TR) have been measured by the authors: TR Optimism, TR Innovativeness, TR Discomfort, and TR Insecurity. A self-administered close-ended questionnaire is developed and distributed among the students studying accounting in various public universities in Bangladesh. Six hundred eight responses are recorded and used to test this study's hypothetical relationships. Structural Equation Modeling (SEM) has been used to test the data's statistical relevance. Findings reveal that TR Optimism and TR Innovativeness have a positive and significant relationship with AI Adoption. TR Insecurity and TR Discomfort have a negative and significant relationship with AI Adoption. This asserts a significant relationship between technological readiness and the adoption of AI in the accounting profession. The value of the R2 is 33.60% which denotes 33.60% of the variability of the adoption of AI can be explained by four variables used in this study. The policymakers can facilitate both the universities and corporates by guiding them with financial incentives, a technical workforce, and a competitive environment to promote AI-based learning for the accounting students to contribute to the country's development.

Chapter 9 reviews that the agile Internet of things supported by artificial intelligence has also injected new impetus into economic and social development and profoundly changed people's production and lifestyle. Consequently, China's FinTech ecosystem will gradually move towards a new ecosystem of "AI + Finance," according to the author. This chapter aims to study how the agile Internet of things supported by artificial intelligence can improve the business efficiency of China's financial technology ecosystem. Case studies were used for discussion. In addition, the scientific econometric analysis was conducted through CiteSpace. Finally, this chapter offers suggestions for policymakers to build a sustainable FinTech ecosystem for enterprises in emerging economies.

Chapter 10 presents that the international aviation industry is projected to increase because of the exponential growth in air passenger volume and a significant emphasis on improving customer experience. Continuous advancements in wireless technology, as well as an increasing desire for smart airport construction, are driving market expansion, according to the author's review. In recent years, the aviation sector has seen unparalleled growth in passenger volume, and the major companies in the aviation sector, in particular, are using data-driven techniques to make business choices. In addition, the Internet of Things (IoT) plays an important role in data collection in the aviation sector by providing statistical summaries to aid airport management. The authors conclude that aviation firms may use data summaries to gain meaningful information while eliminating human intervention.

CONCLUSION

The rise of FinTechs, which use smartphones, the Internet of Things (IoT), data analytics, artificial intelligence (AI) and machine learning (ML), distributed ledgers (blockchain), and other technologies to disrupt the way financial institutions operate and service their customers, has completely disrupted the way financial institutions operate and service their customers (Ashta & Herrmann, 2021). As a result, FinTechs are always recognized for their ability to innovate and contribute to long-term sustainability. Moreover, policymakers and regulators are well aware of FinTechs' significance in assisting policy formulations to move to a more sustainable future. Fintech is on the rise, and digital financial services (trading, investment firms, etc.) are a big part of it. Legacy companies can successfully implement their digital transformation objectives by embracing agile development.

Sandeep Kautish
Lord Buddha Education Foundation, Nepal

Guneet Kaur
Independent Researcher, UK

REFERENCES

Alshehhi, A., Nobanee, H., & Khare, N. (2018). The impact of sustainability practices on corporate financial performance: Literature trends and future research potential. *Sustainability*, *10*(2), 494. doi:10.3390u10020494

Ashta, A., & Herrmann, H. (2021). Artificial intelligence and fintech: An overview of opportunities and risks for banking, investments, and microfinance. *Strategic Change*, *30*(3), 211–222. doi:10.1002/jsc.2404

Beerbaum, D. (2021). *Applying Agile Methodology to Regulatory Compliance Projects in the Financial Industry: A Case Study Research*. Academic Press.

Bofondi, M., & Gobbi, G. (2017). The big promise of FinTech. *European Economy*, *1*(2), 107-119.

Chow, T., & Cao, D. B. (2008). A survey study of critical success factors in agile software projects. *Journal of Systems and Software*, *81*(6), 961–971. doi:10.1016/j.jss.2007.08.020

Dewantari, D., Raharjo, T., Hardian, B., Wahbi, A., & Alaydrus, F. (2021, November). Challenges of Agile Adoption in Banking Industry: A Systematic Literature Review. In *2021 25th International Computer Science and Engineering Conference (ICSEC)* (pp. 357-362). IEEE. 10.1109/ICSEC53205.2021.9684622

Macchiavello, E., & Siri, M. (2020). Sustainable Finance and Fintech: Can Technology Contribute to Achieving Environmental Goals? A Preliminary Assessment of 'Green FinTech'. *Technological Forecasting and Social Change, 1*(174), 121–172.

Nguyen, V. H. (2021, December). An Agile Approach for Managing Microservices-Based Software Development: Case Study in FinTech. In *European, Mediterranean, and Middle Eastern Conference on Information Systems* (pp. 723-736). Springer.

Sharma, M., Luthra, S., Joshi, S., & Joshi, H. (2022). Challenges to agile project management during COVID-19 pandemic: an emerging economy perspective. *Operations Management Research*, 1-14.

Shing, A., & Serret, A. (2021). *Sustainable Finance and FinTech: A necessary marriage.* Retrieved 12 May 2022, from https://www.pwc.com/mu/en/about-us/press-room/sustainable-finance.html

Chapter 1
Unlocking IoT:
AI–Enabled Green FinTech Innovations

Babita Jha
ⓘD https://orcid.org/0000-0001-8586-0250
Christ University (Deemed), India

Pratibha Giri
Christ University (Deemed), India

Deepak Jha
Lingaya's Vidyapeeth, Faridabad, India

Usha Badhera
ⓘD https://orcid.org/0000-0002-6379-3613
Jaipuria Institute of Management, Jaipur, India

ABSTRACT

Meeting ESG (environmental, social, and governance) standards is becoming an essential goal for businesses, one that is supported by both investors and customers. FinTech can help companies evaluate and reduce their environmental effect, as well as investors channel their operations toward more sustainable assets. Embracing sustainability has become one of the priorities for many fintech companies today. Green fintech innovations have provided technologically enabled solutions for financial services that help in increasing the flow of financial resources for sustainable development. Recognizing the importance of green fintech in today's scenario, this chapter will initially focus on the components of the fintech ecosystem and IoT and AI-enabled fintech innovations in India, drivers of green fintech potentials of green fintech IoT, and AI-enabled green fintech from global perspective and has highlighted the green fintech solutions provided by the topmost companies.

DOI: 10.4018/978-1-6684-4176-3.ch001

INTRODUCTION

The financial crisis, which began in 2009 and continues to this day, had a great impact on the development of Fintech. Due to changes in market conditions, many Fintech innovations have emerged. As a result, the Fintech industry's emergence in the modern period is becoming more competitive (Arner et al., 2015). Fintech (financial technology) is one of the most commonly used buzzwords in the financial industry today (Mello, 2018). Fintech refers to a relatively new movement within the financial sector in which digital start-ups or existing IT corporations take use of society's rising digitization and connectivity to produce creative digital solutions to financial services (Gomberet al., 2017). Mobile payments, cryptocurrency, crowdsourcing, and other similar services are examples (Gozmann et al., 2018; Gomber et al., 2017; Punschmann, 2017).

Fintech has the potential to unlock green finance by disrupting technologies like Block chain, the Internet of Things, and big data, which were created concurrently with the Paris Agreement and the Sustainable Development Goals (Nassiry, D., 2018). The Fintech Ecosystem is a term used to describe the ecosystem of financial technology. Fintech ecosystems are intricate and dynamic. They've quickly grown to be one of the most important and difficult areas of the financial services business.

Fintech transformation has been implemented in different phases. In Fintech 1.0 the major focus was on transmission media and computers configurations. The financial technology products, such as SWIFT and ATMs, are result of these technologies. The Internet of Things was one of the related technologies during Fintech 2.0, but more data technologies like Big Data, AI, are utilized during Fintech 3.0 (Leong, K., and Sung A., 2018). Fintech 4.0 is the era of BigTech digital finance platforms (Arner, D. W.,et al., 2017).

AI research was first proposed in the 1950s by Alan Turing, while the name Artificial Intelligence was coined in 1955 by John McCarthy. Education, engineering, finance, healthcare, and marketing are just a few of the domains where AI has had a big impact. Artificial intelligence (AI) makes objects to extract, analyze, and respond instinctively like human mind, and does all this with higher accuracy, speed and correctly (Forbes, 2021).

Artificial intelligence (AI) is a disruptive technology that is in combination with robotics, is revolutionizing the operating model of all businesses (Ruiz-Real et al., 2021). AI in the financial sector retrieves requirements of the business for financial firms, agencies and markets and connects them with technological proficiencies (Golić, 2019). The major role of AI in Fintech are simulation, analysis, computations, predictions, forecasting, planning, optimizing, fault detections and recommendations (Cao, 2018). Artificial Intelligence and Big Data technology utilized in green insurance is priced smartly considering environmental risk for example Alipay for personal carbon account, AntForest to convert virtual tree plantation to real one, digital agricultural system where sensors collect real time ground data which is of high volume, velocity and variety and it is the transmitted to actuators to operate smartly and data is sent to AI for analysis and utilized by financial institutions for real time decision making (Yang, 2020).

The main elements of IoT are focused towards identifying, finding, communicate, compute, services and semantics(Fuqahaet al., 2021). The Internet of Devices (IoT) links, sensors, actuators, and other smart systems to establish communication between individual and object andobject-to-object (Uckelmannet al., 2011). The restriction guidelines of regulatory bodies for sustainability during digital transformation are implementable by the growth of AI and IoT in finance (Guoand Polak, 2021). Artificial intelligence (AI) assisted agile IoT is the way forward for Green Fintech (Pustokhina et al., 2021). Recognizing the importance of Green Fintech in today's scenario, this chapter will initially focus on the components of the Fintech ecosystem and IOT and AI Enabled Fintech Innovations in India. The next part of the chapter deals with the meaning of Green Fintech, Drivers of Green Fintech and Potentials of Green Fintech. This chapter has given special focus on the IOT and AI enabled Green Fintech from Global Perspective and has highlighted the Green Fintech solutions provided by the topmost companies. At the end part of the chapter, the focus is given on the challenges towards the way of Green Fintech and accordingly strategies and recommendations for the success of Green Finance are discussed.

The following are the components of the Fintech ecosystem:

Fintech providers are being considered as the next golden goose by venture capitalists, angel investors, and private equity firms.

- Traditional financial institutions - Banks and financial service providers are figuring out how to work with Fintechs.
- Technology –Technological advancements like AI, IoT, big data analytics, cloud computing are used for lowering operational costs.
- Regulatory bodies and the government – Appropriate legislation safeguards end users are also establishing criteria for Fintech to follow.
- Institutions of higher learning and research – Institutes with a curriculum focusing on Fintech companies in India are helping to address the acute scarcity of bright and equipped workers.
- Incubators - Several well-known corporations in India are launching Fintech incubators to help startups test and develop their products.
- Users - The most crucial cog in the Fintech wheel is still the end user.

IOT - AI ENABLED FINTECH INNOVATIONS IN INDIA

It has become progressively easy to acquire financial services in India due to the growing adoption of "digital" during the last few years. Fintech, a commonly used phrase in the modern digital age, has played a role in shifting consumer banking behaviors. India had a surge in technology usage in financial services around the year 2015. Fintech businesses in India were valued at Rs 1,920 billion in 2019, according to Research and Markets, and are predicted to grow at a CAGR of 22.7 percent to Rs 6,207 billion by 2025.

The modern financial business began in the following year:

- The ATM was first introduced in 1967. (Automated Teller Machine)
- The financial services business transforms from analogue to digital between 1967 and 1987.
- From 1987 to 2008, the financial services business was largely changed into a digital industry, aided by the internet's arrival around the year 2000 (Arner et al., 2015).

India has observed several Fintech innovations over the last decades. These innovations include the following:

Payment Services: Making payments has never been easier. You may have a lot of different payment wallets without having to go through the laborious process of obtaining a bank account. All you need is a smartphone and a mobile phone number to buy nearly anything within your budget. PayTM, Freecharge, and MobiKwik have radically changed the Indian payment landscape. When you go out, physical wallets are no longer required. Simply bring your phone with you and scan away!

Digital Loan: Fintech innovation is being used to carve out a niche in the lending industry. Customers have traditionally had to go through lengthy cycles and paperwork in order to obtain a loan. Companies such as Union Bank of India, Profectus Capital, Bank of India, UCO Bank, SIDBI, and others are disrupting the traditional technique. Customers with inconsistent employment and bank account statements can now apply for loans. Fintech is allowing new lending models to emerge, including flow-based, vertical-based, and ecosystem-based lending.

Insurance: Insurance is another industry that is moving away from paper. Aggregators such as Policybazaar and Coverfox have developed to assist clients in selecting from a variety of service providers by comparing their products and purchasing the most appropriate one.

Savings and Wealth Management - Fintech such as Scripbox and Funds India assist people in saving and investing their money. These systems offer a similar selection of alternatives.

Payments: Notable remittance platforms include Oxigen and Payworld, which have made inbound and outbound remittances straightforward and cost effective. Fintechs in this area supply card swipe machines to facilitate cashless payments at the point-of-sale. New firms such as Mswipe, PineLabs, and ICICI Merchant Services have entered the industry as a result of demonetization, making the market more competitive.

Regtech: Companies in this area help businesses comply with industry regulations such as anti-money laundering and Know Your Customer processes in order to combat fraud. The regulating mechanisms are being improved by notable players IDfy, Avantis, FixNix, and Signzy.

WHAT IS 'GREEN FINTECH,' AND HOW DOES IT DIFFER FROM TRADITIONAL FINANCIAL TECHNOLOGY?

The "Paris Agreement" on climate change (UNFCCC, 2015) and the resolution A/RES/70/1 "Transforming our world: The 2030 Agenda for Sustainable Development" were signed by the world community in 2015, and they essentially represent the difficulties that humanity is confronting today (United Nations, 2015a). Meeting ESG (environmental, social, and governance) standards is becoming a more essential goal for businesses, one that is supported by both investors and customers. Over the last few years, sustainable finance, particularly climate-related financing, has grown in importance at the corporate, governmental, and supranational levels (Macchiavello and Siri, 2020). The globe is shifting toward long-term economic models that might generate $12 trillion in annual economic potential by 2030. Many public, private, and non-governmental entities launched projects in 2017 to accelerate the financial movement for sustainable development. According to Ranchber. (2018), achieving sustainable development and combating climate change will necessitate a faster and more extensive mobilization of financial resources than has previously been seen. One possible answer to this problem has been identified: green Fintech developments.

The term 'Fintech' has become increasingly popular in recent years. The future of financial services is being shaped by two major factors: technology and sustainability. In recent years, the term "green Fintech" has become popular. It, however, lacks a widely accepted definition. It typically refers to businesses or programmes that have a good influence on the environment, such as lowering greenhouse gas emissions or increasing biodiversity. Green Fintech innovations - a novel, technologically enabled solution for financial services developed by start-ups, established technological firms, or traditional financial service providers with the goal of increasing the flow of financial resources for sustainable development - are one example of innovative solutions. It usually refers to businesses or programmes that have a positive environmental impact, such as reducing greenhouse gas emissions or increasing biodiversity. It consists of three main parts:

- Finance that is environmentally friendly
- Eco-friendly financing
- Taking advantage of the chance

Green Fintech can help companies evaluate and reduce their environmental effect, as well as investors channel their operations towards more sustainable assets, using technology such as advanced data analytics, blockchain, and artificial intelligence. Green Fintech can help financial organizations better examine costs and efficiency while also improving data integrity in their green finance operations. Green Fintech can aid in the development of financial regulatory standards, accounting, and auditing services, as well as the prevention of greenwashing. Solutions that extend financing to green start-ups, such as green crowdfunding platforms, or solutions that lower the barrier to consumer action and ensure green investments, such as easily available sustainable financial advising services, are examples of green Fintech breakthroughs (Stockholm Green Digital Finance, 2017). The global 'Green Fintech' ecosystem is fast expanding, yet it is still in its infancy. From planting trees to offering fossil-fuel-free investment options, several Fintech companies are helping to shape this fundamental move toward sustainability. The advancements in sustainable and competitive tech-driven financial products and services, interest in Green Fintech solutions is gradually growing.

ROLE OF FINTECH: GREEN ECONOMY

Fintech is positioned to play a leadership role in the provision of green finance by combining big data analytics and artificial intelligence to encourage consumers and small and medium-sized businesses (SMEs) to make the green transition.

Clean Energy Production

Technology in financial services has the potential to more efficiently channel financial resources to environmentally sustainable firms and incentivize the production of clean energy (for example, green crowd funding platforms; 'energy' tokens on DLT platforms and peer-to-peer exchange networks), or at the very least provide trusted measures of impact and actions to produce it (for example, green crowd funding platforms; 'energy' tokens on DLT platforms and peer-to-peer exchange networks).

Solar Coin, for example, was established to reward solar energy providers while also providing an incentive to others considering solar panel installation.

Offsets for CO2

Approximately 400 of the world's 2,000 largest corporations have committed to achieving net zero emissions. To achieve net-zero emissions, certain Fintech startups, such as CoGo and Almond, have taken a novel method to automate the acquisition of carbon offsets. They use bank account data to track corporate or individual activity, automate offset purchases based on that data, and make recommendations to reduce overall carbon emissions, such as switching to a green energy provider or eating a plant-based diet, as well as encouraging them to spend with brands that share their values.

Sustainability as a Fundamental Value

Even if it isn't part of their primary product, a number of Fintech companies have made sustainability a core value. Bunq is a sustainable challenger bank. For every €100 spent using the card, it pledges to plant a tree. They claim that a user who spends €1,000 per month with their bunq Green Card has a green impact of such magnitude that it only takes 5 years to begin offsetting their annual carbon footprint and become carbon neutral.

Ratings and Investments Based on Environmental, Social, and Governance (ESG) Criteria

The world's largest investment vehicles are paying attention to ESG measures. Customers are increasingly expecting funds with environmental, social, and governance credentials, so it's becoming a top concern when making investment decisions, and it's becoming more significant in middle management's day-to-day activities. Artificial intelligence and distributed ledger technology can also be used by green Fintech companies to help capture and communicate essential data about their social and environmental consequences, lowering research costs and enhancing the price of environmental risk investment opportunities. This technology allows organisations to compare their disclosures with practically real-time data and publicly available environmental data in order to enhance their environmental, social, and governance standards.

Drivers of Green Fintech

Outsourcing, Technology Development, and Digitization: One of the major drivers for general Fintech innovation processes is the changing ecosystems within the financial industry as a result of years of insurance companies and banks outsourcing various operations and divisions (Punschmann, 2017). Instead, established IT corporations have been in charge of a substantial portion of the business process output. Outsourcing has made these players more familiar with the financial business, which they had previously avoided, lowering the barrier to entry and allowing them to develop their own technologically enabled financial services products. These players are aware of technology advances, already work in an innovative and agile environment (in comparison to the banking industry), and hence have a competitive edge in providing innovative financial services. The rise of the Fintech sector has been facilitated by their expertise and knowledge, in combination with the changing role of IT and rising digitization in society. Technological factors have influenced the number of Fintech startups in different nations. Increase in mobile phone subscribers and secure internet servers in a country have lead to more Fintech inventions than it has.

The financial industry's success with digitization is due to the fact that financial products are nearly entirely dependent on data. IT advancements such as big data analytics, the internet of things, and cloud computing have enabled the creation of entirely new products, services, processes, and business models. Technology has also been identified as a driver of general financial advancements, as it allows for more precise risk management.

Unmet Needs and a Market that Isn't Complete - On the other hand, rising digitization's in almost every sector of society has altered how financial service customers engage with and wish to connect with financial service providers. Smartphone and tablets have enabled everyone to be connected at any time and from any location, ready to consume, search, read, and listen. Today's financial service customers expect services to be simple to use, intelligent, and independent of time and place in order to save money. Fintech solutions attempt to address inefficient processes such as slow loan approvals, excessive borrowing costs, and cumbersome application processes Unmet needs or market incompleteness, such as information asymmetries, is what encourages financial innovation, according to research on general financial innovation. Fintech innovations success is based on their ability to better meet these needs than traditional financial service providers. It has been observed from several researches that the number of Fintech innovations is higher in nations where businesses find it harder to obtain financing.

Crowdfunding is one such Fintech innovation. The financial crisis of 2008 caused banks to become more cautious about lending to the real economy, making it difficult for small and medium-sized businesses to obtain loans. Crowdfunding was then proposed as a way to bridge the funding shortfall.

Macroeconomic Factors: Macroeconomic conditions have an impact on both the supply and demand for Fintech technologies. Well-developed economies and capital markets, as well as a large labour force, have a beneficial impact on the supply, or prevalence, of Fintech developments in a country. These are critical enablers for the advancement of these breakthroughs. Simultaneously, as in the case of crowdfunding, demand for these technologies rises as a result of macroeconomic instability, particularly negative economic events, which create market uncertainty and volatility. Countries that were badly damaged by the 2008 financial crisis have a significant demand for Fintech innovation. Furthermore, the financial crisis made the younger, most tech-savvy generation more skeptical of traditional financial service providers and more open and less risk averse to test innovative Fintech solutions, influencing demand for these advances.

Social Difficulties: The worsening of social difficulties (for example, the challenges outlined in the sustainable development objectives) is a related driver that influences the demand and supply of social tech advances. Growth, in combination with a decline in welfare, has created a void that may be filled by innovative organisations by integrating technology and social innovation. Different incentives have been developed particularly to enhance policymakers' dependence on these new solutions to contribute to the resolution of societal concerns.

Potentials of Green Fintech

Green Fintech has the ability to revolutionise the present financial system in all sectors, including payments, investments, financing, advice, and insurance, by, for example, channeling funds towards green ventures and improving data for green company appraisal.

Economic Impact: Because green Fintech enables the change of the financial system, it has a significant impact on the economy as a whole, for example, by enabling the creation of new sustainable business models, startups, and other initiatives.

c2c Transactions: In regions where decentralization is gaining traction, c2c transactions improve value chains by disintermediating them. Energy production and consumption, ride-sharing services, and other services, for example, are all made possible by new green Fintech approaches.

Cross-Industry Ecosystems: Ecosystems that connect green Fintech services to services from other industries such as mobility, energy, and logistics, among others provide for entirely new application areas, such as machine-to-machine payments for mobility services, and so on.

Transparency and Data Models: Because they mix external and internal data sets, data-driven green Fintech solutions provide more transparency about enterprises and value chains, as well as superior decision-making tools.

Innovation: Cooperation between incumbents and non-financial institutions that provide new green Fintech solutions provides for more innovation in this space, allowing for cross-institutional procedures and standards, for example.

IOT - AI ENABLED GREEN FINTECH: GLOBAL PERSPECTIVE

As authorities and businesses consider how to unlock the potential of sustainable financing, there is a global push to investigate the use of emerging financial technology (Fintech) in this context. Satellites, drones, and other digital sensing technologies can be used to monitor compliance with sustainability indicators across investments, lowering monitoring and reporting costs. The first sustainability-linked loan was given by the Dutch ING bank in 2017. If a borrower reduces their environmental impact, it reduces their cost of capital by a percentage, and so the interest on the loan is connected to the company's ESG rating.In Holland, ING Bank has created a computerized tool to assist their commercial real-estate borrowers in identifying energy-saving initiatives for their buildings that deliver the best returns and reduce carbon emissions. The tool is an app that is available to all Dutch customers. The client provides information about the building, such as its age and location, and the software suggests 10 cost-cutting and CO2 emission-reduction strategies for each structure. Loans are then connected to the borrower's performance. In Asia, DBS bank provided the region's first sustainability-linked loan to an IT firm.

The Spatial Finance Initiative has been studying the field of 'spatial finance,' which aims to incorporate geographical data and analysis into financial decision-making. In the United Kingdom (2019), the Financial Conduct Authority (FCA) announced a Green Fintech Challenge to encourage technical advancements in the green finance sector. Successful applicants received variety of benefits, including entrance to the regulatory sandbox, direct support from the regulator, and customized cohort engagement terms, among others.

In Europe, Switzerland's government announced the establishment of a Green Fintech Network in 2020.Carbon Delta, a Swiss firm, has created a Climate Value-at-Risk (VaR) assessment approach for quantifying climate change risks across investment portfolios, allowing climate change to be considered in investment choices. It determines such risks using a combination of publicly available and proprietary data, as well as machine learning. Green capital issuance may be made easier via digital platforms, and access to such financing alternatives can be expanded. Green bond issuing necessitates more auditing and reporting. Investors can use platforms to gain access to external audits and standardised reports. Green Assets Wallet, a blockchain-based platform, validates green pledges and provides a framework for issuers to report on impact, decreasing information gaps and boosting green transaction efficiency and transparency. Tesla stopped accepting Bitcoin payments in May 2021, citing its negative environmental impacts.

Energy X is an online energy firm based in South Korea. Energy X is the creator of a platform powered by artificial intelligence (AI) that allows businesses and individuals to invest in renewable energy projects all around the world. Energy X's online-to-offline network connects investors to low- to mid-risk renewable energy projects through crowdsourcing, private finance, and exchange opportunities. As a result, independent power producers (IPPs) have easier access to investors and contractors, as well as the ability to start projects sooner. HolonIQ named Energy X one of the world's 1,000 most promising climate tech firms.

Major Asian developing countries have recently begun to adopt and expand innovative green finance initiatives. China's Fintech market is the world's largest and fastest-growing Fintech market. China's Fintech investments totaled 25.2 billion USD in 2018, accounting for 46% of all Fintech investments worldwide (Tougaard, 2020). That was greater than the total output of the United States and Europe that year. Some of the world's largest technological companies, such as Alibaba, are examining chances to become leaders in the sustainable energy sector. For example, Alibaba's Fintech branch, Ant Financial Services, has formed the Green Digital Finance Alliance with the United Nations Environment Programme (UNEP). The association aims to demonstrate how digital banking and Fintech can help change the financial system to be more environmentally friendly.

Tokyo's commitment to environmental stewardship is shown in its goal of achieving net-zero carbon emissions by 2050. Given this commitment, as well as Japan's position in driving the global agenda as the only Asian member of the G7, it's no surprise that the city's green finance market continues to grow. Domestically, the volume of sustainability, social, and green bonds sold increased 47 times between 2016 and 2020, totaling more than 2,100 billion yen. The Tokyo Metropolitan Government (TMG) established the Green Finance Subsidy Program for Tokyo Market Entry in 2021 to help Tokyo's green finance momentum. Foreign asset managers and Fintech companies focused on sustainability can receive subsidies to launch and expand new enterprises in Tokyo under this revolutionary new scheme.

Malaysia launched its latest financial sector blueprint for 2022-2026. Malaysia's financial blueprint plan is similar to that of a number of other Asian banks that have made climate change risk management a priority and implemented greener methods to decrease their carbon footprint. Solarvest is collaborating with organisations such as Malaysian Technology Development Corp, Telekom Malaysia Bhd, Malaysia Global Innovation and Creativity Centre, OCBC Bank (Malaysia) Bhd, Inti International

University and Colleges, Junior Chamber International Malaysia, JCI Creative Young Entrepreneurs Award, and others to accelerate the country's green agenda and digital revolution by seeking out bright and innovative ideas from aspiring entrepreneurs.

To speed decarbonization, the Japanese government aims to employ data visualisation strategically. Positioning Japan as a model country for climate-related financial disclosure is a part of this approach, and visualisation will play a key role here. The Japanese government has created the world's first platform for comparing climate-related data from different companies side by side. This visualisation aims to give investors with the information they increasingly value, allowing Japanese companies to attract more overseas funding.

Between 2015 and 2030, India will require at least $2.5 trillion to accomplish its climate change goals (Ahmad,2020). Several efforts around the world demonstrate the role Fintech can play in advancing sustainable financing. India, behind China, is the second largest emerging market for green bonds, according to the latest Economic Survey. In its latest 'Report on Trend and Progress of Banking in India (2018-19),' the Reserve Bank of India advocated for "policy action to establish an enabling environment that fosters the green finance eco-system in India." Indian regulators such as the Reserve Bank of India (RBI) and the Securities and Exchange Board of India (SEBI) are developing frameworks to encourage financial sector innovation.

IOT – AI LINKED LONG-TERM FINANCIAL SOLUTIONS: TOPMOST COMPANIES

Millenials are driving demand for greener products while also demanding more transparency in how businesses integrate environmental, social, and corporate governance (ESG) into their products, services, and policies. To screen investments, a rising range of analytical methods and platforms are being used. While traditional ESG Data players give significant metrics for understanding those risks, there has been an increase in the number of AI players supporting the demand for alternative data over the previous five years. Artificial intelligence (AI) and machine learning algorithms have the ability to scrape any publicly available data about non-listed products in order to assist fund managers in finding stable alternative funds. Truvalue Labs is a Fintech firm with origins in environmental, social, and governance (ESG) reporting analytics. The firm's tools use artificial intelligence to analyse and interpret large amounts of unstructured data, allowing investors to make better decisions across their entire portfolio. Fintech businesses are increasingly reacting to this increased need for transparency and knowledge by giving information and a better understanding of investment supply chains. Following are some of the Start Ups or Fintechs that have embraced transparent and environmentally-safe approaches in doing business:

Aspiration

This challenger bank in the United States focuses on two values: environmental protection and avoiding oil firms that pollute the environment. It believes that every modest action has the potential to make a huge difference. It has incorporated an app in which a portion of each customer's money is used to plant trees. This app has a strong value proposition, with the goal of removing millions of pounds of CO_2 from the atmosphere by planting 100 million trees.

TreeCard

TreeCard, a finance business, primarily serves European customers. The project aims to minimise plastic use and reforest the planet – the company seeks to reduce plastic use and reforest the planet. TreeCard is a project based on a credit card constructed of recycled plastic bottles and cherry wood sourced in a sustainable manner. In addition, 80% of its proceeds go to reforestation efforts.

Starling Bank

Starling Bank is one of the leading Fintech enterprises in the UK today, according to an independent service quality survey. Their desire to become green and adopt more environmentally friendly solutions draws a large number of people to their services. The bank has no branches, uses no paper, and runs on renewable energy. It was also the first bank in the country to use recycled plastic debit cards. Starling also joined the Tech Zero taskforce, together with other leading Fintech firms, to help reduce carbon emissions.

Triodos Bank

Triodos is also one of the UK's Fintech startups working to make the banking sector more environmentally friendly and resource efficient. People are more concerned than ever before about their impact on the environment. Furthermore, according to Triodos' study, ethical options are a top priority for its investors. As a result, the bank exclusively invests in sustainable businesses and makes information about all of the companies with which it works public, displaying one of their core values: transparency. As a result, all stakeholders can see how their money is helping to avert a climate disaster.

Stripe

Stripe is a payment processing service for Internet businesses. Stripe Climate was created to allow all forward-thinking businesses to contribute to making the world more climate neutral. Companies can donate a portion of their earnings to technology that remove carbon from the atmosphere with only a few clicks. In exchange, such companies receive a green emblem that shows clients their involvement in several green projects and, as a result, their core principles. Stripe, on the other hand, distributes money to carbon-reduction firms on a regular basis. All for a good cause: reducing global temperature rise to avoid catastrophic climate change impacts.

Almond

Almond is a green Fintech company based in the United Kingdom. One of its goals is to assist businesses in increasing sales and developing stronger relationships with their customers. However, they have another environmental objective in mind: promoting and assisting people in achieving a carbon-balanced lifestyle. That's why Almond created a free software for Android and iOS users that encourages people to live greener lives. Users can, for example, search for environmentally friendly alternatives, avoid purchasing unsustainable goods and services, and measure their carbon footprint. Furthermore, when customers shop with partner brands, they earn offsetting incentives that are used to plant trees and conserve the rainforest.

Clim8

Clim8 is one of the London Fintech startups that demonstrate a commitment to a long-term future. It helps fund clients grow their investments while also safeguarding the environment (charging a fee as a percentage of assets under management for that). What can you put your money into? In fact, Clim8 is involved in a large variety of environmental programmes aimed at combating climate change. Clean water, energy, technology, sustainable food, smart mobility, and the circular economy are all good investments. All of this contributes to the UN's Paris Climate Agreement's climate goals. By the way, you can begin funding with just £25.

Trine

Trine, like Clim8, is a top Fintech company located in Sweden that allows clients to benefit while creating a positive social and environmental effect. Solar energy is the main focus, and the results are astounding. Because of the money invested by 12 thousand Trine investors, almost 2.5 million people now have access to power. What is the mechanism behind it? You create an account, pick a loan, and determine how much money you're willing to provide – at least £25. Once the loan is fully funded and solar items are distributed, you get your money back with interest. Trine's goal is to help clients obtain three times their money back.

PensionBee

PensionBee is a well-known online pension company that assists you in taking charge of your retirement. Although it may not be the first company that comes to mind when thinking about top Fintech businesses, one of its projects demands your attention. PensionBee started its fossil-fuel-free investment plan in 2020. Its goal is to stop funding oil, gas, coal, and tobacco companies, as well as weapons makers. Additionally, for a 0.75 percent annual charge, its clients can make socially responsible investments. Your money will be invested in firms whose values are aligned with the Paris Agreement in this way.

Bettervest

It's a crowd-funding website specialising in renewable energy and energy efficiency. Private, public, and non-governmental entities interested in installing renewable energy solutions or improving their energy efficiency can submit a project to the digital platform, together with information on the amount of funding they require. Following that, users can pool their funds to invest in the project for as little as €50. (Source: bettervest, n.d.)

SDG

SDG Investments is a digital platform that connects investors with initiatives that support the UN's Sustainable Development Goals. Investors specify which SDGs they want to invest in and how much money they have available, while projects specify which SDGs they contribute to. The actors are then paired up based on their stated objectives.

Raise Green

Raise Green allows you to look for green businesses in your neighborhood. You can have micro-ownership of these initiatives while also supporting businesses and the cause. Green startups are frequently self-funded, but this one is backed by IBM. Both companies collaborated to create a powerful marketplace. Raise Green is transparent, allowing you to know how many kWh of clean energy your investments have generated.

Tumelo

It is another Fintech business promoting green behaviors. Its goal is to empower customers to behave smarter and more strategically when it comes to investing without relying on a financial advisor. It gives investors access to a one-of-a-kind dashboard that allows them to have more transparency and involvement with the companies in which they have stock, as well as improve the depth and quality of client conversations. It also gives investors a better picture of the prospects available in various sectors and businesses.

Tomorrow

Tomorrow is a mobile banking start-up established in Germany. The business owner pays a modest fee to your bank when clients use their card at a store or online, known as an interchange fee (0.2 percent of the transaction). Tomorrow, a portion of the interchange charge will be used to cover transaction costs, and the remaining amount (0.13 percent of the transaction) will be invested in climate-related programmes.

GREEN FINTECH: CHALLENGES

Transitioning to an economy which has a policy on legal, technology, and market changes requires positive human perception, budget, and willingness to create products that are and communicate green.

Mindset: According to a research by the World Resources Institute (WRI), less than half of the world's top banks have committed to prioritising green energy over fossil fuels. Fintech faces both a possibility and a difficulty in this regard. They must inform clients and business partners about the rationale for going green. Education, marketing, and in-app promotions should suffice, but it will take some time.

A Sense of Business: Another issue for many countries is that they have money to invest but lack understanding about the potential economic and environmental consequences. This lack of understanding may lead to the emergence of Fintech, but not green technology financing.

Funding: Green Fintech companies face additional legal hurdles, which raise development expenses in comparison to other companies. This limits access to growth finance because investors view these businesses as long-term investments.

The term of profitability is extended in this situation, as is the patience of certain well-heeled individuals.

Lack of Access to Funding: Fintech innovators have a hard time getting money to develop their ideas due to a lack of access to cash and the involvement of venture capitalists (Haddadd and Hornuf, 2018). Fintech startups are reticent to seek funding from venture capitalists and business angels, according to Zilgalvis (2014).

Hybrid Missions: Arena et al. (2018) investigated financial mechanisms that can be used to fund social tech start-ups, which are businesses that address social problems through technology. According to the authors, when seeking money, particularly from profit-hungry equity investors such as venture capitalists, the worry is not only of losing control over their idea, but also of losing control over the mission that drives the idea. Because innovations driven by hybrid missions are regarded to generate an unfavourable risk/return relationship for investors, both financial returns and societal demands are deemed to be unfavorable.

Information Asymmetry: Information asymmetries relate to the scarcity of historical and financial information about a startup that an investor needs to make a choice. Higher risks for the investor are associated with this uncertainty, which may be mitigated by a request for high interest rates or big shares of equity. The information asymmetries in social tech start-ups are stronger than in traditional high-tech start-ups, because most investors are unfamiliar with the unique qualities of such inventions.

Regulatory Frameworks: They are a set of rules that govern how things are done. Regulatory implications of Fintech advances have become a more prominent concern in recent years (Zavolokina et al., 2016). For new entrants to the financial industry, regulatory barriers are difficult to overcome (Gomber et al., 2017). Fintech innovators must keep a watch on regulatory developments since they may jeopardise the heart of their business models (Haddadd and Hornuf, 2018).

GREEN FINTECH ECOSYSTEM: STRATEGY, RECOMMENDATIONS AND SOLUTIONS

IOT-AI enabled Fintech and green finance in general could benefit from a high-level systemic support structure in a variety of ways. Many countries, particularly those in the European Union, might implement specific engagement laws to help corporations, especially in the early stages of a company's development and expansion. The development of funding instruments is an excellent place to start. There is a whole ecosystem that supports Fintech businesses; now it's time to help green businesses.

To promote IOT-AI linkedgreen Fintech technologies dedicated working groups within local governments (in each country) can be formed. It is critical to have a thorough understanding of the local ecosystems, people, and difficulties. Green Finance (through open banking, for example) and collaboration between universities and other higher education institutions will start the blood flowing. Main street financial institutions may be able to lessen the barriers to entry for startups.

A change in Fintech investment trends also appears to be a smart idea. There are plenty fascinating individuals with much more fascinating ideas. Financing them could usher in a new generation of solutions that are both practical and environmentally friendly. The mentality is shifting. Globally, sustainable assets range from 5% to 25%, according to Harvard Business Review and each year this number is increasing

As part of the solution, climate bonds and certifications are being used. These solutions, as demonstrated on the Climate Bonds Initiative page, can standardise credentials and build worldwide market confidence.

WAY FORWARD

The pandemic's disruption has highlighted how delicate humanity's relationship with the environment is, as well as the importance of preserving biodiversity and natural capital. Private investors may not be willing to invest in these areas because they are too small-scale, too risky, and/or not profitable enough. Natural capital finance requires a standardised set of measures and procedures for evaluating the environmental consequences, risks, and interdependencies of economic and financial activities.ESG frameworks can be integrated with other investor criteria to create weighting systems, which can then be used to evaluate green credentials. Investors can also be provided with information in more simply digestible formats, allowing them to make more educated judgments. The Fintech industry is well-positioned to participate in this field, and it will continue to make major efforts to reduce environmental consequences for the benefit of people and the environment.

CONCLUSION

In present times of digital transformation technologies like Artificial Intelligence (AI), big data, blockchain and IoT are contributing significantly in achieving green finance goals. There is a huge financial data generated from mobile and social footprints of consumers that is utilized for finding financial solution for emerging issues. AI and IoT are contributing in innovations related to decision making, extracting sensor information's, real time monitoring and in execution of sustainable finance.(Boșcoianu et. al., 2020; Musleh Al-Sartawi et. al., 2021; Shihadeh 2020).

Green finance is gaining attention around the world as a viable approach to address the needs of both environmentalism and business at the same time. Green Fintech is expected to account for a growing share of the worldwide Fintech business, which is expected to reach almost 500 billion dollars by 2025.

Companies are being encouraged to investigate Green Fintech due to political, demographic, and legal factors. Green Fintech's key consumers, Millennials and Generation Z, are particularly concerned about sustainability issues, and an emphasis on environmental, social, and corporate governance can help these new businesses grow and prosper post-pandemic.Sustainability has become a key factor in the middle of a digitization tsunami that is affecting the whole financial sector. Despite its challenges, Green Fintech has a lot of potential to not only help the EU achieve its Sustainable Development Goals, but also to act as a catalyst for green innovations that will help address climate change and make net-zero pathways and clean energy more accessible, measurable, and bankable.

REFERENCES

Ahmad, S. (2020). Reimagining sustainable financing through Fintech. *Business Line*. Available at: https://www.thehindubusinessline.com/opinion/reimagining-sustainable-financing-through-Fintech/article30878735.ece

Al-Fuqaha, Guizani, Mohammadi, Aledhari, & Ayyash. (n.d.). Internet of Things: A Survey on Enabling Technologies, Protocols, and Applications. *IEEE Communications Surveys and Tutorials*. . doi:10.1109/COMST.2015.2444095

Arena, M., Bengo, I., Calderini, M., & Chiodo, V. (2018). Unlocking Finance for social tech start-ups: Is there a new opportunity space? *Technological Forecasting and Social Change, 127*, 154–165. doi:10.1016/j.techfore.2017.05.035

ArnerD. W.BuckleyR. P.CharambaK.SergeevA.ZetzscheD. A. (2021). BigTech and Platform Finance: Governing Fintech 4.0 for Sustainable Development. Available at SSRN doi:10.2139/ssrn.3915275

Biswas, S., Carson, B., Chung, V., Singh, S., & Thomas, R. (2020). *AI-Bank of the future: Can Banks meet the AI Challenges*. McKinsey & Company. Available at:https://www.mckinsey.com/industries/financial-services/our-insights/ai-bank-of-the-future-can-banks-meet-the-ai-challenge

Boșcoianu, M., Ceocea, C., Vladareanu, V., & Vladareanu, L. (2020). Special purpose vehicles for sustainable finance of innovation in Romania-the case of intelligent robotic systems. *Periodicals of Engineering and Natural Sciences, 8*(3), 1418–1424.

Brue, M. (2021). *Keeping An "AI" On Fintech: AI-Based Use Cases Poised To Take Financial Services To The Next Level.* Available at: https://www.forbes.com/sites/moorinsights/2021/10/26/keeping-an-ai-on-Fintech-ai-based-use-cases-poised-to-take-financial-services-to-the-next-level/?sh=690d13a34b9f

CaoL. (2020). *AI in finance: A review.* Available at SSRN 3647625.

Golić, Z. (2019). Finance and artificial intelligence: The fifth industrial revolution and its impact on the financial sector. *Zbornik radova Ekonomskog fakulteta u Istočnom Sarajevu*, (19), 67-81.

Gomber, P., Koch, A., & Siering, M. (2017). Digital finance and research: Current research and future research directions. *Business Economics (Cleveland, Ohio)*, *87*, 537–580.

Gozmann, D., Libenau, J., & Mangan, J. (2018). The Innovation Mechanisms of Fintech Start-Ups: Insights from SWIFT's Innotribe Competition. *Management Information Systems*, *35*(1), 145–179. doi:10.1080/07421222.2018.1440768

Guo, H., & Polak, P. (2021). Artificial intelligence and financial technology Fintech: How AI is being used under the pandemic in 2020. The Fourth Industrial Revolution: Implementation of Artificial Intelligence for Growing Business Success, 169-186.

Haddad, C., & Hornuf, L. (2019). The emergence of the global Fintech market: Economic and technological determinants. *Small Business Economics*, *53*(1), 81–105. doi:10.100711187-018-9991-x

Leong, K., & Sung, A. (2018). Fintech (FinancialTechnology): What is it and how to use technologies to create business value in Fintech way? *International Journal of Innovation, Management and Technology*, *9*(2), 74–78. doi:10.18178/ijimt.2018.9.2.791

Macchiavello & Siri. (2020). *Sustainable Finance and Fintech: Can Technology Contribute to Achieving Environmental Goals? A Preliminary Assessment of 'Green Fintech'.* European Banking Institute Working Paper Series 2020 – no. 71. Available at *SSRN*: https://ssrn.com/abstract=3672989 doi:10.2139/ssrn.3672989

Mello, M. (2018). *US Fintech Sector: short-run and long-run performance of initial public offerings* (Doctoral dissertation).

Musleh Al-Sartawi, A. M., Razzaque, A., & Kamal, M. M. (Eds.). (2021). *Artificial Intelligence Systems and the Internet of Things in the Digital Era. EAMMIS 2021* (Vol. 239). Lecture Notes in Networks and Systems.

Nassiry, D. (2018). *The role of Fintech in unlocking green finance: Policy insights for developing countries* (No. 883). ADBI Working Paper.

Punschmann, T. (2017). Fintech. *Business & Information Systems Engineering, 59*(1), 69–76. doi:10.100712599-017-0464-6

Pustokhina, I. V., Pustokhin, D. A., Mohanty, S. N., García, P. A. G., & García-Díaz, V. (2021). Artificial intelligence assisted Internet of Things based financial crisis prediction in Fintech environment. *Annals of Operations Research*, 1–21.

Ranchber, S. (2018). *Stimulating Green Fintech Innovation for Sustainable Development: An Analysis of the Innovation Process*. Academic Press.

Ruiz-Real, J. L., Uribe-Toril, J., Torres, J. A., & De Pablo, J. (2021). Artificial intelligence in business and economics research: Trends and future. *Journal of Business Economics and Management, 22*(1), 98–117. doi:10.3846/jbem.2020.13641

Shihadeh, F. (2020). Online Payment Services and Individuals' Behaviour: New Evidence from the MENAP. *International Journal of Electronic Banking, 2*(4), 275–282. doi:10.1504/IJEBANK.2020.114763

Stockholm Green Digital Finance. (2017). *Unlocking the potential of green Fintech*. Author.

Tougaard, W. E. (2020). *Greening China - How Fintech drives Green Finance in China*. Available at: https://www.china-experience.com/china-experience-insights/how-Fintech-accelerates-chinas-sustainable-finance-ambitions

UNFCCC. (2015). *Paris Agreement. FCCC/CP/2015/10/Add.1*. Available at: https://unfccc.int/files/essential_background/convention/application/pdf/english_paris_agreement.pdf

United Nations. (2015a). *Transforming our world: the 2030 Agenda for Sustainable Development*. Available at: http://www.un.org/ga/search/view_doc.asp?symbol=A/RES/70/1&Lang=E

Yang, X. (2020). Fintech in Promoting the Development of Green Finance in China against the Background of Big Data and Artificial Intelligence. In *2020 4th International Seminar on Education Innovation and Economic Management (SEIEM)*. Francis Academic Press.

Zavolokina, L., Dolata, M. & Schwabe, G. (2016). The Fintech phenomenon: antecedents of financial innovation perceived by the popular press. *Financial Innovation, 2*(16).

Zilgalvis, P. (2014). The Need for an Innovation Principle in Regulatory Impact Assessment: The Case of Finance and Innovation in Europe. *Policy and Internet*, 6(4), 377–392. doi:10.1002/1944-2866.POI374

ADDITIONAL READING

Anshari, M., Almunawar, M. N., Masri, M., & Hamdan, M. (2019). Digital marketplace and FinTech to support agriculture sustainability. *Energy Procedia*, *156*, 234–238. doi:10.1016/j.egypro.2018.11.134

Davis, K., Maddock, R., & Foo, M. (2017). Catching up with Indonesia's fintech industry. *Law and Financial Markets Review*, *11*(1), 33–40. doi:10.1080/1752144 0.2017.1336398

Deng, X., Huang, Z., & Cheng, X. (2019). FinTech and sustainable development: Evidence from China based on P2P data. *Sustainability*, *11*(22), 6434. doi:10.3390u11226434

Iqbal, S., Taghizadeh-Hesary, F., Mohsin, M., & Iqbal, W. (2021). Assessing the role of the green finance index in environmental pollution reduction. *Estudios de Economía Aplicada*, *39*(3), 12. doi:10.25115/eea.v39i3.4140

Khare, A., Khare, K., & Baber, W. W. (2020). Why Japan's digital transformation is inevitable. In *Transforming Japanese Business* (pp. 3–14). Springer. doi:10.1007/978-981-15-0327-6_1

Kim, J. (2018). Leverage the financing role of banks for low-carbon energy transition. *Financing for Low-Carbon Energy Transition*, 189–210.

Lee, I., & Shin, Y. J. (2018). Fintech: Ecosystem, business models, investment decisions, and challenges. *Business Horizons*, *61*(1), 35–46. doi:10.1016/j.bushor.2017.09.003

Puschmann, T., Hoffmann, C. H., & Khmarskyi, V. (2020). How green FinTech can alleviate the impact of climate change—The case of Switzerland. *Sustainability*, *12*(24), 10691. doi:10.3390u122410691

Taghizadeh-Hesary, F., & Yoshino, N. (2019). The way to induce private participation in green finance and investment. *Finance Research Letters*, *31*, 98–103. doi:10.1016/j.frl.2019.04.016

Chapter 2
Review of the Blockchain Technology and Consensus Algorithms for IoT-Based Banking

Guneet Kaur
Cointelegraph, UK

ABSTRACT

The internet of things (IoT) is a global network that connects devices and people, yet it still confronts various challenges. This chapter explores the challenges banks face and how blockchain technology (integrated with IoT devices) can help address them. The chapter has also conducted a review of the different consensus mechanisms employed by the blockchain systems to find out which consensus method should be deployed by IoT-based banks. The underlying consensus method was first created for permissionless blockchain on a trustless network model using proof-of-work, which is a mathematical challenge that demands a lot of computing power. The findings of the study revealed that considering the regulatory requirements such as permissioned blockchains are best suitable for banks due to know your client (KYC) and anti-money laundering (AML) regulatory requirements. Additionally, for such a blockchain network, the practical byzantine fault tolerance (PBFT) and proof of authority (PoA) consensus methods ensure business resiliency.

DOI: 10.4018/978-1-6684-4176-3.ch002

INTRODUCTION

Banking and financial services organizations are the backbone of many countries' economic prosperity, and information technology (IT) aids in the management and scaling of services for banking institutions. Knowledge and information processing are the lifeblood of the financial industry. Products are developed, promoted, and distributed via IT systems and applications. Because IT drives all economic activity, an efficient banking system will allow money to move faster, resulting in increased growth and more substantial balance sheets, contributing to economic growth. Digital account opening; application programming interfaces (APIs); video collaboration, peer-to-peer (P2P) payments; and cloud computing are the top five technologies used by banks nowadays. Moreover, retail banking, business, and corporate banking, and investment banking are the three primary categories of banking services (Ramalingam & Venkatesan, 2019).

- Retail banking- Provides savings, deposits, and loans to individual consumers.
- Business and corporate banking- Provides current accounts, payments, cash management, trade finance, guarantees, and foreign exchange (FOREX) services to small, medium, and large businesses.
- Investment banking- Advisory, investment research, brokerage, mergers & acquisitions, and wealth management are all examples of investment banking services.

Banks rely on IT infrastructure to handle their own data processing and link to their various ATM/POS terminals. Retail banks use consumer-facing ATM/POS devices as edge data interfaces to collect multiple forms of banking customer data. The IT infrastructure of a bank is made up of a mix of hardware and software-based systems that store, process, and communicate banking-related data. Branch connectivity is available 24 hours a day, seven days a week, and any downtime is unacceptable. Large data centers can accommodate various databases and software applications for financial products. With the Internet of Things (IoT) power, digital banking brings the above infrastructure closer to acquiring client data, and ATM/POS terminals/mobile banking are evolving. For instance, IoT-based video capturing devices might be used to collect data on customer experience in retail banking and open up new avenues for improvement.

While the big banks are aggressively innovating in many areas to combat competition from so-called "challenger" banks and fintech start-ups, they have mostly left the IoT to other industries, such as retail and manufacturing. Furthermore, the present IoT architecture is based on the server/client model, which is a centralized concept (Atlam et al., 2018). In this arrangement, all devices cannot communicate with one another and must instead communicate through a centralized gateway. For many years, the centralized model has been used to link a wide range of computing devices, and it will continue to support small-scale IoT networks in the future, but it will not be able to meet the needs to expand the IoT system. In addition, data manipulation is a risk with the centralized architecture. However, collecting data in real-time does not guarantee that it is put to excellent and appropriate use. In contrast, payments, enhanced operability (to allow open banking), and better mobile services are essential for banking organizations to survive the fintech competition. Many of these difficulties could be solved with a decentralized IoT solution. Blockchain is one of the most widely used decentralization techniques (Qian et al., 2018). In this context, this chapter focuses on '*how blockchain can address various challenges faced by the banks and what consensus algorithms should be adopted to implement a IoT-based banking system.*'

The remainder of this chapter is divided into the following sections. First, the background on IoT and blockchain is covered in Section 2. Section 3 highlights the primary challenges that banks are now facing and how blockchain could help solve these issues and several consensus techniques are discussed in Section 4. Finally, section 5 discusses the application of consensus algorithms in IoT-based banking, while section 6 investigates potential study discrepancies and suggestions for improvement before section 7 concludes.

RELATED WORK

Several papers have looked into using a blockchain system in the IoT. This chapter will discuss the existing work in this area to find the research gap.

The phrase "Internet of Things" was first coined in 1998 by Kevin Ashton at the Massachusetts Institute of Technology (MIT), and it was characterized as allowing people and things to be connected anytime, anywhere, with anything and anyone, ideally via any path/ network and any service" (Sundmaeker et al., 2010). The Internet of Things has progressed through five stages, beginning with the connection of two computers, then expanding to a vast number of computers with the advent of the World Wide Web. The mobile Internet, which connects mobile devices to the Internet, is followed by the people-Internet supported by social networks. Finally, the IoT emerged as the universe of networked devices (Perera et al., 2014). The Internet of Things is growing at a breakneck speed, influencing every aspect of daily life. Connected items are definitely paving the way for new applications in various industries. For example, banking, insurance, and transportation services will undoubtedly benefit from these technologies' ability to collect, process, and communicate a large amount of data quickly and autonomously (Wünderlich et al., 2013).

Casino et al. (2019) provided that the huge amounts of data generated by the Internet of Things are believed to be of significant business value, and data mining methods can be used to extract hidden information from the data. Classification, clustering, association analysis, time series analysis, and outlier analysis were reviewed in a systematic approach by Casino et al. (2019) in terms of knowledge, technique, and application. In addition, the most recent application cases were examined. As more devices become connected to the Internet of Things, they recommend that a vast volume of data should be examined and that current algorithms be changed to adapt to big data. Ammirato et al. (2019) provided an adequate reason for using an IPS (Intelligent Protection System) to oversee security management operations as part of an IoT trial for banking physical security. Although they did not extrapolate their findings from the Italian banking security system, the literature analysis and scarcity of research urged them to look into the usage of the Internet of Things for bank physical security in a broader sense.

Khanboubi et al. (2019) identified seven IoT-based digital trends that directly affect financial services: mobile banking, M-banking, crowd-based financing, virtual money, high-frequency trading firms, cyber criminality, big data, and IT analytics. Suseendran et al. (2020) explored IoT use-cases in banking and found that biometrics (voice/touch) can enable account access via the digital channel more accessible from anywhere. They further provided that the customer can sign in remotely using any touch screen device and be marked on paper with Wet Ink using a new Wet Ink technology. New daily leasing models have enabled digital assets throughout the world, effectively turning traditional items and services into digital assets. The rented resources could be fastened or disabled remotely by the bank for delineations. Mohaghar et al. (2021) researched and prioritized IoT applications in the Iranian banking industry based on business continuity indicators. According to the findings, IoT-based financial services, such as transmitting immediate reporting, smart ATMs, non-contact electronic payments, and electronic checks have been discovered for Iranian banks. Then, based on the capacities of Iranian banks, these appropriate services are prioritized.

Vimal Jerald et al. (2015) proposed an IoT-based integrated smart environment. Agriculture, banking, household appliance monitoring, security and emergency, surveillance, education, health care, meteorology, government e-services, and traffic surveillance are among the domains where radio frequency identification (RFID) technology is being used to connect diverse objects and devices. They also discussed how RFID technology and sensor networks are used to connect many sectors. It also proposed the creation of an IoT information Kendra, which infers and processes data retrieved from various smart environment sectors. The operation of cloud-based computing and data center and an administration and management center linked to the IoT information Kendra are also covered. Furthermore, Bansal et al. (2020) discussed the breadth of IoT in the banking industry and how various transformations could potentially lead to game-changing changes in traditional banking practices. They concluded that banking institutions should integrate IoT into their systems to enhance their market share by providing services tailored to a client's needs based on real-time data processing. In the future, IoT will be able to develop technologies that will allow physical items to communicate with one another and make intelligent decisions on their own. In contrast, Alti & Almuhirat (2021) developed an evaluation model that can collect incoming sensor performance data from work environments, analyze data from diverse employers, and determine their performance while tailoring multi-criteria decision-making. For practically all training programs and decision-making managers, the experimental results revealed that an IoT-based solution provides significantly superior performance than existing tools in the literature.

Majeed et al. (2021) examined the role of blockchain in enabling IoT-based smart cities in depth. The evolution of blockchain technology is first presented in terms of constituent technologies, consensus algorithms, and blockchain platforms. Secondly, they examined and assessed a variety of blockchain-enabled smart applications. Third, they provided case studies of real-world blockchain deployment in smart cities. Lastly, they outlined the most important prerequisites for integrating blockchain with smart cities, followed by open research challenges, root causes, and potential remedies. In addition to it, Dineshreddy & Gangadharan (2016) described an architecture for the banking and finance sector that uses the Internet of Things to manage mobile devices, wearable sensors, household gadgets, and other sensing devices for various insurance and retail applications, banking, and investments. By evaluating customers' data, they offered a case study of how different banking applications flow with IoT intelligence. They also proposed the architecture to several banks and financial industry applications. However, supporting legacy IT infrastructure is a big problem in integrating IoT technologies in banks. As a result, it must be rebuilt in order to simplify complicated systems and successfully accommodate modern technology. Identity management, energy-efficient sensing, greening IoT, scalability, security and privacy, communication mechanisms, integration of smart components, and global cooperation are some of the technical difficulties surrounding the internet of things. Data sharing between heterogeneous elements (interoperability), successfully handling ambiguous information, and service adaptability in a dynamic system environment are among the scientific problems.

The literature review identified essential research gaps in existing IoT–blockchain-based retail banking facilities. In such a situation, there is a lack of discussion about consensus algorithms that can help solve issues in retail banking such as remittances, fraud, and contract management. As a result, by reviewing blockchain technology and the characteristics of a consensus algorithm for IoT-based retail banks, this chapter contributes to closing these research gaps.

BLOCKCHAIN TECHNOLOGY AND ITS BENEFITS FOR BANKING ORGANIZATIONS

Features of Blockchain Technology

Blockchain is an *immutable distributed ledger* that is spread among the network's devices. Immutability refers to the inability to change or alter anything. This is one of the essential blockchain aspects for ensuring that the technology stays - a permanent, unchangeable network. A blockchain is a chain of indestructible blocks, also known as distributed ledger technology (DLT) (Acharjamayum et al., 2018). A public ledger contains the details of a transaction and the participants. These blocks hold the records linked together using hash (a 256-bit number wedded to the nonce) values. A genesis block is the first block in a blockchain (Samaniego et al., 2016). If a new block is added, the previous block's hash value is input and validated using the backtracking method, which is immediately available to all network participants. The acquired data is decentralized in blockchain network nodes (Urmila et al., 2019). The *network is decentralized*, so there is no governing authority or one individual in charge of the infrastructure. Instead, the network is maintained by a collection of nodes, making it decentralized.

There is a block header and a block body in each block. The following can be found in the block header:

- Block version- indicates software version and validation rules.
- Merkle Tree root hash- represents the transaction's hash value as well as a summary of all transactions.
- Timestamp- Since January 1970, the current universal time has been used as the timestamp.
- N-Bits- refers to the number of bits needed to verify something. Parent block hash- contains the hash value that denotes the previous block.
- Nonce- stores any 4-byte number that starts at 0 and increases for every transaction's hash.

The block body covers all transaction records. The block size determines the maximum number of transactions that can be made. This blockchain continues to expand as new blocks are added to it regularly. For user security, public-key cryptography and distributed consensus procedures are used. The purpose of blockchain is to enable the recording and distribution of digital data without modifying it. In this sense, a blockchain serves as the foundation for immutable ledgers or transaction records that can't be changed, erased, or destroyed. Blockchain is a hybrid of three cutting-edge technologies:

- Keys used in cryptography.
- A peer-to-peer network with a distributed ledger.
- A computer system for storing network transactions and records.

Two keys are used in cryptography: private and public keys, which aid in the practical completion of transactions between two parties (Iyer & Dannen, 2018). These two keys are unique to each person and are used to create a secure digital identity reference. Cryptocurrencies (digital currencies) developed on blockchain networks rely on public and private keys, which are part of a more considerable discipline of cryptography known as Public Key Cryptography (PKC) or Asymmetric Encryption (Huang et al., 2021). The public and private keys, generally symbolized by a padlock (public key) and the actual key (the private key) to open the padlock, are used in PKC. Additionally, the most significant component of blockchain technology is secure identity. This identity is known as a 'digital signature' in the crypto world, and it is used for authorizing and managing transactions. The peer-to-peer network is combined with the digital signature; many people acting as authorities use the digital signature to reach a consensus on transactions and other issues. It is verified mathematically when they approve a transaction, resulting in a successful secured transaction between the two networked parties. To summarize, blockchain users use cryptographic keys to conduct various forms of digital transactions through a peer-to-peer network. When combined with decentralization, cryptography adds another degree of *security* for consumers.

In addition to the above, consensus algorithms are at the heart of any blockchain. Every blockchain has a consensus mechanism in place to assist the network in making choices. The consensus is a decision-making mechanism for the network's active nodes in their most basic form. The nodes can reach an agreement immediately and relatively quickly in this case. A consensus is required for a system to work smoothly when millions of nodes are validating a transaction (Nguyen & Kim, 2018). It's similar to a voting system in which the majority wins, and the minority is forced to support it. The network is trustless due to the consensus. Nodes may not trust each other, but the algorithms at the heart of the system may be trusted. As a result, every network choice is a win-win situation for the blockchain. It's one of the advantages of blockchain technology. There are numerous blockchain consensus algorithms in use around the world (these will be discussed later in this chapter). Each has its own distinct method of making decisions and perfecting prior techniques' errors. On the internet, blockchain architecture establishes a world of justice.

Written contracts help all businesses, regardless of size or industry. Unfortunately, they are frequently inconvenient and a source of legal and corporate strife. Traditional contracts can be replaced with smart contracts as a solution in the blockchain world. Furthermore, a smart contract on the blockchain aims to make business and trading between anonymous and identified participants easier, without an intermediary. A smart contract is a software that runs on the blockchain. It's a collection of code (its functions) and data (its state) stored on the blockchain at a specific address. On a particular blockchain, smart contracts are a type of account. This indicates that they have a balance and can send transactions across the network. However, they are not controlled by a user; instead, they are deployed to the network and run according to a set of instructions. User accounts can then engage with a smart contract by sending transactions that cause the smart contract to perform a function. Smart contracts, like conventional contracts, can set rules and have them enforced automatically through programming. By default, smart contracts cannot be deleted, and interactions with them are irreversible.

Major Challenges in Banking and How Blockchain can Address Them

Payments and Remittances

Remittances have long been a part of a "financial inclusion assemblage" (Schwittay, 2011) that includes public agencies, philanthropic groups, business players, and consortia working toward inclusion and, more recently, digitization. Simultaneously, the "migration-development nexus" concept portrays remittances as an untapped sector of an informal value transfer (Faist, 2008) that could burst in size if more people had access to formalized financial institutions as well as mobile and digital technology. Furthermore, the value of cross-border payments is expected to rise from almost $150 trillion in 2017 to more than $250 trillion by 2027, a rise of more than $100 trillion in only ten years (Bank of England, 2022). Even though many fintech businesses have emerged that provide cheaper costs, there is still a desire for safe financial services at a reasonable price. Blockchain, which was originally designed for cryptocurrencies, may meet that demand. Interoperability, or the mutual visibility of ledgers, standards, payment infrastructures, and individual clients and transactions, is crucial to implementing blockchain technologies in correspondent banking.

Since their debut, payments and remittances have been critical use cases for blockchain technologies. The original blockchain, Bitcoin, claimed to administer a distributed payment network without the need for centralized accounting, clearing, or settlement entity (Rella, 2019). BitPesa was the first application of blockchain technology. BitPesa, which was founded in 2013 and was inspired by the success of Kenya's M-Pesa (Omwansa and Sullivan, 2012), manages payments between two fiat currencies by matching them with payments from the originating currency to Bitcoin and from Bitcoin to the currency of the destination country (McKay, 2014). BitPesa has since expanded its geographical reach to include eight African countries, and it has shifted its focus away from P2P remittances and toward business-to-business (B2B) operations, thus losing its original focus on remittances (DuPont, 2019, p. 19). On the other hand, Ripple remained focused on cross-border payments, but it moved its emphasis from peer-to-peer to interbank transfers, intending to replace correspondent banking (Rosner & Kang, 2015). Ripple, which is older than Bitcoin, began in 2004 as a mutual credit network similar to a hawala, a time bank, or a Local Exchange Trading System (LETS) (Rella, 2019). Ripple's primary purpose was to create a platform for scaling up LETS and other alternative currencies (Fugger, 2004). Ripple evolved into the XRP Ledger, a distributed ledger system that integrates the mutual credit network with the crypto asset XRP and a distributed currency exchange between 2012 and 2013 (Rella, 2020). Ripple is also the corporation's name that provides payment services based on the XRP Ledger and other technologies. Ripple has been focusing on interbank payments since 2015 to become a competitor to Society for Worldwide Interbank Financial Telecommunication (SWIFT), and it now has 200 customers in 40 countries (Rella, 2019).

Know-Your-Customer/ID Fraud

Know-your-customer tools aid banks in combating fraud, which has emerged as one of the most significant concerns facing financial institutions and their clients. ID vulnerabilities, remote deposit fraud, and identity theft are the most serious dangers. As a result, banks should strengthen their security measures to safeguard critical data. Money laundering is as difficult to combat as fraud, which is why banks adopted anti-money laundering (AML) laws to mitigate risk. Ripple also claims to address another source of correspondent banking de-risking, namely KYC-AML compliance expenses, in addition to transaction costs. Ripple has promised to provide greater transparency of funds transfers than SWIFT can provide in several hearings and public discussions. Ripple explained the visibility of transactions on the XRP Ledger in answer to the UK payment system regulator, saying, "Unlike payments conducted through correspondent banking today, which are opaque at best, Ripple Ledger provides comprehensive end-to-end transaction traceability" (Gifford, 2015, p. 13). This is a significant shift from the initial concerns about anonymity and privacy that ushered in blockchain technologies and cryptocurrencies (Swartz, 2018).

Contract Management

The relationship between a banker and a consumer is based on a contract between the two parties. It is governed by contract law because it is a contractual relationship. On the other hand, contract law does not provide the consumer with the necessary protection against the bank (Plato-Shinar, 2012). In this context, blockchain technology could be a valuable tool for completing smart contracts such as loans or building funding (it is not just for quick and painless transactions or account opening. The main benefit of blockchain is that all records can be processed without an intermediary, resulting in a higher level of trust. Banks, for example, might assert their treaty rights without resorting to judicial action by merging blockchain and IoT. If a client agrees, more favorable terms and conditions may be provided to them. Nonetheless, there are still certain limitations and flaws. For example, the primary impediment to banking embracing blockchain for smart contracts is legal jurisdiction.

CONSENSUS ALGORITHMS

A consensus mechanism is a fault-tolerant mechanism used in computer and blockchain systems to achieve the necessary agreement among distributed processes or multi-agent systems, such as cryptocurrencies, on a single data value or a single network state (Ferdous et al., 2020). Consensus algorithms decide how the blockchain works and protect the block from unauthorized users, which is the root of the blockchain transaction. There are a variety of consensus mechanism algorithms, each of which operates on a different set of principles. These are explained in below sub-sections.

Proof-of-Work (PoW)

Bitcoin was the first to use proof of work as a crypto consensus technique. The concepts of proof of work and mining are intertwined. The network demands a large amount of computing power, which is why it's termed "proof of work" (Bach et al., 2018). Virtual miners worldwide compete to be the first to solve a math challenge to protect and verify proof-of-work blockchains. The winner updates the blockchain with the most recent verified transactions and is paid with a set amount of cryptocurrency by the network. Proof of work provides many benefits, especially for a simple but precious cryptocurrency like Bitcoin. It's a tried-and-true method of keeping a decentralized blockchain safe. As a cryptocurrency's value rises, more miners are enticed to join the network, increasing its power and security. Because of the computing power required, tampering with the blockchain of a valuable cryptocurrency is unfeasible for any individual or group. On the other hand, it's a time-consuming procedure that may struggle to scale to handle many transactions that smart-contract compatible blockchains like Ethereum can generate (Gramoli, 2020). As a result, new options have emerged, the most prominent known as proof of stake.

Proof-of-Stake (PoS)

The Ethereum developers knew from the start that proof of work would have scalability issues that would need to be addressed and, indeed, as Ethereum-powered decentralized finance (or DeFi) protocols have grown in popularity, the blockchain has struggled to keep up, causing fees to skyrocket (Kim, 2018). Staking in a proof of stake system is similar to mining in a proof of work system in that it is the method by which a network participant is chosen to add the most recent batch of transactions to the blockchain in exchange for some coin (Gao & Nobuhara, 2017).

Proof of stake blockchains use a network of "validators" who contribute or "stake" their own crypto in exchange for a chance to validate new transactions, update the blockchain, and earn a reward. The network chooses a winner based on the quantity of crypto each validator has in the pool and the length of time they've had it there, thus rewarding those who have put the most effort into it. Other validators can attest to the accuracy of the latest block of transactions once the winner has confirmed it. In addition, the blockchain is updated when a certain amount of attestations have been made. All validators earn a reward in the native cryptocurrency, which is dispersed proportionally to each validator's stake by the network. Becoming a validator is a significant duty requiring a high level of technical expertise. Validators must stake a certain amount of crypto (for example, 32 ETH for Ethereum's upcoming version), and validators might lose some of their stake through a process known as slashing if their node goes down or if they validate a "bad" block of transactions (Bach et al., 2018). Even if that sounds like too much responsibility, you may still participate in staking by joining a staking pool controlled by someone else, earning incentives for bitcoin that would otherwise be idle. Delegating is a term used to describe this process, and tools provided by exchanges like Coinbase can make it smooth and straightforward.

Delegated Proof-of-Stake (DPoS)

Delegated proof of stake is similar to PoS, with the addition of a vote and delegation mechanism to encourage users to protect the network with their staked collateral (Yang et al., 2019). To participate in the PoS and DPoS consensus mechanisms, users must stake their coins. On the other hand, a successful block production requires network users to elect witnesses or delegates, and only the delegates and voters who are elected can validate transactions. Block producers or witnesses are terms used to describe elected delegates. When a delegated proof of stake is employed, users can vote on delegates by combining all of their coins into a centralized staking pool then linking those coins to a certain delegate (Saad et al., 2020). It is vital to remember that the funds are not physically transferred from one wallet to another when a user links to a delegate. Therefore, it is critical that when delegates are finally elected, they can agree on which transactions should be refused and authorized. Stake-delegated proof blockchains have a couple of drawbacks, despite their benefits in terms of inclusivity and protecting users from double-spending. For instance, if just a small number of users are allowed to function as witnesses, the network may become centralized (Saad et al., 2020). Weighted voting is also a possibility in which people with a little stake in the currency elect not to vote.

Proof of Importance (PoI)

New Economic Movement (NEM) or 'UtopianFuture' was the first to introduce Proof of Importance, a blockchain consensus algorithm (Krishnamurthi & Shree, 2019). The Proof of Importance technique is used to identify which network participants (nodes) are qualified to add a block to the blockchain, a process called 'harvesting' by NEM (Krishnamurthi & Shree, 2019). Nodes can receive transaction fees within a block in return for harvesting it. Accounts with a higher significance score are more likely to be selected to harvest a block. Proof of Importance is a novel consensus method since, unlike previous consensus mechanisms like proof of stake, it aims to consider one's overall support for the network. Proof of stake, for example, can be used to argue that it rewards currency hoarders. Nodes are confined to 'mining' a percentage of transactions that reflects their share in a coin under the proof of stake architecture. Proof of stake miner who owns 10% of a cryptocurrency, for example, would be allowed to mine 10% of the network's blocks. The drawback of this consensus approach is that it encourages network nodes to keep their coins rather than spend them. It also creates a scenario where "the rich get richer," as large coin holders can mine a higher percentage of the network's blocks. Proof of Importance aims to solve the flaws that plague the proof of stake concept by determining an account's overall network support. This is accomplished by considering three factors: vesting, transaction partners, and the quantity and amount of transactions in the previous 30 days.

Practical Byzantine Fault Tolerance (PBFT)

Barbara Liskov and Miguel Castro proposed Practical Byzantine Fault Tolerance in the late 1990s as a consensus technique (Hao et al., 2018). Asynchronous (no upper bound on when the response to the request will be received) systems were created with pBFT in mind. It is designed to have a reduced overhead time. Its purpose was to address several issues with existing Byzantine Fault Tolerance methods. Distributed computing and blockchain are two examples of application areas. BFT (Byzantine Fault Tolerance) is a distributed network feature that allows it to attain consensus (agreement on the same value) even when some nodes in the network fail to reply or respond with inaccurate information (Zhang & Li, 2018). The goal of a BFT mechanism is to protect against system failures by utilizing collective decision-making (both right and faulty nodes) to reduce the influence of faulty nodes. Byzantine Generals' Problem is the source of BFT. The Byzantine Generals Problem explains how difficult it is for decentralized systems to agree on a single truth (Chondros et al., 2012) Until the invention of Bitcoin, the Byzantine Generals Problem plagued money for millennia. To overcome the Byzantine Generals Problem, Bitcoin employs a Proof-of-Work method and a blockchain. There are four phases to the pBFT consensus rounds (Hao et al., 2018):

- A request is sent from the client to the primary(leader) node.
- The request is disseminated to all secondary (backup) nodes by the primary (leader) node.
- The nodes (main and secondary) provide the desired service and then respond to the client.
- When the client receives 'm+1' responses with the same result from different nodes in the network, the request is successfully fulfilled, where m is the maximum number of defective nodes allowed.

A view change protocol can be used to replace the primary(leader) node if a predetermined amount of time has passed without the leading node broadcasting a request to the backups (secondary). If necessary, a majority of the honest nodes can vote on the current leading node's legitimacy and replace it with the next in line. However, due to the large communication overhead that grows exponentially with each additional node in the network, the pBFT consensus model only works efficiently when the number of nodes in the distributed network is minimal.

Sybil assaults, in which one entity (person) controls several identities, are vulnerable to the pBFT methods (Sukhwani et al., 2017). Sybil attacks get more difficult to carry out as the number of nodes in the network grows. However, because pBFT techniques have scalability concerns, they are employed in conjunction with other mechanisms. Furthermore, because of the overhead of communication (with all the other nodes at every step), pBFT does not scale effectively. For example, the number of nodes in the network grows as $O(n^k)$, where n is the number of messages and k is the number of nodes (Fan, 2018).

Proof of Authority (POA)

Proof-of-Authority is a novel class of Byzantine fault-tolerant consensus algorithms widely utilized in practice to provide higher performance than standard PBFT. Parity and Geth, two well-known Ethereum permissioned setting clients, are now using it (De Angelis et al., 2018). Intuitively, the algorithms work in rounds, with an elected party serving as the mining leader and proposing new blocks on which distributed consensus is reached (Al Asad et al., 2020). The PoA consensus mechanism makes use of the value of identities, which implies that block validators stake their own reputation rather than money. As a result, validating nodes that are arbitrarily designated as trustworthy individuals safeguard PoA blockchains. The Proof of Authority concept allows businesses to protect their anonymity while making use of blockchain technology's benefits. Additionally, PoA, unlike PBFT, involves fewer message exchanges and delivers superior performance (Dinh et al., 2017). However, the practical repercussions of such performance enhancements are unclear, particularly in terms of availability and consistency guarantees in a realistic, eventually synchronous network topology like the Internet (De Angelis et al., 2018).

Proof of Elapsed Time (PoET)

Proof of elapsed time is a consensus technique developed by Intel Corporation (The Hyperledger Sawtooth project) to determine who creates the next block in permissioned blockchain networks (Bowman et al., 2021). PoET uses a lottery method that distributes the chances of winning evenly among network participants, ensuring that each node has an equal chance of winning. The PoET algorithm assigns each node in the blockchain network a random wait time, and each node must sleep for that length. The node with the least wait time will be the first to wake up and win the block, allowing it to add a new block to the blockchain. PoET's workflow is similar to Bitcoin's proof of work, but it uses less energy because it allows a node to sleep and transition to other jobs for a set period.

PoET is a scalable and efficient consensus and block creation algorithm. The procedure is ideal for use on private blockchain networks, and it is specifically designed for controlled commercial environments (Kumar et al., 2019). Validators are chosen and accepted to ensure that the network is resistant to both external and internal threats. On these networks, however, there are attack vehicles that use Intel processor vulnerabilities. Furthermore, it is heavily reliant on Intel technology. Despite the fact that the method is open source and can be ported to other platforms, the alterations would render these networks practically incompatible or cause major incompatibility issues.

APPLICATION OF BLOCKCHAIN NETWORK AND RELATED CONSENSUS ALGORITHM(S) IN IOT-BASED BANKING

Mingxiao et al. (2017) provided that public, private, and permissioned blockchains are the three types of blockchains, as explained below.

A public blockchain is available to everyone in a public space. Anyone can join the nodes and contribute in order to receive the rewards if they follow the rules (Mohan, 2019). There are no node-to-node trust relationships. The public blockchain is entirely decentralized and open. On the public blockchain, no transaction can be modified or cancelled. The consensus algorithms PoW, PoS, and DPoS are popular candidates for public blockchains.

The blockchain owner has the ultimate authority to update the information in a private blockchain and the rest of the nodes have restricted read access. In comparison to the public blockchain, the private blockchain has the advantages of being easy to modify and having a cheap transaction cost (Dinh et al., 2017). Only a few high-credit nodes are required for transaction verification on the private blockchain. Private blockchain is used in more secure networks like intranets. Crash defects are more crucial to fix than Byzantine faults. Organizations can employ the PBFT consensus method depending on the network size.

Permissioned blockchain is one in which the primary nodes are pre-specified by the participants and the blockchain is made up of several parties (Helliar et al., 2020). Members of the permissioned blockchain do not have complete faith in one another. According to the regulations, each participant chooses their own consensus node. Therefore, most consensus nodes must be able to recognize transactions. The consortium blockchain falls between public and private blockchains in terms of openness and centralization. The permissioned blockchain is appropriate for a semi-closed network developed by multiple businesses. Because there may be disagreements between different firms, and certain nodes may turn malevolent, it is preferable to employ PBFT in this situation (Mingxiao et al., 2017).

Therefore, it is vital to evaluate the sort of blockchain network employed in the system when choosing a consensus protocol. The blockchain network should allow participants to check the history of a digital value and its associated transaction records in the banking business. Regulatory requirements such as KYC and AML provide additional reasons to prefer permissioned blockchains for financial applications (Lewis et al., 2017), as transactions on a fully public, permissionless blockchain are anonymous and open to all. In contrast, private blockchains can limit participants to those who have been pre-approved and trusted. It is also feasible to put rules in place in permissioned blockchains to allow varied access levels to the information in the ledger. Regulators, for example, might be able to see all the information of a transaction in the ledger but not add any. In contrast, users would only see certain elements of transactions based on their access level. As an IoT system grows and improves, the number of IoT devices in a network might grow. In this situation, the consensus algorithm is supposed to guarantee stable operation. Therefore, it is essential to consider network node failure while creating blockchain solutions for IoT systems. The breakdown of individual devices' hardware should not fail the entire system. In the case of a centralized banking system, power, wealth, and resources are concentrated in the hands of a few people. The PBFT mechanism in blockchain can make the system transparent, responsible, and corrupt-free. Similarly, the PoA consensus method allows a system of verifiable banks, each of which functions as its own validator, to maintain greater efficiency in transaction verification and achieve agreement without giving up a significant amount of influence, privacy, or power in the process by requiring a majority to affirm the state of the blockchain. Hence, PBFT (Mingxiao et al., 2017) and PoA (De Angelis et al., 2018) consensus algorithms are recommended for IoT-based banking businesses.

LIMITATIONS OF THE STUDY AND FUTURE WORK

In banking, IoT devices must provide sensitive and private information about clients, which, by law, must be kept secret and confidential. The majority of IoT devices rely on existing centralized server data management technology, which does not guarantee authenticity or security. Therefore, this study reviewed the benefits of blockchain technology, a decentralized network system that disperses data transactions across nodes. Moreover, with its consensus mechanism, blockchain can solve significant banking difficulties by allowing for decentralized computing of IoT data. Therefore, the use of IoT and blockchain technology in conjunction with a consensus algorithm may be the best option for developing safe distributed e-banking systems.

However, the study involves a qualitative review of consensus algorithms and blockchain's application in banking, which means that the findings cannot be statistically verified, and it is challenging to investigate causality. Therefore, future studies could concentrate on data analysis to assess the performance of consensus algorithms for e-banking systems. Additionally, the structure and semantics of technical and non-technical data transferred in the e-banking system to provide security guarantees can be analyzed.

CONCLUSION

Blockchain is a revolutionary technology generating a lot of attention in the banking sector because of its decentralization, immutability, and data integrity qualities. The underlying consensus method was first created for permissionless blockchain on a trustless network model using proof-of-work, which is a mathematical challenge that demands a lot of computing power. Because this approach has poor performance, alternative consensus algorithms such as proof-of-stake were developed. Moreover, considering the challenges faced by banks, such as payments/remittance, KYC/ID fraud, and contract management, it is evident that blockchain technology is a valuable tool to ensure instant clearance of funds, security, end-to-end transaction traceability, and implement smart contracts so that transactions can be processed without an intermediary.

Furthermore, the study discovered that it is critical to consider the type of blockchain network that a bank will deploy when selecting a consensus protocol. The reasons to prefer permissioned blockchains for financial applications include regulatory requirements such as Know-Your-Client (KYC) and Anti-money laundering (AML). In addition, the number of IoT devices in a network may increase as an IoT system grows and improves. Therefore, the chosen consensus algorithms should ensure business resiliency. As a result, the findings of the study provided that the Practical Byzantine Fault Tolerance (PBFT) and Proof of Authority (PoA) is efficient for permissioned blockchains (the type of blockchain network suitable for banks). Finally, this chapter proposes to develop a blockchain system with these consensus algorithms that shall improve IoT-based banking systems more efficiently.

REFERENCES

Acharjamayum, I., Patgiri, R., & Devi, D. (2018, November). Blockchain: a tale of peer to peer security. In *2018 IEEE Symposium Series on Computational Intelligence (SSCI)* (pp. 609-617). IEEE. 10.1109/SSCI.2018.8628826

Alti, A., & Almuhirat, A. (2021). An Advanced IoT-Based Tool for Effective Employee Performance Evaluation in the Banking Sector. *Ingénierie des Systèmes d Inf.*, *26*(1), 103–108. doi:10.18280/isi.260111

Al Asad, N., Elahi, M. T., Al Hasan, A., & Yousuf, M. A. (2020, November). Permission-Based Blockchain with Proof of Authority for Secured Healthcare Data Sharing. In *2020 2nd International Conference on Advanced Information and Communication Technology (ICAICT)* (pp. 35-40). IEEE. 10.1109/ICAICT51780.2020.9333488

Ammirato, S., Sofo, F., Felicetti, A. M., & Raso, C. (2019). A methodology to support the adoption of IoT innovation and its application to the Italian bank branch security context. *European Journal of Innovation Management*, *22*(1), 1–28. doi:10.1108/EJIM-03-2018-0058

Atlam, H. F., Alenezi, A., Alassafi, M. O., & Wills, G. B. (2018). Blockchain with Internet of Things: Benefits, challenges, and future directions. *International Journal of Intelligent Systems & Applications*, *10*(6), 1–10. doi:10.5815/ijisa.2018.06.05

Bach, L. M., Mihaljevic, B., & Zagar, M. (2018, May). Comparative analysis of blockchain consensus algorithms. In *2018 41st International Convention on Information and Communication Technology, Electronics and Microelectronics (MIPRO)* (pp. 1545-1550). IEEE. 10.23919/MIPRO.2018.8400278

Bank of England. 2022. *Cross-border payments*. Available at: https://www.bankofengland.co.uk/payment-and-settlement/cross-border-payments

Bansal, M., Oberoi, N., & Sameer, M. (2020). IoT in Online Banking. *Journal of Ubiquitous Computing and Communication Technologies*, *2*(04), 219–222. doi:10.36548/jucct.2020.4.005

Bowman, M., Das, D., Mandal, A., & Montgomery, H. (2021). On Elapsed Time Consensus Protocols. *IACR Cryptol.*, 86.

Casino, F., Dasaklis, T. K., & Patsakis, C. (2019). A systematic literature review of blockchain-based applications: Current status, classification and open issues. *Telematics and Informatics*, *36*, 55–81. doi:10.1016/j.tele.2018.11.006

Chondros, N., Kokordelis, K., & Roussopoulos, M. (2012, December). On the practicality of practical byzantine fault tolerance. In *ACM/IFIP/USENIX International Conference on Distributed Systems Platforms and Open Distributed Processing* (pp. 436-455). Springer. 10.1007/978-3-642-35170-9_22

De Angelis, S., Aniello, L., Baldoni, R., Lombardi, F., Margheri, A., & Sassone, V. (2018). *PBFT vs proof-of-authority: Applying the CAP theorem to permissioned blockchain*. Academic Press.

Dineshreddy, V., & Gangadharan, G. R. (2016, March). Towards an "Internet of Things" framework for financial services sector. In *2016 3rd International Conference on Recent Advances in Information Technology (RAIT)* (pp. 177-181). IEEE.

Dinh, T. T. A., Wang, J., Chen, G., Liu, R., Ooi, B. C., & Tan, K. L. (2017, May). Blockbench: A framework for analyzing private blockchains. In *Proceedings of the 2017 ACM International Conference on Management of Data* (pp. 1085-1100). 10.1145/3035918.3064033

DuPont. (2019). *Cryptocurrencies and blockchains*. John Wiley & Sons.

Fan, X. (2018, October). Scalable practical byzantine fault tolerance with short-lived signature schemes. In *Proceedings of the 28th Annual International Conference on Computer Science and Software Engineering* (pp. 245-256). Academic Press.

Faist, T. (2008). Migrants as transnational development agents: An inquiry into the newest round of the migration–development nexus. *Population Space and Place, 14*(1), 21–42. doi:10.1002/psp.471

Ferdous, M. S., Chowdhury, M. J. M., Hoque, M. A., & Colman, A. (2020). *Blockchain consensus algorithms: A survey.* arXiv preprint arXiv:2001.07091.

Fugger, R. (2004). *Money as IOUs in social trust networks & a proposal for a decentralized currency network protocol.* http://ripple. sourceforge. net

Gao, Y., & Nobuhara, H. (2017). A proof of stake sharding protocol for scalable blockchains. *Proceedings of the Asia-Pacific Advanced Network, 44*(1), 13–16.

Gramoli, V. (2020). From blockchain consensus back to Byzantine consensus. *Future Generation Computer Systems, 107,* 760–769. doi:10.1016/j.future.2017.09.023

Hao, X., Yu, L., Zhiqiang, L., Zhen, L., & Dawu, G. (2018, May). Dynamic practical byzantine fault tolerance. In *2018 IEEE Conference on Communications and Network Security (CNS)* (pp. 1-8). IEEE.

Helliar, C. V., Crawford, L., Rocca, L., Teodori, C., & Veneziani, M. (2020). Permissionless and permissioned blockchain diffusion. *International Journal of Information Management, 54,* 102136. doi:10.1016/j.ijinfomgt.2020.102136

Huang, K., Mu, Y., Rezaeibagha, F., Zhang, X., & Chen, T. (2021). Building blockchains with secure and practical Public-Key cryptographic algorithms: Background, motivations and example. *IEEE Network, 35*(6), 240–246. doi:10.1109/MNET.101.2100088

Iyer, K., & Dannen, C. (2018). Crypto-economics and game theory. In *Building Games with Ethereum Smart Contracts* (pp. 129–141). Apress. doi:10.1007/978-1-4842-3492-1_6

Kim, S. G. (2018). A study on the blockchain 2.0 ethereum platform analysis for DApp development. *The Journal of Korea Institute of Information, Electronics, and Communication Technology, 11*(6), 718–723.

Khanboubi, F., Boulmakoul, A., & Tabaa, M. (2019). Impact of digital trends using IoT on banking processes. *Procedia Computer Science, 151,* 77–84. doi:10.1016/j.procs.2019.04.014

Krishnamurthi, R., & Shree, T. (2019). A Brief Analysis of Blockchain Algorithms and Its Challenges. *Architectures and Frameworks for Developing and Applying Blockchain Technology*, *1*(2), 69–85. doi:10.4018/978-1-5225-9257-0.ch004

Kumar, M. A., Radhesyam, V., & SrinivasaRao, B. (2019, January). Front-End IoT Application for the Bitcoin based on Proof of Elapsed Time (PoET). In *2019 Third International Conference on Inventive Systems and Control (ICISC)* (pp. 646-649). IEEE. 10.1109/ICISC44355.2019.9036391

Lewis, R., McPartland, J., & Ranjan, R. (2017). Blockchain and financial market innovation. *Economic Perspectives*, *41*(7), 1–17.

Majeed, U., Khan, L. U., Yaqoob, I., Kazmi, S. A., Salah, K., & Hong, C. S. (2021). Blockchain for IoT-based smart cities: Recent advances, requirements, and future challenges. *Journal of Network and Computer Applications*, *181*, 103007. doi:10.1016/j.jnca.2021.103007

McKay, C. (2014). *Digital Currencies and Financial Inclusion: Revisited. CGAP*. Available online at: https://www.cgap.org/blog/digital-currencies-and-financial-inclusion-revisited

Mingxiao, D., Xiaofeng, M., Zhe, Z., Xiangwei, W., & Qijun, C. (2017, October). A review on consensus algorithm of blockchain. In 2017 IEEE international conference on systems, man, and cybernetics (SMC) (pp. 2567-2572). IEEE. doi:10.1109/SMC.2017.8123011

Mohaghar, A., Sadeghi Moghadam, M. R., Ghourchi Beigi, R., & Ghasemi, R. (2021). IoT-Based Services in Banking Industry Using a Business Continuity Management Approach. *Journal of Information Technology Management*, 16–38.

Mohan, C. (2019, June). State of public and private blockchains: Myths and reality. In *Proceedings of the 2019 international conference on management of data* (pp. 404-411). 10.1145/3299869.3314116

Nguyen, G. T., & Kim, K. (2018). A survey about consensus algorithms used in blockchain. *Journal of Information Processing Systems, 14*(1), 101-128.

Omwansa, T. K., & Sullivan, N. P. (2012). *Money, real quick: The story of M-PESA*. Guardian Books.

Perera, C., Liu, C. H., Jayawardena, S., & Chen, M. (2014). A survey on internet of things from industrial market perspective. *IEEE Access: Practical Innovations, Open Solutions*, *2*, 1660–1679. doi:10.1109/ACCESS.2015.2389854

Plato-Shinar, R. (2012). The Banking Contract as a Special Contract: The Israeli Approach. *Touro Law Review*, *29*, 721.

Ramalingam, H., & Venkatesan, V. P. (2019, October). Conceptual analysis of Internet of Things use cases in Banking domain. In TENCON 2019-2019 IEEE Region 10 Conference (TENCON) (pp. 2034-2039). IEEE. doi:10.1109/TENCON.2019.8929473

Rella, L. (2019). Blockchain technologies and remittances: From financial inclusion to correspondent banking. *Frontiers in Blockchain*, *2*, 14. doi:10.3389/fbloc.2019.00014

Rella, L. (2020). Steps towards an ecology of money infrastructures: Materiality and cultures of Ripple. *Journal of Cultural Economics*, *13*(2), 236–249. doi:10.1080/17530350.2020.1711532

Rosner, M. T., & Kang, A. (2015). Understanding and regulating twenty-first century payment systems: The ripple case study. *Michigan Law Review*, *114*, 649.

Saad, S. M. S., & Radzi, R. Z. R. M. (2020). Comparative Review of the Blockchain Consensus Algorithm Between Proof of Stake (POS) and Delegated Proof of Stake (DPOS). *International Journal of Innovative Computing*, *10*(2), 1–18.

Samaniego, M., Jamsrandorj, U., & Deters, R. (2016, December). Blockchain as a Service for IoT. In 2016 IEEE international conference on internet of things (iThings) and IEEE green computing and communications (GreenCom) and IEEE cyber, physical and social computing (CPSCom) and IEEE smart data (SmartData) (pp. 433-436). IEEE. doi:10.1109/iThings-GreenCom-CPSCom-SmartData.2016.102

Sundmaeker, H., Guillemin, P., Friess, P., & Woelfflé, S. (2010). Vision and challenges for realising the Internet of Things. *Cluster of European research projects on the internet of things*. *European Commision*, *3*(3), 34–36.

Suseendran, G., Chandrasekaran, E., Akila, D., & Kumar, A. S. (2020). Banking and FinTech (Financial Technology) Embraced with IoT Device. In *Data Management, Analytics and Innovation* (pp. 197–211). Springer. doi:10.1007/978-981-32-9949-8_15

Sukhwani, H., Martínez, J. M., Chang, X., Trivedi, K. S., & Rindos, A. (2017, September). Performance modeling of PBFT consensus process for permissioned blockchain network (hyperledger fabric). In *2017 IEEE 36th Symposium on Reliable Distributed Systems (SRDS)* (pp. 253-255). IEEE.

Qian, Y., Jiang, Y., Chen, J., Zhang, Y., Song, J., Zhou, M., & Pustišek, M. (2018). Towards decentralized IoT security enhancement: A blockchain approach. *Computers & Electrical Engineering*, *72*(1), 266–273. doi:10.1016/j.compeleceng.2018.08.021

Urmila, M. S., Hariharan, B., & Prabha, R. (2019, July). A Comparitive Study of Blockchain Applications for Enhancing Internet of Things Security. In *2019 10th International Conference on Computing, Communication and Networking Technologies (ICCCNT)* (pp. 1-7). IEEE. 10.1109/ICCCNT45670.2019.8944446

Vimal Jerald, A., Rabara, S. A., & Bai, T. D. P. (2015). Internet of things (IoT) based smart environment integrating various business applications. *International Journal of Computers and Applications*, *128*(8), 32–37. doi:10.5120/ijca2015906622

Wünderlich, N. V., Wangenheim, F. V., & Bitner, M. J. (2013). High tech and high touch: A framework for understanding user attitudes and behaviors related to smart interactive services. *Journal of Service Research*, *16*(1), 3–20. doi:10.1177/1094670512448413

Yang, F., Zhou, W., Wu, Q., Long, R., Xiong, N. N., & Zhou, M. (2019). Delegated proof of stake with downgrade: A secure and efficient blockchain consensus algorithm with downgrade mechanism. *IEEE Access: Practical Innovations, Open Solutions*, *7*, 118541–118555. doi:10.1109/ACCESS.2019.2935149

Zhang, L., & Li, Q. (2018, July). Research on consensus efficiency based on practical byzantine fault tolerance. In *2018 10th International Conference on Modelling, Identification and Control (ICMIC)* (pp. 1-6). IEEE. 10.1109/ICMIC.2018.8529940

ADDITIONAL READING

Arjun, R., & Suprabha, K. R. (2020). Innovation and Challenges of Blockchain in Banking: A Scientometric View. *International Journal of Interactive Multimedia & Artificial Intelligence*, *6*(3), 11–23. doi:10.9781/ijimai.2020.03.004

Buitenhek, M. (2016). Understanding and applying blockchain technology in banking: Evolution or revolution? *Journal of Digital Banking*, *1*(2), 111–119.

Gorkhali, A., Li, L., & Shrestha, A. (2020). Blockchain: A literature review. *Journal of Management Analytics*, *7*(3), 321–343. doi:10.1080/23270012.2020.1801529

Hassani, H., Huang, X., & Silva, E. (2018). Banking with blockchain-ed big data. *Journal of Management Analytics*, *5*(4), 256–275. doi:10.1080/23270012.2018.1 528900

Peters, G. W., & Panayi, E. (2016). Understanding modern banking ledgers through blockchain technologies: Future of transaction processing and smart contracts on the internet of money. In *Banking beyond banks and money* (pp. 239–278). Springer. doi:10.1007/978-3-319-42448-4_13

Xiong, H., Chen, M., Wu, C., Zhao, Y., & Yi, W. (2022). Research on Progress of Blockchain Consensus Algorithm: A Review on Recent Progress of Blockchain Consensus Algorithms. *Future Internet*, *14*(2), 47. doi:10.3390/fi14020047

KEY TERMS AND DEFINITIONS

Consensus Algorithms: A consensus algorithm allows distributed processes or systems to agree on a single data value in computer science.

Distributed Ledger: A distributed ledger is a record of consensus that includes a cryptographic audit trail that nodes maintain and validate. It might be either decentralized or centralized in nature.

Internet of Things: The internet of things (IoT) is a collection of interconnected devices that are connected to a network and/or to one another and exchange data without requiring human-machine interaction.

Merkle Tree: In computer science, Merkle trees, also known as Binary hash trees, are a common type of data structure.

Node: Nodes are network stakeholders and equipment that have been permitted to maintain track of the distributed ledger and act as communication hubs for various network tasks.

Nonce: A number or value that can only be used once is referred to as a nonce. Nonces are frequently employed in cryptographic hash algorithms and authentication procedures.

Peer-to-Peer Network: Peer-to-peer networking is a distributed application architecture in which jobs or workloads are divided across peers.

Permissioned Blockchain: Permissioned blockchains are distributed ledgers that are not open to the public.

Public-Key Cryptography: A combination of keys known as a public key and a private key is associated with an entity that needs to authenticate or sign or encrypt data using public-key cryptography.

Smart Contract: A self-executing contract in which the conditions of the buyer-seller agreement are put directly into lines of code is called a smart contract.

Chapter 3
Blockchain Platform to Resolve Security Issues in IoT and Smart Networks

Pawan Whig
Vivekananda Insitute of Professional Studies, India

Arun Velu
Equifax, USA

Rahul Reddy Nadikattu
University of the Cumberlands, USA

ABSTRACT

IoT provided a unified operating picture across a wide range of modern-day applications. The operating image is accomplished thanks to improvements in wireless sensor network devices that can interact over a network, exchanging data and executing various analyses. The only way to share information and authenticate data in the internet of things is through a central server, which raises security and privacy problems. Device spoofing, incorrect authentication, and a lack of data exchange dependability are all possibilities. A central server idea is abolished, and blockchain technology is used as part of IoT to solve such security and privacy problems. This chapter examines the potential security and privacy concerns associated with component interaction in the internet of things, as well as how the distributed ledger-based blockchain technology might help. Here, in this chapter, the authors discuss the application of BC to certain areas and categories. Various IoT and IoT with BC problems were also highlighted in order to better comprehend blockchain technology's role.

DOI: 10.4018/978-1-6684-4176-3.ch003

INTRODUCTION

Nearly every chief information officer's list of game-changing technologies set to change sectors includes block chain and artificial intelligence (AI) (Whig et al., 2022). Both technologies have a lot of advantages, but they also have their own set of obstacles when it comes to adoption. It's also fair to argue that the excitement around each of these technologies is unparalleled, so some may see the idea of combining these two elements as creating a contemporary day type of IT fairy dirt. All together, there is rational and pragmatic approach to think about this mash-up (Anand et al., 2022).

AI is currently, for all intents and purposes, a centralised process. In order to achieve a dependable business output, an end operator necessity has total faith in the central specialist. By decentralizing the three fundamental components of AI statistics replicas can provide the trust and confidence that end users require to fully adopt and rely on AI-based business operations. Though, all have struggled to instill trust in their passionate but skeptical users. How can a business reassure its consumers that its machine learning has not pushed far off? (Jiwani et al., 2021)

Consider if such AI solutions could provide a "investigative report" that was certified by a second party and having you, without a certainty, when and how companies are using your information after it has been digested. Consider that your data could only be utilised if you provided consent (Alkali et al., 2022).

A blockchain record may be secondhand as a privileges organization scheme, agreeing you to "licensed" personal data to the AI breadwinner based on your footings, requirements, and timescale. The blockchain would function as an access organization system, storage evidence and permits that allow a firm to acquire and utilise a operator's statistics (Chopra & WHIG, 2022a).

Reflect how blockchain technology may be used to provide trustworthy data and provenance for machine learning training models. In this example, we've devised a make-believe mechanism to determine which fruit it is (Madhu & WHIG, 2022).

This issue system that we create is referred to as a perfect, and it is shaped through with a procedure named as exercise. Objective of exercise is to develop an precise perfect that most of the time answers our questions accurately. Of course, we need data to train a model on, which in this case might will be the color along with the sweetness of fruit (Chopra & Whig, 2022).

You may examine an review trail of the indication that led to the prediction of why a certain fruit is categorised as an apple against an carroty using blockchain, as well as trace the provenance of the training data. If apples are the more expensive of the two fruits, a company can show that it isn't "juicing up" its books by labelling produce as apples more often (Chopra & WHIG, 2022b).

The European Union has passed legislation mandating that any decision made by a computer be easily explainable, or face fines of billions of euros. The Overall Data Defense Rule, which went into power in 2018, stretches a correct to an explanations of algorithm choices, as well as the option to opting from some algorithm findings completely (WHIG, 2022).

Every second, massive volumes of data are created – far more data than humans can analyses and utilise as a foundation for forming judgments. AI applications, on the other hand, can analyse big data sets with numerous variables while learning about or linking those factors that are relevant to their goals and aims. As a result, AI continues to be embraced in a variety of sectors and applications, and we are increasingly reliant on its results. It is critical, however, that any AI judgments be double-checked by humans for correctness (George et al., 2021).

The provenance, transparency, comprehension, and explanations of those results and decisions may all be improved by blockchain. The inherent properties of blockchain would enable auditing selections and related data points simpler when they are recorded using blockchain activities. Imbuing blockchain in AI judgement processes might be the missing piece for achieving the transparency required to completely trust AI-derived choices and results. Because blockchain is a fundamental technology that adds confidence to transactions, adding blockchain into AI judgement procedures might be the missing piece needed to provide the transparency required to completely trust the judgments and outcomes produced from AI (Mamza, 2021).

IoT already includes over a billion intellectual, linked gadgets. With hundreds of billions more predicted to be produced, we are on the verge of a change that will affect the electronics sector and many other fields (Pawar, 2021).

Figure 1. IoT blockchain interaction

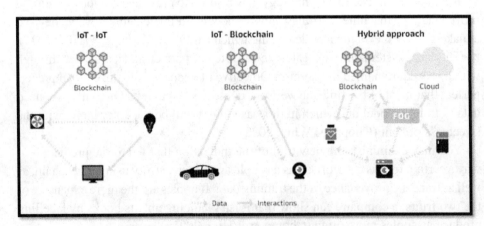

Because of developments in IoT, industries can now acquire data, get vision from the statistics, and make choices founded on the data. As a consequence, around is indeed a high level of "confidence" in the data collected. But the major concern is, do we really understand in which this statistics originated from, and should we really be making choices and dealing founded on the information we can't confirm? (Sinha & Ranjan, 2015)

Does the weather information, for instance, come from the edit in the Atlantic Marine, or did the temperature of the delivery crate not surpass the agreement restriction? There are several IoT use scenarios, however they all share the same trust problem.

IoT combined with block chain can provide genuine confidence in data collected. The fundamental concept is to give gadgets an identity at the moment of manufacture that can be checked and confirmed using blockchain throughout their lifespan. Blockchain abilities based on device identification standard and reputational technology holds a lot of potential for Iot network (Parihar & Yadav, 2020).

Every gadget can have its individual blockchain community important and send encoded test and response messages to other strategies via a expedient identification protocol, ensuring that the device retains switch of its individuality. A expedient with an individuality may also create a record or past, where a blockchain may track (Bhargav & Whig, 2021).

A blockchain network's business logic is represented via smart contracts. When a transaction is suggested, these smart contracts execute themselves according to the network's rules. Smart contracts may play a critical role in IoT networks by automating transaction and interaction coordination and authorization (Khera et al., 2021).

IoT was created with the goal of surfacing data and providing actionable information at the correct moment.

Home automation, for example, are now a thing of the past, and nearly everything is potentially connected. When an IoT device fails, these IoT devices could even take immediate action, such as buying a novel part.

IOT

The individual who came up with the phrase "Internet of Things" Kevin Ashton originated the phrase "Internet of Things" (IoT) in a presentation to Proctor & Gamble in 1999. In the supply-chain management sector, he pioneered RFID (used in bar code detectors). He also founded Zensi, a firm that specialises in energy sensing and monitoring (Velu & Whig, 2021).

Any device having built-in sensors and the capacity to collect and send data over a network without user intervention qualifies as a "Thing" in the Internet of Things. The integrated technology in the item allows it to interact with internal states as well as the external world, which aids in decision-making.

In a word, the internet of things (IoT) is a concept that links all of your gadgets to the internet and allows them to interact with one another. The Internet of Things is a vast net of interconnected plans that collect and exchange information about how they are utilised and the surroundings in which they function (Whig, 2019a).

Each of your gadgets will learn from the experiences of other devices in the same way that people do. IoT aims to increase human interdependence by allowing people to connect, participate, and cooperate with objects (Whig, 2019b).

SECURITY ISSUES

By 2027, it is expected that there will be more than 41 billion linked devices. Hackers are taking advantage of this expansion by attacking a variety of companies and sectors with simple cyber-attacks that originate from Internet of Things (IoT) devices with inadequate security, paralysing and defeating certain firms (Verma, 2019).

Figure 2. Various security issues in Iot

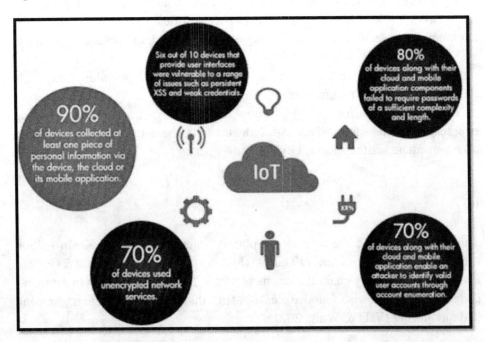

Worse, these hackers are expanding their attacks on linked devices as a result of the increase in remote workers and their connected devices caused by the coronavirus. Almost every firm is at danger since IoT is used by 63 percent of businesses, 92 percent of industrial organisations, and 82 percent of healthcare organisations. Despite the fact that IoT devices have demonstrated productivity benefits for organisations, connecting them to your network expands the attack surface and gives hackers new access opportunities (Reddy, 2019).

As new devices are developed and deployed in a variety of settings, the Internet of Things (IoT) continues to expand. Because of this extensive adoption, IoT security has become a serious issue for businesses, as the devices they install are likely to contain a number of security flaws, including:

Old Operating Systems: IoT devices do not always use the most recent version of the operating systems on which they operate. This implies that the operating systems of IoT devices may have publicly known vulnerabilities that attackers might exploit to gain control of or harm these IoT devices (Chouhan, 2019).

In contrast to desktop PCs, IoT devices rarely include built-in antivirus and other security measures. This raises the likelihood that they may be infected with malware, allowing the attacker to exploit them in an attack or get access to sensitive data collected and processed by these devices.

Difficult to Patch or Upgrade: All software requires regular updates to update functionality or fix security gaps. Because of the unusual deployment situations of IoT devices, they seldom receive upgrades. As a result, the gadgets are extremely vulnerable to targeted assaults.

Insecure Passwords: There are a variety of password-related concerns with IoT devices. Device makers frequently utilise weak default passwords that users do not update prior to or after deployment. Manufacturers may also put hardcoded passwords in their systems that consumers cannot alter. These weak passwords put IoT devices at danger. As a result, attackers may quickly enter into these devices using readily guessable passwords or simple brute-force assaults (Rupani & Sujediya, 2016).

Unreliable Deployment Regions: IoT devices are frequently designed to be placed in public and distant locations where an attacker may physically obtain access to the devices. This physical access might allow the attacker to circumvent the devices' existing protections.

Use of Insecure Protocols: Because of their lack of built-in security, several network protocols, such as Telnet, have been formally deprecated. IoT devices, on the other hand, are notorious for employing insecure protocols, putting their data and security at danger (Srivastava et al., 2020).

ATTACKS ON IOT

Because of the widespread use of IoT devices on corporate networks, they pose a serious danger to company cybersecurity. Unfortunately, these gadgets frequently have weaknesses that may be exploited. Cybercriminals have taken advantage of these flaws and have carried out a variety of attacks on various IoT devices, including:

Figure 3. Different attacks on IoT

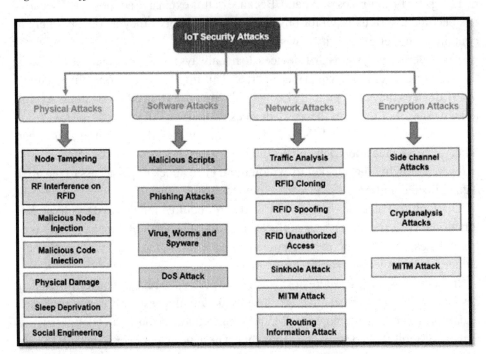

Direct Manipulation: Printers (and other IoT devices) are a frequent way for employees to get access to a company's network. Because everyone has to be able to use the printer, these devices are rarely protected by firewalls and have high permissions. People can take advantage of this by getting initial network access through a printers and then expanding their access through the business network (Reddy, n.d.).

Botnets based on IoT devices: Iot systems are World wide web computers that are well-suited to launching automated assaults. An IoT device that has been infected with botnet malware can be used to launch Distributed Denial of Service (DDoS) attacks, try to gain unauthorised access to user accounts via credential stuffing, spread malicious activity or other ransomware, or perform other malicious actions against an organization's information systems.

IoT Data Breach: Because IoT devices are frequently used to process sensitive data, execute essential tasks, or connect to cloud subscription services, they are a great target for hackers. For example, an attacker might get access to potentially sensitive data or other important information via exploiting Internet-connected cameras and/or the user's cloud service (Chanda & Rupani, 2022).

Companies are increasingly adopting IoT devices, which represent a serious danger to them as well as other companies. IoT devices having privileged responsibilities, such as controlling industrial machinery or monitoring a critical site, can be hacked and exploited to steal sensitive data or disrupt business operations. Botnets, which are made up of IoT devices, are also growing more prevalent and causing substantial damage through DDoS and other assaults.

BLOCK CHAIN

You may see a world where contracts are recorded in digital code and preserved in clear, shareable records which are safeguarded from removal, alteration, and modification by blockchain. Every contract, procedure, duty, and imbursement would have a numeric recording and signature that can be identified, authenticated, archived, and shared in this environment. Lawyers, brokers, and bankers may no longer be required as middlemen. People, corporations, machines, and computers would be able to do business and engage with each extra without restriction (Nadikattu et al., 2020b).

Almost everybody has caught the argument that blockchain would transform commercial and reshape organisations and frugalities. Many barriers—technical, governance, organisational, and even societal—will have to collapse if there is to be a blockchain revolution, according to our experience researching technology innovation. It would be a mistake to dive headfirst into blockchain technology without first knowing how it will spread.

We believe that true blockchain-led corporate and government change is still several years away. This is due to the fact that block chain is not a "disruptive" skill that can attack a outdated business perfect with a low cost key and swiftly overrun existing businesses. Blockchain is a foundational technology, with the ability to build new economic and social institutions on top of it. However, while blockchain will have a huge influence, it determination income decades for it to pervade our financial and social substructure. As waves of technical and institutional change acquire speed, adoption will be gradual and steady, rather than abrupt (Ruchin & Whig, 2015).

Both blockchain and the Internet of Things (IoT) are frequently touted as significant digital transformation technologies. But what if you used a mix of the two? End of 2019, Gartner identified blockchain adoption in conjunction with IoT adoption as a DX sweet spot, particularly in the United States. And nothing has changed.

Since about 2014, blockchain technology, a kind of Distributed Ledger Technology, has gotten a lot of attention in fields other than cryptocurrency (Kaushik et al., 2018).

Blockchain is intended to serve as the foundation for apps that include transactions and interactions. IoT activities are examples of these. As a result, blockchain technology may enhance not just IoT compliance, but also IoT features and cost-efficiency.

BLOCKCHAIN AND IOT

The dispersed record of a blockchain is interfere proof, reducing the essential for the parties complicated to trust one another, according to Andres Ricaurte, senior vice president and worldwide head of payments at an IT services business. Because of blockchain encryption, it is nearly difficult for anybody to alter existing data records. Furthermore, storing IoT data on blockchain adds another layer of protection to prevent hostile attackers from getting access to the network (Saini et al., 2017).

Figure 4. Benefit of block chain

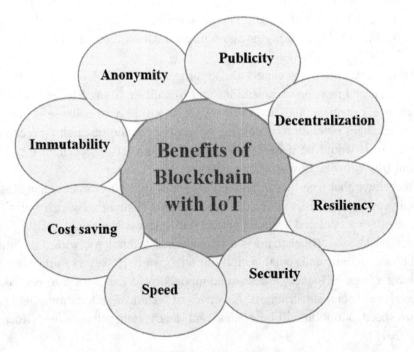

One of the most tough difficulties for IoT providers, according to Vipul Parekh, senior director at management consulting firm Alvarez & Marsal, is securing information throughout the IoT ecosystem. Because of security weaknesses in IoT devices, they are an easy target for distributed-denial-of-service attacks, malicious attackers, and data breaches (Velu & Whig, n.d.).

According to Parekh, the integration of IoT with blockchain offers up new opportunities for all interested parties by reducing inefficiencies, improving safety, and increasing transparency while enabling secure engine to mechanism transactions. The combination of these technologies enables a physical asset to be monitored from the time raw materials are mined, for example, and along the supply chain until it reaches the end customer.

Increased security. Blockchain technology integrates security by allowing trusted parties to verify and approve transactions, as well as encryption while data is being sent and stored. Blockchain technology gives visibility into who has access, who is transacting, and a record of all interactions. Furthermore, blockchain provides a layer of security through encryption, the elimination of single points of failure, and the capacity to rapidly identify the weakest link in the whole network (Ajay Rupani, 2019).

Cost savings. The entire ecosystem may be made more proactive at a lower cost by automating the transaction validation and processing processes on blockchain.

Transactional speed. This is especially true for supply chain transactions involving many suppliers, manufacturers, distributors, and customers. Because the blockchain functions as a shared ledger to some extent, untrusted parties may exchange data directly with one another, reducing manual processes and boosting transaction speed.

"While at Amazon, we handled this problem using a strategy known as 'working backwards,' in which we began with the consumer and moved backwards to the solution," Rossman explained. "Blockchain is an example of a technology that seems like a transformative technology, but substantial adoption outside of cryptocurrencies has not fulfilled the expectations. Let us begin with the consumer and move backwards to see how blockchain might help the Internet of Things."

Costs, security, privacy, and data sharing are all issues that must be addressed in IoT implementations.

According to Rossman, blockchain is encrypted and safe by design, with multiple independent nodes validating modifications to the chain prior to upgrades to avoid malicious acts. This is designed to be secure. The blockchain can be viewed and confirmed by all stakeholders, which helps to enhance data access and trust without adding cumbersome and expensive bureaucratic layers. This significantly increases accessibility, trust, and affordability.

CASE STUDY

Smart contracts/supply chain According to John Thielens, CTO of Cleo, IoT and blockchain may be integrated for quality assurance in the supply chain. Perishable commodities, such as wine or rare delicacies, are frequently exposed to changing temperatures and light exposures as they travel through transportation and warehousing networks. "By integrating IoT and blockchain, we can record the path of perishable commodities from manufacturer to retailer," Thielens explained. "At the case or pallet level, location and temperature data may be gathered and put into the blockchain, providing the ability to verify the history of the product as it goes through the supply chain and refuse accepting the goods and transferring it (Nadikattu et al., 2020a).

Figure 5. Flow chart of smart contract

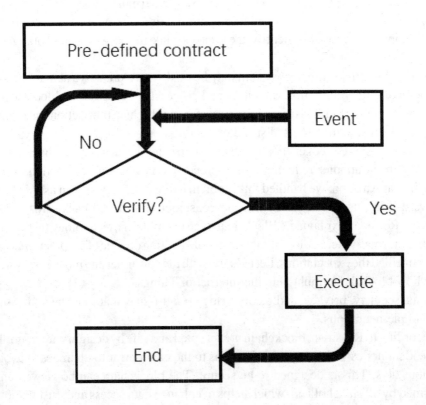

Aside from storing data, certain blockchain models enable companies to store and operate immutable algorithms in a distributed and decentralised manner, according to Carvahlo. These algorithms, often known as smart contracts, allow businesses to automatically codify business and domain rules (Whig & Ahmad, 2018).

IoT devices, such as temperature sensors, can continually check the temperature of shipments and communicate data to a running smart contract, which can notify stakeholders of any temperature decline in real time," Carvahlo explained. "Because the smart contract is operating on top of blockchain, the underlying temperature data are saved in an immutable data structure, which aids in data tampering prevention."

Figure 6. Blockchain in transportation

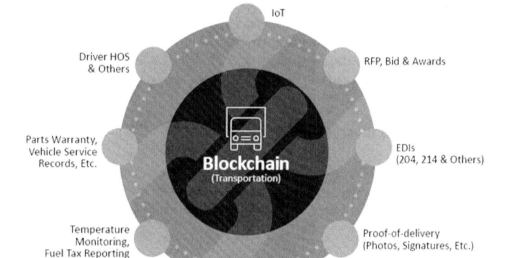

Leasing a truck According to the Gartner Inc. study "Integrating Blockchain With IoT Strengthens Trust in Multiparty Processes," IoT sensors installed in leased vehicles may record critical events on a blockchain to assist monitor fleet whereabouts and returns, as well as to enable more meaningful invoicing methods (Ahmad & Whig, 2011).

"With IoT sensors on board vehicles, truck leasing firms may charge renters' costs based on the torque of the loads rather than distance, as is now the practise," according to the study. "The blockchain distributed ledger technology enables people to share a single, shared version of the truth. There is no single body in charge of the data, and truckers and leasing firms can all be independent.

Field service and oil operations According to the Garter research, IoT sensors on oil and water wells may help oil firms control the performance of hauling businesses that pick up and distribute oil and water from wells and carry it to various destinations, including environmental waste dumping grounds.

"The IoT sensors on the wells assist oil firms in scheduling truck pickups and allowing them to monitor the amount of material picked up and delivered to avoid fraud and false representations," according to the article. "The blockchain distributed ledger technology records critical events in the logistics chain and provides a shared single version of independently verifiable truth throughout the entire logistics chain."

According to the Gartner study, using blockchain in this use case may help oil firms save money and run their pickup and delivery operations more effectively. Furthermore, by providing regulators with access to data such as the volume of water transported to a water dumping site vs the amount taken up from a water well, blockchain distributed ledger technology will assist the oil firm in managing its compliance reporting obligations (Pawan Whig Anupam Priyam, 2018; Whig, 2017).

DIFFICULTIES OF INTEGRATING

According to Paul Brody, global novelty frontrunner, blockchain skill at EY, one of the most difficult aspects of combining blockchain with IoT is the restrictions associated with the low battery life of some IoT devices (Kautish et al. 2022; Moorthy et al. 2022)

Figure 7. Integrating blockchain technology with IoT

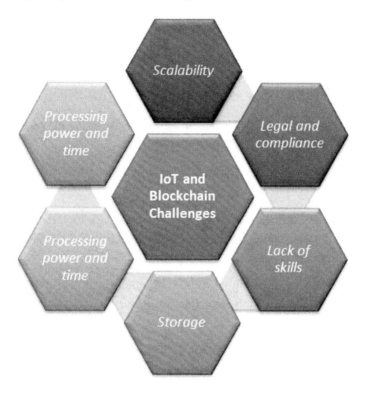

"Some IoT devices are always linked to electricity and Wi-Fi, so there aren't really any significant constraints," he explained. "However, many IoT devices are not. And you can't run a compute- and bandwidth-intensive blockchain transaction system on a little device. As a result, they may need to employ some form of server-based architecture (Sharma et al. 2022; Madhu et al. 2022; Rajawat et al. 2022).

CONCLUSION

We examined studies from many areas, including smart contracts, smart transport, and smart vehicle applications that used Edge, Fog, Cloud computing, and Blockchain technology to solve security and privacy issues. Despite this, a number of technological and security problems in IoT remain unresolved. Several obstacles in using Blockchain technology in the IoT sector are mentioned in this review article, and how those challenges are being solved is described. Existing Blockchain and IoT articles were examined in terms of several aspects in order to demonstrate their strengths and limitations. Furthermore, the study provides a general overview of Blockchain components as well as numerous industry standards. This book chapter will be benefited doing research in the same field.

REFERENCES

Ahmad, S. N., & Whig, P. (2011). *On the Performance of ISFET-based Device for Water Quality Monitoring*. Academic Press.

Ajay Rupani, P. (2019). The development of big data science to the world. *Engineering Reports*, 2(2), 1–7.

Alkali Y. Routray I. Whig P. (2022). Study of various methods for reliable, efficient and Secured IoT using Artificial Intelligence. Available at SSRN 4020364. doi:10.2139/ssrn.4020364

Anand, M., Velu, A., & Whig, P. (2022). Prediction of Loan Behaviour with Machine Learning Models for Secure Banking. *Journal of Computing Science and Engineering: JCSE*, 3(1), 1–13.

Bhargav, R., & Whig, P. (2021). More Insight on Data Analysis of Titanic Data Set. *International Journal of Sustainable Development in Computing Science*, 3(4), 1–10.

Chanda, P. K., & Rupani, A. (n.d.). *A Review of Technology Paradigm for Near-Field Communication Sensors and Cloud-Based Smart Campus Management System*. Academic Press.

Chopra, G., & Whig, P. (2022a). A clustering approach based on support vectors. *International Journal of Machine Learning for Sustainable Development*, 4(1), 21–30.

Chopra, G., & Whig, P. (2022b). Using machine learning algorithms classified depressed patients and normal people. *International Journal of Machine Learning for Sustainable Development*, 4(1), 31–40.

Chopra, G., & Whig, P. (2022). Energy Efficient Scheduling for Internet of Vehicles. *International Journal of Sustainable Development in Computing Science*, 4(1).

Chouhan, S. (2019). Using an Arduino and a temperature, humidity sensor, Automate the fan speed. *International Journal of Sustainable Development in Computing Science, 1(2)*.

George, N., Muiz, K., Whig, P., & Velu, A. (2021). Framework of Perceptive Artificial Intelligence using Natural Language Processing (PAIN). *Artificial & Computational Intelligence*.

Jiwani, N., Gupta, K., & Whig, P. (2021). Novel HealthCare Framework for Cardiac Arrest With the Application of AI Using ANN. *2021 5th International Conference on Information Systems and Computer Networks (ISCON)*, 1–5.

Kaushik, S., Chouhan, Y. S., Sharma, N., Singh, S., & Suganya, P. (2018). Automatic fan speed control using temperature and humidity sensor and Arduino. *International Journal of Advanced Research*, *4*(2), 453–467.

Kautish, S., Reyana, A., & Vidyarthi, A. (2022). SDMTA: Attack Detection and Mitigation Mechanism for DDoS Vulnerabilities in Hybrid Cloud Environment. *IEEE Transactions on Industrial Informatics*.

Khera, Y., Whig, P., & Velu, A. (2021). efficient effective and secured electronic billing system using AI. *Vivekananda Journal of Research*, *10*, 53–60.

Madhu, G., Govardhan, A., & Ravi, V. (2022). DSCN-net: A deep Siamese capsule neural network model for automatic diagnosis of malaria parasites detection. *Multimed Tools Appl*. doi:10.1007/s11042-022-13008-6

Madhu, M., & Whig, P. (2022). A survey of machine learning and its applications. *International Journal of Machine Learning for Sustainable Development*, *4*(1), 11–20.

Mamza, E. S. (2021). Use of AIOT in Health System. *International Journal of Sustainable Development in Computing Science*, *3*(4), 21–30.

Moorthy, T. V. K., Budati, A. K., Kautish, S., Goyal, S. B., & Prasad, K. L. (2022). Reduction of satellite images size in 5G networks using Machinelearning algorithms. *IET Communications*, *16*, 584–591. https://doi.org/10.1049/cmu2.12354

Nadikattu, R. R., Mohammad, S. M., & Whig, P. (2020a). *Novel economical social distancing smart device for covid-19*. *International Journal of Electrical Engineering and Technology*.

Nadikattu, R. R., Mohammad, S. M., & Whig, P. (2020b). *Novel economical social distancing smart Device for COVID-19* (SSRN Scholarly Paper ID 3640230). Social Science Research Network. Https://Papers. Ssrn. Com/Abstract

Parihar, V., & Yadav, S. (n.d.). *Comparison estimation of effective consumer future preferences with the application of AI*. Academic Press.

Pawar, V. S. (2021). IoT architecture with embedded AI. *International Journal of Sustainable Development in Computing Science*, *3*(4), 11–20.

Rajawat, A. S., Bedi, P., Goyal, S. B., Kautish, S., Xihua, Z., Aljuaid, H., & Mohamed, A. W. (2022). Dark Web Data Classification Using Neural Network. *Computational Intelligence and Neuroscience.*

Reddy, R. (2019). Purification of indoor air using a novel pseudo PMOS ultraviolet photocatalytic oxidation (PP-UVPCO) sensor. *International Journal of Sustainable Development in Computing Science, 1*(3).

Reddy, R. (n.d.). Role of information science during COVID-19. *COVID-19, 149.*

Ruchin, C. M., & Whig, P. (2015). Design and Simulation of Dynamic UART Using Scan Path Technique (USPT). *International Journal of Electrical, Electronics & Computing in Science & Engineering.*

Rupani, A., & Sujediya, G. (2016). A Review of FPGA implementation of Internet of Things. *International Journal of Innovative Research in Computer and Communication Engineering, 4*(9).

Saini, D., Rupani, A., Sujediya, G., & Sharma, T. (2017). An ISFET automated output calibration system implementation on reconfigurable FPGA device with MATLAB artificial intelligence interfacing. *2017 3rd International Conference on Applied and Theoretical Computing and Communication Technology (ICATccT)*, 354–358.

Sharma, C., Sharma, S., Kautish, S., Alsallami, S. A., Khalil, E. M., & Mohamed, A. W. (2022). A new median-average round Robin scheduling algorithm: An optimal approach for reducing turnaround and waiting time. *Alexandria Engineering Journal, 61*(12), 10527–10538.

Sinha, R., & Ranjan, A. (2015). Effect of Variable Damping Ratio on design of PID Controller. *2015 4th International Conference on Reliability, Infocom Technologies and Optimization (ICRITO)(Trends and Future Directions)*, 1–4.

Srivastava, J., Bhagat, R., & Kumar, P. (2020). Analog inverse filters using OTAs. *2020 6th International Conference on Control, Automation and Robotics (ICCAR)*, 627–631.

Velu, A., & Whig, P. (2021). Protect Personal Privacy And Wasting Time Using Nlp: A Comparative Approach Using Ai. *Vivekananda Journal of Research, 10*, 42–52.

Velu, A., & Whig, P. (n.d.). *Studying the Impact of the COVID Vaccination on the World Using Data Analytics.* Academic Press.

Verma, T. (2019). A comparison of different R2R D/A converters. *International Journal of Sustainable Development in Computing Science, 1*(2).

Whig, P. (2022). More on Convolution Neural Network CNN. *International Journal of Sustainable Development in Computing Science*, *1*(1).

Whig, P. (2017). Temperature and Frequency Independent Readout Circuit for PCS System. *SF J Material Res Let*, *1*(3), 8–12.

Whig, P. (2019a). A Novel Multi-Center and Threshold Ternary Pattern. *International Journal of Machine Learning for Sustainable Development*, *1*(2), 1–10.

Whig, P. (2019b). Exploration of Viral Diseases mortality risk using machine learning. *International Journal of Machine Learning for Sustainable Development*, *1*(1), 11–20.

Whig, P., & Ahmad, S. N. (2018). Comparison analysis of various R2R D/A converter. *Int J Biosen Bioelectron*, *4*(6), 275–279.

Whig, P., Nadikattu, R. R., & Velu, A. (2022). COVID-19 pandemic analysis using application of AI. *Healthcare Monitoring and Data Analysis Using IoT: Technologies and Applications*, 1.

Whig, Priyam, & Ahmad. (2018). Simulation & performance analysis of various R2R D/A converter using various topologies. *International Robotics & Automation Journal*, *4*(2), 128–131.

ADDITIONAL READING

Bhatia, V., & Whig, P. (2013). A secured dual tune multi frequency based smart elevator control system. *International Journal of Research in Engineering and Advanced Technology*, *4*(1), 1163–2319.

Dannen, C. (2017). *Introducing Ethereum and Solidity: Foundations of Cryptocurrency and Blockchain Programming for Beginners* (1st ed.). Apress. doi:10.1007/978-1-4842-2535-6

DavidsonS.De FilippiP.PottsJ. (2016). *Disrupting Governance: The New Institutional Economics of Distributed Ledger Technology*. Social Science Research Network. doi:10.2139/ssrn.2811995

Rupani, A., Whig, P., Sujediya, G., & Vyas, P. (2017). A robust technique for image processing based on interfacing of Raspberry-Pi and FPGA using IoT. *2017 International Conference on Computer, Communications and Electronics (Comptelix)*, 350–353. 10.1109/COMPTELIX.2017.8003992

Sharma, A., Kumar, A., & Whig, P. (2015). On the performance of CDTA based novel analog inverse low pass filter using 0.35 μm CMOS parameter. International Journal of Science. *Technology & Management, 4*(1), 594–601.

Singh, A. K., Gupta, A., & Senani, R. (2018). OTRA-based multi-function inverse filter configuration. *Advances in Electrical and Electronic Engineering, 15*(5), 846–856. doi:10.15598/aeee.v15i5.2572

Whig, P., & Ahmad, S. N. (2012). Performance analysis of various readout circuits for monitoring quality of water using analog integrated circuits. *International Journal of Intelligent Systems and Applications, 4*(11), 103. doi:10.5815/ijisa.2012.11.11

Whig, P., & Ahmad, S. N. (2014). Simulation of linear dynamic macro model of photo catalytic sensor in SPICE. *COMPEL: The International Journal for Computation and Mathematics in Electrical and Electronic Engineering*.

KEY TERMS AND DEFINITIONS

AI: Artificial intelligence (AI) is the ability of a computer or a robot controlled by a computer to do tasks that are usually done by humans because they require human intelligence and discernment.

Big Data: Big data is a combination of structured, semi structured, and unstructured data collected by organizations that can be mined for information and used in machine learning projects, predictive modeling, and other advanced analytics applications.

Bitcoin: *Bitcoin* (₿) is a decentralized digital currency that can be transferred on the peer-to-peer *bitcoin* network.

Blockchain: A blockchain platform allows users and developers to create novel uses of an existing blockchain infrastructure.

Crypto: A cryptocurrency is an encrypted data string that denotes a unit of currency.

Ethereum: *Ethereum* is a technology that's home to digital money, global payments, and applications.

Holochain: Holochain is an eco-aware peer-to-peer network.

IoT: The term IoT, or Internet of Things, refers to the collective network of connected devices and the technology that facilitates communication between devices and the cloud, as well as between the devices themselves.

Machine Learning: Machine learning is a branch of artificial intelligence (AI) and computer science which focuses on the use of data and algorithms to imitate the way that humans learn, gradually improving its accuracy.

NFT: NFT, known as non-fungible tokens (NFTs), these cryptographic assets are based on blockchain technology and have unique identification codes and metadata that set them apart from each other.

Smart Contracts: A *smart contract* is a computer program or a transaction protocol which is intended to automatically execute, control or document legally.

Chapter 4

Gender Diversity in FinTech:
An Effort Towards Creating an
Inclusive and Sustainable Industry

Farjana Nur Saima
ⓘD https://orcid.org/0000-0001-8389-6858
Bangladesh University of Professionals, Bangladesh

Md. H Asibur Rahman
ⓘD https://orcid.org/0000-0003-1045-1115
Bangladesh University of Professionals, Bangladesh

Ratan Ghosh
ⓘD https://orcid.org/0000-0002-2506-8357
Bangaladesh University of Professionals, Bangladesh

ABSTRACT

This study explores gender diversity in fintech usage for creating an equitable and sustainable fintech industry in Bangladesh. A closed-ended structured questionnaire was developed and distributed to fintech users by email and social media platforms. A total of 527 complete responses were documented. SPSS and SmartPLS have been used for analyzing data. Moreover, structural equation modeling (SEM) has been employed to test the study's hypotheses. Results reveal that perceived ease of use, perceived credibility, and perceived usefulness have a significant positive relationship with satisfaction. Furthermore, satisfaction has a positive and significant relationship with loyalty. While investigating the role of gender diversity on fintech, there is no moderating effect of gender on the effects of perceived ease of use, perceived credibility, and satisfaction on loyalty. However, the relationship between perceived usefulness and satisfaction is moderated by gender. Satisfaction is a significant predictor of ensuring fintech loyalty of both males and females.

DOI: 10.4018/978-1-6684-4176-3.ch004

INTRODUCTION

The dominance of Artificial Intelligence (AI), Big Data, and Blockchain Technology has revolutionized our traditional lifestyle. The epoch-making technological innovations of the 21st century have made peoples' life more convenient and brought socio-economic progress. Such a digital technology, Fintech, has emerged with the potential to bring sustainable development by creating an inclusive financial service system. According to World Bank (2018), *"Financial inclusion means that individuals and businesses have access to useful and affordable financial products and services that meet their needs-transactions, payments, savings, credit, and insurance- delivered responsibly and sustainably."* World Bank estimated that 1.7 billion adults (with women 1 billion) yet to have a basic financial transaction account (Kapadia, 2020, p.5). These unbanked people are mostly from developing countries (Demirguç-Kunt *et al*., 2018). Fintech will help to achieve the UN Sustainable Development Goal (SDG)1 (terminating extreme poverty) and SDG5 (ensuring gender equality). It will unlock the door of enormous socio-economic opportunities for financially unserved or underserved communities. They will be better able to manage their financial life (i.e., collect money from distant sources, transfer and store funds) through Fintech. Thus, it can positively impact society by reducing poverty and empowering women. Suri and Jack (2016) documented a 22% reduction in the poverty level of women-headed Kenyan households due to mobile money usage. The G20 High-Level Principles for Digital Financial Inclusion formulated by the Global Partnership for Financial Inclusion (GPFI) is also promoting the digital financial system that provides an economical way for the financially excluded communities, especially the women, to conduct their necessary financial transactions (e.g., making payment, saving for kids' school, sending/receiving remittances, getting a loan or buying insurance) (Global Partnership for Financial Inclusion, 2016). Inclusive Fintech can make financial products and services accessible, affordable and appropriate for the underserved segments of society (Kapadia, 2020, P. 10).

Though Fintech can drive the growth of financial inclusion and reduce income inequality, this projection may not be applied equally to low-income countries. According to Demir *et al*. (2020), the probable reasons behind this might be the lack of a well-established infrastructure, proper consumer protection regulations, and essential financial literacy among households in low-income countries. However, the financial inclusion penetration rate has shown an uptick since 2011 in developed and developing countries. 1.2 billion adults have opened a bank or mobile money account since 2011 (The World Bank, 2018), but a wide gender gap exists in accessing financial service accounts globally (Delaporte & Naghavi,2019). In developing countries, women are 9% less likely to own a bank account than men (Demirguç-Kunt *et al*., 2018). Closing the gender gap is now a paramount concern to achieving the Universal Financial Goal 2020. Focusing on a gender-inclusive financial system will also foster the financial growth of the mobile industry. As per the Global System for Mobile Communications (GSMA), the revenue of the mobile industry could be increased to $140 billion over the period 2019-2023 in low and middle-income countries by reducing the existing mobile gender gap (GSMA, 2021).

Bangladesh has already achieved the status of a lower-middle-income country in 2015 and set the target of becoming a developed country by 2041. For this purpose, Bangladesh is working towards achieving the Digital Bangladesh Vision 2021 (launched in 2009) aligned with SDGs. The core philosophy of Digital Bangladesh is to enhance socio-economic benefits by connecting the citizens meaningfully, providing doorstep services, preparing skilled human resources for the 21st century, and making a productive and competitive market through the adoption of digital technology (Rogers, 2018). Since 2010, the shift from a manual to an automated payment system, cash to the card, or other payment systems has unleashed the potential of the digital financial system in Bangladesh (Financial Institutions Division, 2019). Moreover, the Mobile Financial System (MFS) operation has continued in Bangladesh since 2011. Currently, MFS service is being provided by 15 banks approved and regulated by Bangladesh Bank (Hazra and Priyo, 2020). Bangladeshi MFS providers like Bkash, Nagad, Rocket, to name a few, have succeeded, including a broad range of customers under the umbrella of the digital financial system. Financial account ownership and mobile money account have increased since 2014, as estimated by the World Bank in 2017 (Alliance for Financial Inclusion, 2020). Huge mobile and internet penetration rates are the primary reasons behind such a surge. Bangladesh Telecommunication Regulatory Commission (BTRC) reported that mobile phone and mobile internet subscriptions have risen by 67% and 221%, respectively, from 2012 to August 2019 (Hazra and Priyo, 2020). Again, the recent COVID-19 pandemic hit has pushed up the mobile phone, internet, and mobile money usage rate. Amid the COVID-19 pandemic, BTRC reported 1 million new mobile phone users and 2.9 million new internet users in September 2020 (The Business Standard, 2020). Between 2019 and 2020, a 20% growth rate has been seen in MFS account registration and 7% in daily transactions through MFS (Alliance for Financial Inclusion, 2020).

Figure 1. Ownership of financial account and the transactions through digital methods (in percentage) Source: Author's creation from Global Findex Database (2017)

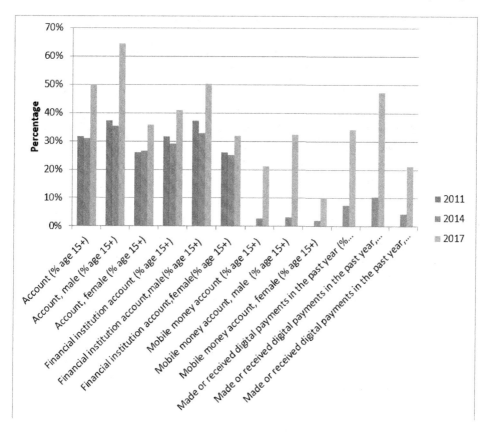

During the pandemic, the government's safety net disbursement through MFS fueled such growth (Saima *et al.*, 2022). However, the picture is not rosy as it seems. Despite the mobile penetration rate being approximately 65 million in Bangladesh, these people are still unbanked (Rogers, 2018). There is a huge gender gap in mobile phone subscription, mobile internet, and mobile money usage rate. The GSMA consumer survey 2020 reveals that in Bangladesh, smartphone ownership for females was 21% compared to the rate of males (39%); internet usage rate of females was 19% compared to male (33%), and the rate was 14% for female and 40% for male in mobile money usage (GSMA, 2021). The recent Global Findex Database also documented the gender-wise account ownership in the financial institutions and MFS from 2011 to 2017. (see Figure-1). The study's objective is to investigate the role of fintech for a gender-based sustainable fintech solution in Bangladesh. This study has proposed a framework incorporating Perceived Credibility (PU), Satisfaction (SAT) and Loyalty (LOY) with perceived ease of use (EU) and usefulness (PU) from TAM.

THEORETICAL BACKGROUND

Behavioral intention to adopt or continue Fintech usage has been analyzed from different theoretical lenses such as Theory of Planned Behavior (TPB)(Ajzen, 1991), Theory of Reasoned Action (TRA) (Fishbein and Ajzen, 1975), Technology Acceptance Model (TAM) (Davis, 1989), (TAM) 2 (Venkatesh and Davis, 2000), Innovation Diffusion Theory (IDT) (Rogers, 1995), Unified Theory of Acceptance and Use of Technology (UTAUT) (Venkatesh *et al.*, 2003), Task Technology Fit (TTF)(Goodhue and Thompson, 1995), Information Systems Success Model (ISS) (DeLone and McLean, 1992, 2004), Expectation Confirmation Theory (ECT) (Oliver, 1980) etc. One widely used model in the information technology context is the TAM (Davis, 1989), adapted from the TRA and TPB. According to TAM, two constructs- perceived ease of use and perceived usefulness can explain why the users adopt a particular technology (Yen and Wu, 2016). This model has also been used to analyze the post-adoption behavior of consumers. However, it has been criticized for failing to account for other important constructs suggested being incorporated to extend the model (Ajibade, 2018; Legris et al., 2003). But, the incorporation of the external variable will be fruitful if those are context specific such as target group, geographical location, technology type etc. (Moon and Kim, 2001; Popy and Bappy, 2020). Therefore, external variables like Credibility, Satisfaction have been added to determine the loyalty towards Fintech in this study. Previous studies such as (Akturan and Tezcan, 2012; Albashrawi and Motiwalla, 2017; Azad, 2016; Hanafizadeh et al., 2012; Hsu et al., 2011; Himel et al., 2021; Koenig-Lewis et al., 2010; Yen and Wu, 2016) extended TAM to investigate the factors responsible for MFS or M-banking usage. Mere adoption is not adequate to escalate the benefits of Fintech. A paramount concern for creating a sustainable Fintech industry is to confirm Fintech users' loyalty which is embedded in the users' perceived credibility and Satisfaction on using such innovation (Saima *et al.*, 2022). Thus, in line with the study's objective, three additional variables, Perceived Credibility, Satisfaction and Loyalty, have been included in the research model. The study's main objective is to determine the gender difference in Fintech loyalty. Thus, we also included gender variables in the model to identify gender impacts on the relationships between the variables in the proposed framework. A summary of previous empirical evidence related to the moderating role of gender on the usage of Fintech/MFS/M-banking/ Internet Banking has also been presented in Table-1 below.

Table 1. Summary of previous empirical evidence related to moderating role of gender on the usage of Fintech/MFS/M-banking/internet banking

Authors	Sample	Theory/Variables	Analysis Technique	Findings Related to Effects of gender
Oliveira et al. (2014)	194 mobile phone users from a public university in Portugal, Lisbon.	Integrated Task Technology Fit (TTF) Model, Unified Theory of Acceptance and Usage of Technology (UTAUT), and Initial Trust Model (ITM) to investigate the adoption of M-banking	Partial Least Squares (PLS)	Gender does not have any significant moderating effect on the behavioral intention to adopt m-banking.
Sharma et al. (2015)	110 Omani Internet banking users	Applied TAM to investigate the determinants of internet banking adoption	Compared results of Multiple Linear Regression (MLR) and neural network model	MLR result shows gender as a non-significant predictor of internet banking adoption, whereas neural network result is reverse.
Azad (2016)	314 Bangladeshi M-banking users	Incorporated social influence (SI), Compatibility (COM) and demographic variables (namely age, education and gender) into the original TAM to investigate M-banking adoption.	Artificial neural network approach as well as the principal component analysis (PCA)	Gender does not influence M-banking adoption.
Yen and Wu (2016)	368 Taiwanese MFS users	Integrated additional variables namely perceived enjoyment, perceived mobility, personal habit and into the original TAM to investigate intention to continue MFS usage	Structural Equation Modeling (SEM)	Gender has a moderating effect on the relationship between variables in the projected model.
Lwoga and Lwoga, 2017	292 M-payment users from Morogoro and Dar es Salaam, Tanzania	Integrated TAM with other factors such as user-centric factors, security factors, system characteristics, and gender to investigate M-payment usage intention.	SEM and multigroup analysis	Behavioral intention to use M-payment varies with gender.
Vasudeva and Chawla (2019)	524 M-banking users from the state of Punjab in India.	M-banking usage, Loyalty, Gender, Age, Income	Moderated Multiple Regression Analysis	Gender moderates the relationship between M-banking usage and loyalty.

Continued on following page

Table 1. Continued

Authors	Sample	Theory/Variables	Analysis Technique	Findings Related to Effects of gender
Tariq et al., 2021	392 Pakistani MFS users	Applied UTAUT 2 to investigate MFS adoption.	PLS	Gender is found to have moderating effect only in the rural sample.
Nurlaily et al., (2021)	406 Indonesian Fintech users	Adopted the Theory of Planned Behavior (TPB) to investigate the Fintech continuance intention	Generalized Structured Component Analysis (GSCA)	In the female user group, gender moderates the impact of perceived risk on the Fintech continuance intention.

RESEARCH FRAMEWORK & HYPOTHESES DEVELOPMENT

Following Albashrawi and Motiwalla (2017), this study proposed a framework incorporating Perceived Credibility, Satisfaction and Loyalty with perceived ease of use and usefulness from TAM. Figure-2 presents the proposed research framework of this study.

Effect of Perceived Ease of Use on Satisfaction

Perceived ease of use indicates how comfortably the users can use technology. It refers to the degree of effort a user has to use technological innovation. If a user faces difficulties operating a digital device, he is less likely to adopt and or continue using that. According to Kim, Choi and Han (2009), the higher the users' perception of ease regarding technology use, the higher the acceptance rate of that technology. Generally, technology users look for a comfortable and user-friendly interface of digital devices. Thus, the positive perception of ease of use leads to greater Satisfaction. Hew et al. (2016) stated that users accept an information system well if it can be operated and handled easily. Consumers who have more mobile phone literacy than others are expected to face fewer operating problems and get accustomed to M-banking quickly (Koenig-Lewis et al., 2010). Albashrawi and Motiwalla (2017) hypothesized a positive link between perceived ease of use with Satisfaction in mobile banking. Similarly, this study formulated the following hypothesis-

H1: *There is a positive effect of perceived ease of use on Satisfaction.*

Figure 2. Research framework

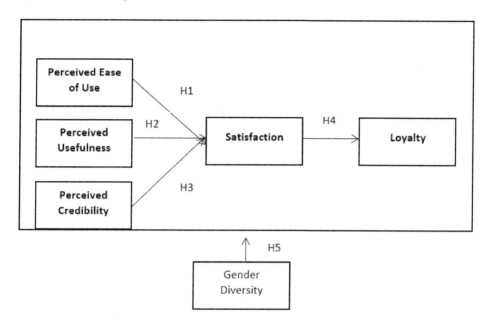

Effect of Perceived Usefulness on Satisfaction:

Perceived usefulness refers to how much a user can improve his performance using particular information technology (Davis et al., 1989). Here, it indicates how Fintech usage will improve the users' way of doing financial transactions. People are assertive about using MFS as completing banking transactions through MFS is useful (Luarn and Lin, 2005). Despite having some limitations like low computing power and small screen size in MFS, it may be useful due to its easy manipulation and clear, interactive interface (Yen & Wu, 2016). The higher the perception of usefulness, the higher the intention to adopt M-banking (Yang, 2009). Previous studies (Albashrawi and Motiwalla, 2017; Bhattacherjee, 2001; Humbani and Wiese, 2019; Saima et al., 2022) draw a positive link between perceived usefulness with Satisfaction in the context of MFS continuance. Similarly, this study formulates the following hypothesis-

H2: *There is a positive effect of perceived usefulness on Satisfaction.*

Effect of Perceived Credibility on Satisfaction

Credibility is defined by Wang et al. (2003) as the degree of belief a user has in the security and privacy of a digital system. One potential reason for not adopting a digital financial system is the fear of losing money and personal information to hackers or third parties. M-banking users worry about security and privacy threats (Luarn and Lin, 2005). Sagib and Zapan (2014) found that assurance and security can alter the Satisfaction of M-banking users in the context of Bangladesh. As a positive link exists between Satisfaction and credibility (Reji Kumar and Ravindran, 2012), the service providers need to create a system that can combat such threats to increase Satisfaction in MFS usage (Saima et al., 2022). Thus, this study formulates the following hypothesis-

H3: *There is a positive effect of perceived credibility on Satisfaction.*

Effect of Satisfaction on Loyalty

Loyalty denotes the repeated use of a particular digital system. Here, it refers to the tendency of users to use Fintech applications continuously for carrying out daily financial transactions. Users' Satisfaction will lead to Loyalty towards the Fintech applications. To create a sustainable Fintech industry, the users must keep taking the Fintech service. Loyalty can be established in the case of higher Satisfaction in M-banking (Sagib and Zapan, 2014). Similarly, this study hypothesizes a positive link of Satisfaction with Fintech users' loyalty.

H4: *There is a positive effect of Satisfaction on loyalty.*

The Moderating Role of Gender

Gender is a significant trait by which behavioral intention can differ. According to psychologists, males and females possess heterogeneous psychological characteristics that alter their reactions and decision-making. While confronting a barrier, males and females take different coping strategies (Yen and Wu, 2016). For example- a male is likely to avoid or withdraw to release stress, whereas a female tends to talk to and seek support from others (McDonald and Korabik, 1991). In the studies of consumers' behavioral intention, gender is perceived to be an influential factor (Saad and Gill, 2000). In the case of using electronic or digital communication systems, the purpose of usage differs between males and females (Mante and Piris, 2002). A similar conclusion may be attributed to the intention of M-banking adoption (Vasudeva and Chawla, 2019). Hamza and Shah (2014) found that the willingness to complete financial transactions using MFS is higher among males than females. Empirical evidence on the effect of gender on Fintech adoption is inconclusive. Some of the previous studies, such as (Lwoga and Lwoga, 2017; Nurlaily et al., 2021; Vasudeva and Chawla, 2019; Yen and Wu, 2016), found a significant effect of gender, whereas studies such as (Azad, 2016; Oliveira et al., 2014) found insignificant effect. Besides, Tariq et al. (2021) found the significance of gender for the partial sample only. Thus, it can be assumed that the ease of use, usefulness, credibility, Satisfaction and loyalty towards Fintech will be differently perceived by males and females in Bangladesh. So, the following hypothesis related to moderating effects of gender is formed.

H5: *Gender has a moderating effect on the relationships between the variables in the proposed framework.*

RESEARCH METHODOLOGY

Sampling and Data Collection

Data was taken from actual MFS users in Bangladesh between January 05, 2022, and January 31, 2022. The period is marked by the third wave of the COVID-19 pandemic in Bangladesh, characterized by infection outbreaks with COVID-19 virus Omicron strains. To ensure the research's credibility and collect data exclusively from MFS users, an initial screening question regarding whether or not they use MFS was asked the respondents. Therefore, we used purposive sampling. COVID-19 limits resulted in lockdowns. Thus, to contact as many individuals as possible while keeping social distance, a Google Form was utilized to produce an online survey sent out via email and social media (e.g., Facebook, Imo, and WhatsApp). However, participation in the survey was entirely voluntary. Finally, 527 responses were found to be accurately completed and, therefore, were considered the sample for the study. The sample size was sufficient for a countrywide survey, as the minimum sample size required for such a study is 384 respondents (Krejcie and Morgan, 1970).

Research Measurement Items

In the first section of the questionnaire, the research objectives are described. The second portion of the questionnaire asked about the demographics of the respondents. The last part had 19 questions to measure the constructs. All constructs were assessed using instruments derived from prior research and included three or four items (see Table 2). Certain language changes have been made to the items to reduce ambiguity. Using a five-point Likert scale, participants must answer each question on a scale of 1 (strongly disagree) to 5 (strongly agree).

Table 2. Sources of construct measurements

No.	Constructs	Measurement items	Sources
1	Perceived Ease of Use (EU)	EU1-EU3	Saji and Paul (2018)
2	Perceived Credibility (PC)	PC1-PC2	Luarn and Lin (2005)
		PC3-PC4	Boonsiritomachai and Pitchayadejanant (2017)
3	Perceived Usefulness (PU)	PU1-PU4	Venkatesh and Davis (2000)
4	Satisfaction (SAT)	SAT1-SAT4	(Bhattacherjee, 2001)
5	Loyalty (Loy)	Loy1-Loy4	(Le, 2021)

ANALYSIS OF FINDINGS

Demographic Profile

Males comprised 68.31% of responses, while females made up 31.69%. Table 3 provides relevant information about the respondents' profiles.

Table 3. Profile of the respondents

Particulars	No of Response	Percentage	Particulars	No of Response	Percentage
Gender			**Age**		
Male	360	68.31%	15-24 years	296	56.17%
Female	167	31.69%	25-34 years	220	41.74%
Profession			Above 35 years	11	02.09%
Student	284	53.89%	**Education**		
Service	227	43.07%	HSC or below	114	21.63%
Housewife	09	1.71%	Undergraduate/ Honors	223	42.31%
Business	07	1.33%	Graduate/Masters	190	36.05%

Measurement Model

The constructs' Convergent Validity was evaluated using item loading and Average Variance Extracted (AVE). To ensure AVEs higher than 0.50, item *Loy4* was deleted from the model. Table 4 shows the constructs Outer Loadings, Cronbach's Alpha, Composite Reliability (CR), Dijkstra–indicator Henseler's (rho A) and Average

Variance Extracted (AVE), which are higher than the recommended cut-off values. Accordingly, enough reliability had been observed at the item and construct level (Henseler et al., 2015; Hair et al., 2019).

Table 4. Convergent validity, internal consistency, and reliability

Factor/Construct	Items	Loading	AVE	CR	Cronbach's Alpha	rho_A
Ease of Use	EU1	0.879	0.742	0.896	0.827	0.833
	EU2	0.842				
	EU3	0.862				
Perceived Credibility	PC1	0.774	0.596	0.855	0.776	0.778
	PC2	0.791				
	PC3	0.775				
	PC4	0.747				
Perceived Usefulness	PU1	0.911	0.795	0.939	0.914	0.915
	PU2	0.876				
	PU3	0.920				
	PU4	0.857				
Satisfaction	SAT1	0.862	0.669	0.889	0.833	0.851
	SAT2	0.880				
	SAT3	0.687				
	SAT4	0.830				
Loyalty	Loy1	0.894	0.778	0.913	0.857	0.858
	Loy2	0.883				
	Loy3	0.868				

The discriminant validity of a latent construct is the degree to which it differs from another (Hair et al., 2019). All square roots of AVE (diagonal components) are greater than inter-construct correlation coefficients (off-diagonal elements), as presented in Table 5. Therefore, satisfactory discriminant validity is indicated (Fornell and Larcker, 1981).

Table 5. Fornell-Larcker criterion to assess discriminant validity

	EU	LOY	PC	PU	SAT
1. Ease of Use (EU)	0.861				
2. Loyalty (Loy)	0.570	0.882			
3. Perceived Credibility (PC)	0.420	0.479	0.772		
4. Perceived Usefulness (PU)	0.283	0.459	0.262	0.892	
5. Satisfaction (SAT)	0.644	0.714	0.500	0.456	0.818
Mean	3.792	4.211	3.844	3.999	4.054
Standard Deviation	0.800	0.756	0.732	0.936	0.749

Besides, we also assessed discriminant validity with a relatively new approach, the Heterotrait-Monotrait ratio of correlations (HTMT) (Henseler et al., 2014). The constructs fulfill the required criterion at HTMT 0.85 (Hair et al., 2019; Kline, 2015), as shown in Table 6. Moreover, item cross-loadings were assessed and found satisfactory to demonstrate the constructs' discriminant validity. In conclusion, all the latent constructs tested in this study showed exceptionally high reliability and validity, allowing us to assess the structural model.

Table 6. Heterotrait-Monotrait ratio to assess discriminant validity

	EU	Loy	PC	PU	SAT
1. Ease of Use (EU)					
2. Loyalty (Loy)	**0.674**				
3. Perceived Credibility (PC)	**0.523**	**0.575**			
4. Perceived Usefulness (PU)	**0.318**	**0.518**	**0.297**		
5. Satisfaction (SAT)	**0.771**	**0.833**	**0.613**	**0.513**	

The Structural Model

The structural model coefficients for the links between the constructs were estimated using a set of regression equations. Collinearity must be looked at to ensure it doesn't cause the regression results to be biased when looking at structural relationships. The variance inflation factor (VIF) is often used to look at the collinearity of exogenous components (Hair et al., 2019; Memon et al., 2017). The VIF scores observed for the latent constructs in this study were significantly lower than the threshold (lower than 3.0 or close to it) recommended in Hair *et al.* (2019), indicating that the study was free of collinearity concerns.

The bootstrapping approach (resampling =5,000, minimum) was used in our investigation to determine the statistical significance of the path coefficients (Hair et al., 2017). We investigate the links between exogenous and endogenous variables using t-values, a 0.05 (p<05) significance level, and Bias Corrected Confidence Intervals (BCI LL-UL) to report the implications of the predicted interactions (Hair et al., 2019).

Full Sample Analysis Results

As expected, all exogenous factors exhibit a positive and statistically significant association with endogenous variables when the full sample is considered. Here, ease of use (**H1:** EU → SAT, β= 0.471, t= 11.972, p < 0.05, BCI LL: 0.405, UL: 0.533); perceived usefulness (**H2:** PU → SAT, β= 0.262, t= 6.188, p < 0.05, BCI LL: 0.190, UL: 0.330), and perceived credibility (**H3:** PC → SAT, β= 0.234, t= 5.460, p < 0.05, BCI LL: 0.163, UL: 0.303) were significantly and positively related to satisfaction. Besides, satisfaction (**H4:** SAT→ Loy, β= 0.715, t= 21.546, p < 0.05, BCI LL: 0.654, UL: 0.764) was significantly and positively related to Loyalty to use MFS. Figure 3 and Table 7 demonstrate the results of causal interactions.

This research found that R^2 of Satisfaction (SAT) toward MFS = 0.540 and Loyalty to use MFS= 0.511, indicating that the independent variables (e.g., EU, PU, and PC) can explain 54.00% variability in Satisfaction (SAT) toward MFS and 51.10% variability of Loyalty to use MFS (available in Figure 3).

Table 7. Results of complete sample for causal relationships

H	Relations	Beta	Std. Dev.	T-stat	P value	BCI LL	BCI UL	f^2	VIF	Decision	
H1	EU → SAT	0.471	0.039	11.972	0.000	0.405	0.533	0.383	1.263	Accepted	
H2	PU → SAT	0.262	0.042	6.188	0.000	0.190	0.330	0.133	1.117	Accepted	
H3	PC → SAT	0.234	0.043	5.460	0.000	0.163	0.303	0.095	1.247	Accepted	
H4	SAT→ Loy	0.715	0.033	21.546	0.000	0.654	0.764	1.041	1.000	Accepted	
	R^2										
	Loyalty to use MFS 0.511 (51.10%)										
	Satisfaction toward MFS 0.540 (54.00%)										

The effect size, denoted by f², is the amount to which an exogenous variable contributes to the R². f² values more than 0.35, 0.15, and 0.02 indicate a large, medium, and minor influence, respectively, while f² values less than 0.02 indicate no effect (Cohen, 1988).

Figure 3. Structural Model representing R2, beta coefficient & t- values for path coefficients

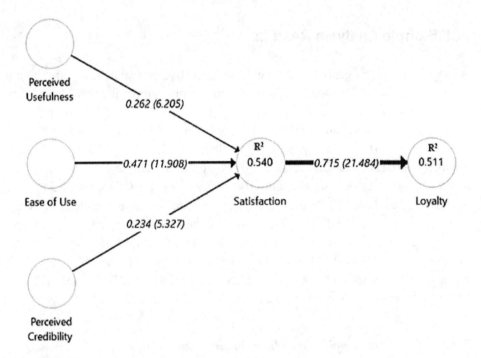

Here, EU → SAT (H1: f² > 0.35) and SAT→ Loy (H4: f² > 0.35) largely affect the corresponding R². Besides, we noticed a small effect for PU → SAT (H2: f² > 0.02) and PC → SAT (H3: f² > 0.02), (available in Table 7).

Hair *et al*. (2017) acknowledged "in the structural model, Q² values larger than zero for a specific reflective endogenous latent variable indicate the path model's predictive relevance for a particular dependent construct" (p. 202). In this investigation, SAT (Q²= 0.355) Loy (Q²= 0.390) indicated an adequate predictive relevance. Finally, the study data were self-assessed, there was a possibility of method-related variance/bias. The "Harman single-factor test" found that a single factor accounted for about 27.70% of the total variation, which was less than the

50% maximum allowed. This implies that this investigation is free from common method bias (Podsakoff et al., 2003).

Female vs. Male Sample Analysis Results

We split up the data set into two groups based on the gender of the respondents. Then, using a similar bootstrapping approach (minimum resampling = 5,000), we examined the statistical significance of the path coefficients for each of the categories, namely the female and male groups. For both males and females, we found all the relationships were significant. However, when looking at the results, it becomes clear that the beta coefficient values were not consistent across the groups. Table 8 demonstrates a comparative result of causal relationships for females and males. Besides, Figure-4 demonstrates a structural model for both females and males in absolute values.

Table 8. Comparative result of causal relationships for female and male

Female (167 responses)						
Relations	**Beta**	**Std. Dev.**	**T-Stat**	**P Values**	**BCI LL**	**BCI UL**
EU → SAT	0.542	0.069	7.900	**0.000**	0.421	0.649
PC → SAT	0.295	0.074	3.997	**0.000**	0.178	0.420
PU → SAT	0.151	0.060	2.518	**0.006**	0.053	0.249
SAT → Loyalty	0.737	0.043	17.237	**0.000**	0.649	0.795
Male (360 responses)						
EU → SAT	0.423	0.050	8.533	**0.000**	0.342	0.506
PC → SAT	0.208	0.052	4.033	**0.000**	0.124	0.293
PU → SAT	0.328	0.057	5.755	**0.000**	0.233	0.423
SAT → Loyalty	0.708	0.045	15.896	**0.000**	0.624	0.772
Female (R²)			**Male (R²)**			
Loyalty to use MFS 0.543 (54.30%)			Loyalty to use MFS 0.501 (50.10%)			
Satisfaction toward MFS 0.596 (59.60%)			Satisfaction toward MFS 0.534 (53.40%)			

Between-Group Analysis: Gender Differences

To assess whether respondents gender impacts using MFS, a multigroup analysis was performed for differences in how the variables were related between the groups by running the previous estimation for the subsamples, e.g., female and male. The results of the multi-group PLS test revealed that the path coefficient between EU and SAT (EU SAT) is larger in the female user sample ($\beta = 0.542$) than in the male user sample ($\beta = 0.423$), β (Female-Male) = 0.119, t-value (|Female vs Male|) = 1.381, and P-value (Female vs Male) = 0.084. It provides evidence that the difference between female users and male users was not significant in terms of the EU → SAT relationship. Similarly, PC → SAT and SAT → Loyalty relationships provided evidence that the difference in female users and male users was not significant. On the other hand, the MGA Analysis allows us to report a significant difference between female and male users when it comes to the PU→ SAT relationship.

Figure 4. Structural model representing R^2, beta coefficient and t- values (females vs. males)

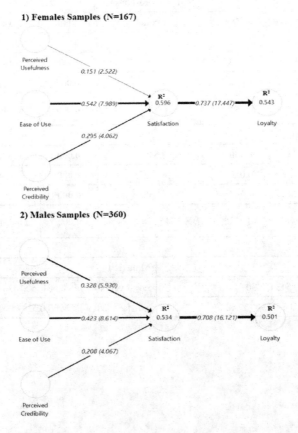

Table 9.

Relation	Beta (Female - Male)	t-Value (IFemale vs MaleI)	p-Value (Female vs Male)	Decision
EU → SAT	0.119	1.381	0.084	Rejected
PC → SAT	0.086	0.964	0.168	Rejected
PU → SAT	-0.178	1.977	0.024	Accepted
SAT → Loyalty	0.029	0.405	0.343	Rejected

DISCUSSION

This study explores gender diversity in fintech usage for creating an equitable and sustainable Fintech industry in Bangladesh. Specifically, this study has statistically identified the gender gap in the post-adoption behavior of Fintech users of Bangladesh. This study has considered three variables, Perceived ease of use (EU), Perceived Credibility (PC) and Perceived Usefulness (PU), to measure the Satisfaction (SAT) of Fintech users. Moreover, Satisfaction (SAT) has been further used to explain the Loyalty (LOY) of fintech users of Bangladesh. The results reveal that EU, PC and PU have a significant positive relationship in explaining SAT.

Moreover, SAT has a positive and significant relationship with LOY. These findings articulate an impressive reflection of the fintech service experience for the users of Bangladesh. MFS is one of the most highly used Fintech services in Bangladesh. As MFS is an easy and secure media for doing financial transactions, it facilitates many unbanked people to get the facility of the modern banking system in the best possible way. People who could not take the formal banking services in rural areas find it easier and trustworthy to use fintech services in Bangladesh.

Moreover, urban people of Bangladesh have fashioned Fintech usage as an alternative to branch banking as it saves time and energy for individuals. Fintech has been an economical and easy way for the government of Bangladesh to bring everyone under formal financial services. To substantiate it, there should not be any gender gap. This is inevitable for the sustainable and inclusive development of the fintech industry. This study has extended the model to check the gender diversity in fintech services of Bangladesh. The results reveal that there is no moderating effect of gender on the relationship between EU→SAT, PC→SAT and SAT→LOY. The only relationship moderated by gender is PU→SAT. The possible reason for such findings can be a limited engagement of females in economic activities. In Bangladesh, the volume, variations, and complexities in economic/ financial transactions are limited for Females than males. That's why increasing fintech usefulness further may not possibly escalate Satisfaction to a greater extent for female users. This is evident in the results, which show PU is less important than EU and PC for females.

Nonetheless, SAT is a significant predictor of ensuring fintech loyalty of both males and females. Using fintech is not a luxury rather a necessity of today's world. Either voluntarily or involuntarily, people are adopting the fintech services. But fintech users, irrespective of gender, will continue using it only if they are satisfied. So, fintech service providers should focus on the basic post-adoption factors such as EU, PU, and PC, improving users' Satisfaction.

CONCLUSION

The study's objective is to investigate the role of fintech for a gender-based sustainable fintech solution in Bangladesh. This study has proposed a framework incorporating Perceived Credibility (PU), Satisfaction (SAT) and Loyalty (LOY) with perceived ease of use (EU) and usefulness (PU) from TAM. Findings reveal that EU, PC and PU have a significant positive relationship with SAT. Additionally, SAT has a positive and significant relationship with LOY. While investigating the role of gender diversity on fintech, there is no moderating effect of EU, PC and SAT on Loyalty. Only the relationship between PU and SAT is moderated by gender. It is found that the female fintech users are not getting usefulness by taking service, leading them to dissatisfied customers. Still, they are continuing fintech usage due to their economic commitment. There is a huge gender gap in the pre-adoption of fintech users. This study has taken responses from the users currently using fintech services in Bangladesh. By analyzing users' post-adoption fintech services behavior, it is highly recommended that fintech servicers focus on retaining existing users and acquiring new customers. In both cases, special focus should be given to female users to increase their service experience. As more and more women are joining and contributing to the economic development of Bangladesh, satisfied female fintech users can help the industry and economy to boost a lot. Future research can be conducted on the various facets of the pre-adoption and post-adoption gender gap of fintech users of Bangladesh. This may help policymakers create a sustainable gender-based fintech solution in Bangladesh.

REFERENCES

Ajibade, P. (2018). Technology acceptance model limitations and criticisms: Exploring the practical applications and use in technology-related studies, mixed-method, and qualitative researches. *LibraryPhilosophy & Practice, 1941*. https://digitalcommons.unl.edu/libphilprac/1941

Ajzen, I. (1991). The theory of planned behavior. *Organizational Behavior and Human Decision Processes*, *50*(2), 179–211. doi:10.1016/0749-5978(91)90020-T

Akturan, U., & Tezcan, N. (2012). Mobile banking adoption of the youth market: Perceptions and intentions. *Marketing Intelligence & Planning*, *30*(4), 444–459. doi:10.1108/02634501211231928

Albashrawi, M., & Motiwalla, L. (2017). Privacy and Personalization in Continued Usage Intention of Mobile Banking: An Integrative Perspective. *Information Systems Frontiers*, *21*(5), 1031–1043. doi:10.100710796-017-9814-7

Alliance for Financial Inclusion. (2020). *Digital financial services supervision in Bangladesh.* Alliance for Financial Inclusion.

Azad, M. A. K. (2016). Predicting mobile banking adoption in Bangladesh: A neural network approach. *Transnational Corporations Review*, *8*(3), 207–214. doi:10.10 80/19186444.2016.1233726

Bhattacherjee, A. (2001). Understanding Information Systems Continuance: An Expectation-Confirmation Model. *Management Information Systems Quarterly*, *25*(3), 351. doi:10.2307/3250921

GSMA Connected Women. (2021). *The Mobile Gender Gap Report 2021.* GSMA.

Davis, F. D. (1989). Perceived Usefulness, Perceived Ease of Use, and User Acceptance of Information Technology. *Management Information Systems Quarterly*, *13*(3), 319–340. doi:10.2307/249008

Delaporte, A., & Naghavi, N. (2019). *The promise of mobile money for further advancing women's financial inclusion* [Blog]. Retrieved February 5 2022, from https://www.gsma.com/mobilefordevelopment/blog/the-promise-of-mobile-money-for-further-advancing-womens-financial-inclusion/

DeLone, W. H., & McLean, E. R. (1992). Information Systems Success: The Quest for the Dependent Variable. *Information Systems Research*, *3*(1), 60–95. doi:10.1287/isre.3.1.60

Demir, A., Pesqué Cela, V., Altunbas, Y., & Murinde, V. (2020). Fintech, financial inclusion and income inequality: a quantile regression approach. *The European Journal of Finance*, 1-22. doi:10.1080/1351847X.2020.1772335

Demirgüç-Kunt, A., Klapper, L., Singer, D., Ansar, S., & Hess, J. (2018). *Measuring financial inclusion and the fintech revolution.* The Global Findex Database, World Bank Group. doi:10.1596/978-1-4648-1259-0

Financial Institutions Division. (2019). *National Financial Inclusion Strategy-Bangladesh*. Retrieved from https://fid.portal.gov.bd/sites/default/files/files/fid.portal.gov.bd/notices/43182ae2_205c_417f_919f_172c5cb60566/Final-Submitted%20to%20FID_NFIS-B-v2.doc#:~:text=National%20Financial%20Inclusion%20Strategy%20(NFIS)%20is%20a%20roadmap%20of%20actions,to%20achieve%20financial%20inclusion%20objectives.&text=Ingraining%20Financial%20Inclusion%20in%20National,3

Fishbein, M., & Ajzen, I. (1975). *Belief, attitude, intention and behaviour: An introduction to theory and research*. Academic Press.

Global Partnership for Financial Inclusion. (2016). *G20 high level principles for digital financial inclusion*. Global Partneship for Financial Inclusion. Retrieved from https://www.gpfi.org/publications/g20-high-level-principles-digital-financial-inclusion

Goodhue, D. L., & Thompson, R. L. (1995). Task-Technology Fit and Individual Performance. *Management Information Systems Quarterly*, *19*(2), 213–236. doi:10.2307/249689

Hair, J. F., Hult, G. T. M., Ringle, C. M., Sarstedt, M., & Thiele, K. O. (2017). Mirror, mirror on the wall: A comparative evaluation of composite-based structural equation modeling methods. *Journal of the Academy of Marketing Science*, *45*(5), 616–632. doi:10.100711747-017-0517-x

Hair, J. F., Risher, J. J., Sarstedt, M., & Ringle, C. M. (2019). When to use and how to report the results of PLS-SEM. *European Business Review*, *31*(1), 2–24. doi:10.1108/EBR-11-2018-0203

Hamza, A., & Shah, A. (2014). Gender and mobile payment system adoption among students of tertiary institutions in Nigeria. *International Journal of Computer and Information Technology*, *3*(1), 13–20. www.ijcit.com/archives/volume3/issue1/Paper030103.pdf

Hanafizadeh, P., Behboudi, M., Koshksaray, A. A., & Tabar, M. J. S. (2012). Mobile-banking adoption by Iranian bank clients. *Telematics and Informatics*, *31*(1), 62–78. doi:10.1016/j.tele.2012.11.001

Hazra, U., & Priyo, A. K. K. (2021). Mobile financial services in Bangladesh: Understanding the affordances. *The Electronic Journal on Information Systems in Developing Countries*, *87*(3), e12166. doi:10.1002/isd2.12166

Hew, T. S., Leong, L. Y., Ooi, K. B., & Chong, A. Y. L. (2016). Predicting drivers of mobile entertainment adoption: A two-stage SEM-artificial-neural-network analysis. *Journal of Computer Information Systems*, *56*(4), 352–370. doi:10.1080 /08874417.2016.1164497

Himel, M. T. A., Ashraf, S., Bappy, T. A., Abir, M. T., Morshed, M. K., & Hossain, M. N. (2021). Users' attitude and intention to use mobile financial services in Bangladesh: An empirical study. *South Asian Journal of Marketing*, *2*(1), 72–96. Advance online publication. doi:10.1108/SAJM-02-2021-0015

Hsu, C. L., Wang, C. F., & Lin, J. C. C. (2011). Investigating customer adoption behaviours in Mobile Financial Services. *International Journal of Mobile Communications*, *9*(5), 477. doi:10.1504/IJMC.2011.042455

Humbani, M., & Wiese, M. (2019). An integrated framework for the adoption and continuance intention to use mobile payment apps. *International Journal of Bank Marketing*, *37*(2), 646–664. doi:10.1108/IJBM-03-2018-0072

Kapadia, S. (2020). *New frontiers for financial inclusion: Gender impact & fintechs align*. Roots of Impact & SDC. Retrieved from https://www.roots-of-impact.org/

Kim, B., Choi, M., & Han, I. (2009). User behaviors toward mobile data services: The role of perceived fee and prior experience. *Expert Systems with Applications*, *36*(4), 8528–8536. doi:10.1016/j.eswa.2008.10.063

Koenig-Lewis, N., Palmer, A., & Moll, A. (2010). Predicting young consumers' take up of mobile banking services. *International Journal of Bank Marketing*, *28*(5), 410–432. doi:10.1108/02652321011064917

Le, M. T. (2021). Examining factors that boost intention and loyalty to use Fintech post-COVID-19 lockdown as a new normal behavior. *Heliyon*, *7*(8), e07821. doi:10.1016/j.heliyon.2021.e07821 PMID:34458639

Legris, P., Ingham, J., & Collerette, P. (2003). Why do people use information technology? A critical review of the technology acceptance model. *Information & Management*, *40*(3), 191–204. doi:10.1016/S0378-7206(01)00143-4

Luarn, P., & Lin, H.-H. (2005). Toward an understanding of the behavioral intention to use mobile banking. *Computers in Human Behavior*, *21*(6), 873–891. doi:10.1016/j. chb.2004.03.003

Lwoga, E. T., & Lwoga, N. B. (2017). User acceptance of mobile payment: The effects of user-centric security, system characteristics and gender. *The Electronic Journal on Information Systems in Developing Countries*, *81*(1), 1–24. doi:10.1002/j.1681-4835.2017.tb00595.x

Mante, E. A., & Piris, D. (2002). SMS use by young people in the Netherlands. *Revista de Estudios de Juventud, 52*, 47-58. Retrieved from https://www.itu.int/osg/spu/ni/ubiquitous/Papers/Youth_and_mobile_2002.pdf#page=45

McDonald, L. M., & Korabik, K. (1991). Sources of stress and ways of coping among male and female managers. *Journal of Social Behavior and Personality*, *6*(7), 185–198.

Moon, J. W., & Kim, Y. G. (2001). Extending the TAM for a World-Wide-Web context. *Information & Management*, *38*(4), 217–230. doi:10.1016/S0378-7206(00)00061-6

Nurlaily, F., Aini, E. K., & Asmoro, P. S. (2021). Understanding the FinTech continuance intention of Indonesian users: The moderating effect of gender. *Business: Theory and Practice*, *22*(2), 290–298. doi:10.3846/btp.2021.13880

Oliveira, T., Faria, M., Thomas, M. A., & Popovič, A. (2014). Extending the understanding of mobile banking adoption: When UTAUT meets TTF and ITM. *International Journal of Information Management*, *34*(5), 689–703. doi:10.1016/j.ijinfomgt.2014.06.004

Oliver, R. L. (1980). A Cognitive Model of the Antecedents and Consequences of Satisfaction Decisions. *JMR, Journal of Marketing Research*, *17*(4), 460–469. doi:10.1177/002224378001700405

Popy, N. N., & Bappy, T. A. (2020). Attitude toward social media reviews and restaurant visit intention: a Bangladeshi perspective. *South Asian Journal of Business Studies*. doi:10.1108/SAJBS-03-2020-0077

Reji Kumar, G., & Ravindran, D. S. (2012). An Empirical Study on Service Quality Perceptions and Continuance Intention in Mobile Banking Context in India. *Journal of Internet Banking and Commerce*, *17*(1), 1–22.

Rogers, E. (1995). *Diffusion of innovations*. Free Press.

Rogers, M. (2018). *Country overview: Bangladesh Mobile industry driving growth and enabling digital inclusion*. GSM Association. Retrieved from https://data.gsmaintelligence.com/api-web/v2/research-file-download?id=30933394&file=Country%20overview%20Bangladesh.pdf

Saad, G., & Gill, T. (2000). Applications of evolutionary psychology in marketing. *Psychology and Marketing, 17*(12), 1005–1034. doi:10.1002/1520-6793(200012)17:12<1005::AID-MAR1>3.0.CO;2-H

Sagib, G. K., & Zapan, B. (2014). Bangladeshi mobile banking service quality and customer satisfaction and loyalty. *Management & Marketing, 9*(3).

Saima, F. N., Rahman, M. H. A., & Ghosh, R. (2022). MFS usage intention during COVID-19 and beyond: an integration of health belief and expectation confirmation model. *Journal of Economic and Administrative Sciences.* doi:10.1108/JEAS-07-2021-0133

Sharma, S. K., Govindaluri, S. M., & Al Balushi, S. M. (2015). Predicting determinants of Internet banking adoption: A two-staged regression-neural network approach. *Management Research Review, 38*(7), 750–766. doi:10.1108/MRR-06-2014-0139

Singh, S., & Srivastava, R. K. (2018). Predicting the intention to use mobile banking in India. *International Journal of Bank Marketing, 36*(2), 357–378. doi:10.1108/IJBM-12-2016-0186

Tariq, B., Najam, H., Han, H., Sadaa, A. M., Abbasi, A. A., Christopher, N., & Abbasi, G. A. (2021). Examining mobile financial services in Pakistan: Rural and urban perspective with gender as a moderator. In *Recent advances in technology acceptance models and theories* (pp. 225–245). Springer. doi:10.1007/978-3-030-64987-6_14

The Business Standard. (2020). *Bangladesh gets 3.9m new mobile, internet subscribers in September.* Retrieved from https://www.tbsnews.net/bangladesh/telecom/bangladesh-gets-39m-new-mobile-internet-subscribers-september-153343

The World Bank. (2018, October 2). *Financial Inclusion Overview.* Author.

Vasudeva, S., & Chawla, S. (2019). Does Gender, Age and Income Moderate the Relationship Between Mobile Banking Usage and Loyalty? *International Journal of Online Marketing, 9*(4), 1–18. doi:10.4018/IJOM.2019100101

Venkatesh, V., & Davis, F. D. (2000). A Theoretical Extension of the Technology Acceptance Model: Four Longitudinal Field Studies. *Management Science, 16*(2), 186–204. doi:10.1287/mnsc.46.2.186.11926

Venkatesh, V., Morris, M. G., Davis, G. B., & Davis, F. D. (2003). User Acceptance of Information Technology: Toward a Unified View. *Management Information Systems Quarterly, 27*(3), 425–478. doi:10.2307/30036540

Wang, Y. S., Wang, Y. M., Lin, H. H., & Tang, T. I. (2003). Determinants of user acceptance of Internet banking: An empirical study. *International Journal of Service Industry Management, 14*(5), 501–519. doi:10.1108/09564230310500192

Yang, A. S. (2009). Exploring adoption difficulties in mobile banking services. *Canadian Journal of Administrative Sciences/Revue Canadienne des Sciences de l'Administration, 26*(2), 136-149. doi:10.1002/cjas.102

Yen, Y. S., & Wu, F. S. (2016). Predicting the adoption of mobile financial services: The impacts of perceived mobility and personal habit. *Computers in Human Behavior, 65*, 31–42. doi:10.1016/j.chb.2016.08.017

ADDITIONAL READING

Alshurideh, M. T., Al Kurdi, B., Masa'deh, R., & Salloum, S. A. (2021). The moderation effect of gender on accepting electronic payment technology: A study on United Arab Emirates consumers. *Review of International Business and Strategy., 31*(3), 375–396. doi:10.1108/RIBS-08-2020-0102

Arnold, J., & Gammage, S. (2019). Gender and financial inclusion: The critical role for holistic programming. *Development in Practice, 29*(8), 965–973. doi:10.1080/09614524.2019.1651251

Belayeth Hussain, A. H. M., Endut, N., Das, S., Chowdhury, M. T. A., Haque, N., Sultana, S., & Ahmed, K. J. (2019). Does financial inclusion increase financial resilience? Evidence from Bangladesh. *Development in Practice, 29*(6), 798–807. doi:10.1080/09614524.2019.1607256

Jaradat, M. I. R. M., & Faqih, K. M. (2014). Investigating the moderating effects of gender and self-efficacy in the context of mobile payment adoption: A developing country perspective. *International Journal of Business and Management, 9*(11), 147. doi:10.5539/ijbm.v9n11p147

Kanwal, M., Burki, U., Ali, R., & Dahlstrom, R. (2021). Systematic review of gender differences and similarities in online consumers' shopping behavior. *Journal of Consumer Marketing, 39*(1), 29–43. doi:10.1108/JCM-01-2021-4356

Liébana-Cabanillas, F., Molinillo, S., & Japutra, A. (2021). Exploring the determinants of intention to use P2P mobile payment in Spain. *Information Systems Management, 38*(2), 165–180. doi:10.1080/10580530.2020.1818897

Singh, N., Kumar, N., & Kapoor, S. (2022). Consumer multihoming predisposition on food platforms: Does gender matter? *Journal of Retailing and Consumer Services, 67,* 103029. doi:10.1016/j.jretconser.2022.103029

Sun, Q., & Xu, B. (2019). Mobile social commerce: Current state and future directions. *Journal of Global Marketing, 32*(5), 306–318. doi:10.1080/08911762.2019.1620902

Talwar, S., Dhir, A., Khalil, A., Mohan, G., & Islam, A. N. (2020). Point of adoption and beyond. Initial trust and mobile-payment continuation intention. *Journal of Retailing and Consumer Services, 55,* 102086. doi:10.1016/j.jretconser.2020.102086

APPENDIX

Table 10.

Ease of Use	
EU1	Learning how to use MFS is much easy for me
EU2	MFS/ mobile banking makes me more skillful in use of technology
EU3	I would find mobile banking much easy to use.
Perceived Usefulness	
PU1	Using MFS applications increases my chances of purchasing things that are important to me.
PU2	Using MFS applications enables me to accomplish the purchasing process more easily.
PU3	I feel safe when I use MFS applications for purchasing things.
PU4	Overall, MFS applications are useful.
Perceived Credibility	
PC1	Using MFS application would not divulge my personal information.
PC2	I would find MFS applications secure in conducting my banking transactions.
PC3	I receive confirmation evidence every time I complete a transaction.
PC4	Every time I use MFS service, I must provide a transaction password.
Satisfaction (SAT)	
SAT1	I feel satisfied with using mobile payment applications.
SAT2	I feel pleased with using mobile payment applications.
SAT3	I feel contented with using mobile payment applications.
SAT4	Overall, I am satisfied with mobile payment applications.
Loyalty (Loy)	
Loy1	I will say positive word-of-mouth about MFS service
Loy2	I will recommend MFS service to others
Loy3	I will encourage others to use MFS service.
Loy4	MFS service will be the first choice to pay for future

Chapter 5
Secure Authentication in Wireless Sensor Networks Using Blockchain Technology

S. B. Goyal

(iD) https://orcid.org/0000-0002-8411-7630
City University, Malaysia

Pradeep Bedi

(iD) https://orcid.org/0000-0003-1708-6237
Galgotias University, India

Anand Singh Rajawat
Shri Vaishnav Vidyapeeth Vishwavidyalaya, India

Divya Prakash Shrivastava
Higher Colleges of Technology, Dubai, UAE

ABSTRACT

A wireless sensor network (WSN) is capable of monitoring, fetching, and transmitting data from one place to another in any condition. The internet of things (IoT) network, a type of WSN, and its protection have always been a big problem. There are lots of risks related to security in this network. Authentication of node identity is an essential security concern. Conventional security algorithms for IoT rely on trustworthy third parties. They might fail at a single stage point. Therefore, in this chapter, the model is proposed as the solution to the security concerns by blockchain concepts. So, in this chapter, a trust model is introduced based on blockchain for WSN for communicating with several nodes without having any risks related to security.

DOI: 10.4018/978-1-6684-4176-3.ch005

INTRODUCTION

In terms of expediting the internet and technology, the Internet of Things has emerged as a major force for promoting economic and social developments (Zawaideh et al., 2018). Wireless Sensor Network (WSNs) as the key technology in the IoT-architecture plays an essential role in fostering IoT development with remarkable real importance and research value. Mobile, ad hoc network sensors (MANETs) are distributed micro-device systems that have the characteristics of the wider range of sensors, rapid deployment, remote monitoring, high-precision monitoring, high tolerance faults, and self-organization (Zeng et al., 2018) (Su et al., 2018). WSNs have been widely used in a variety of fields, including military, smart home, commercial, and others (Prabha et al., 2017). The sensor nodes, even so, share similar restrictions – they are damaged easily and possess limited capacity, computer skill, memory, and range of transmission (Zhang et al., 2017). Besides, an opponent can easily compromise them (Anu and Vimla, 2019). Statistics show that there are mainly two aspects to the threats faced by the WSN (Das and Das, 2015) (Jaint et al., 2019). The external Network attacker on the one hand invades the internal node and regulates it to become an inside malicious node to start a strike. Consequently, it is an urgent security problem for networks of wireless sensors to identify and delete internal malicious nodes. And the healthy development of IoT has a profound impact on how this security threat can be resolved. That is why many scientists were made aware of the safety of the WSN's network (Chen et al, 2013).

Blockchain technology makes great tact of researchers, as the researchers have believed in that technology, this will introduce noticeable changes and changes to industries. In a decentralized fashion, Blockchain technology is very effective for settling trusted communications. Back in 2008, this technology was proposed and disseminated by the cryptography mailing group. Decentralization is the key capability of blockchain technology, which permits transactions directly peer to peer. In distributed systems, this approach is also utilized in the system which requires trust for nodes to do transactions. There are several means adopted by the Blockchain technology like a distributed consensus, time stamping, economic incentives, and data encryption. It is used in solving the problems like insecure data storage, high cost, and inefficiency. The research on this technology is excited to grow rapidly by the quick development and acclaim of blockchain (Pinto et al., 2018).

WNS (Wireless Sensor Network) includes various kinds of small sensing devices, that are being used for monitoring the physical conditions. smart cities, medicine military purpose, and monitoring an environment are the Applications of the WSNs. The Sensing nodes are installed in the required manner (may be static or random) for the prospect of monitoring, recognizing, and fetching information. It has some problems like routing, void holes, connectivity, small memory, throughput, and most dominantly the issues of security. The threats encountered by the WSNs mostly come from two sources. Firstly, the internal nodes of the network become malicious, and secondly, the external attacks on the network.

When a malicious node gets packets of data from a neighboring node, it discards packets directly and stops forwarding the packets of data to its next-hop neighboring node. This produces a "black hole" data in the network and their detection is very hard for the routing nodes in the WSNs.

These malicious nodes may be legitimate internal nodes or external intrusion attackers intercepted by outside attackers. Recently the management of Trust has become a popular way for confirming the safety of the routing network recently. This methodology can build up the routing node to select the reliable relatively routing links effectively. On the other side, its usage is bounded since the trust values of routing nodes that are adjacent can only be accessed by one routing node that that does not follow the distributed multi-hop WSN entirely.

Hence, it is a necessary security enigma for WSNs to keep the ability to identify and disconnect the internal nodes that are malicious, so, it is a major challenge to find the methodology for solving this issue of security for nodes of the sensor. In the WSNs the problem of a malicious node can be solved by utilizing any one of mentioned two categories; (1) either WSN protocol or (2) propose a secure model.

In the proposed article, we appropriate the first one and offer a model of trust for WSNs with the help of blockchain concepts, Lin et al. offered a solution based on LoRaWAN (Long Range Wide Area Networks). By considering the economy and crowdsensing, the Authors unite LoRaWAN and blockchain. They implemented a LoRaWAN server for solving trust problems on lack of network coverage and private network operators. A mechanism for verifying the data existence at a special time on a network is proposed in this study. CMA (Confusion Mechanism Algorithm) is offered for protecting the information of the user by collected information encryption from the sensors. Another use of blockchain is to secure the information of the user and allot incentives based on participation frequency. The outcomes show that the mechanism offered to enhance the participation of users largely from 20% in tradition to 80% in the mode proposed. so, the results fetched may be one-sided as limited data was collected.

The central authority is needed to facilitate the identification and authentication of every device in the conventional protocols of routing. However, the network performance was decreased gradually and some unnecessary calculations were included because of the PoW (Proof of Work) consensus algorithm. In the present work, a structure that is trusted is offered for avoiding malicious attacks and providing the network sensors security with the help of the blockchain concept. Moreover, PoA replaced PoW for avoiding unnecessary computations, which were earlier included due to the PoW.

LITERATURE REVIEW

Recently, researchers have extensively studied the security issues and problems associated with WSN or IoT networks. The processes can be categorized into 2 groups: firstly, the trust model and secondly, the Protocol of WSN. The first method is the most popular. Zawaideh et al. (2018) has enhanced the neighbor weight trust determination algorithm to address the trust problem of node detection malicious in the WSN (NWTD). The algorithm updates the confidence level of nodes regularly and sets a minimum trust threshold for nodes. It can then identify the malicious nodes that are separated. To accept the indirect and direct trust of third-party nodes, Zeng et al. (2018) submitted a framework of trust based on the DS (Dempster-Shafer) evidence theory, aimed at addressing the malicious node detection problem in WSN. It ensured that the network was robust and that the data packet was accurate. Su et al. (2018) has proposed a confidence-based measurement of the belief degree against and has deemed both the levels of internal and external trust in WSN. Prabha et al. (2017) suggested fuzzy logic approach using multiple attributes. A new trust administration scheme based on the D-S theory of proof was proposed by Zhang et al. (2017). The trust model was developed following D-S, and the space-temporal correlation of data collected by adjacent sensor nodes. Finally, the entire degree of confidence was calculated for the compromised users. Anu and Vimala (2019) suggested a new attacker node prediction model oppose fraudulent defamation behavior in current WSNs. Using Beta Distribution, this model demonstrated the implicit legitimacy of third-party entities and the distribution of reputation and integrated confidence values for different types of attacks to obtain reliable protection against malicious nodes. Furthermore, some other sort of procedure technique is popular would use predicated on a WSN, based also on a trust mechanism in the malicious node method. Das and Das (2015) suggested an extension of the LEACH protocol to resolve the relatively low capacities of the WSN to identify power use, distance, and malice nodes in wireless sensor networks. In addition to the number of hops from the sensor nodes to the basic station, Jaint et al. (2019) have launched a new trust-based, multi-viewed trust-routing protocol to ensure network stability, identify malicious nodes, and enhance system safety. Chen et al. (2013) proposed a decentralized node detection technology, based on received signal strength indicators (RSSI). Pinto et al. (2018) proposed a new, machine-learning tactic to use radio devices in wireless network communication. The company has used two classifiers to organize and store actual specimen of connection speed received and to optimize legitimate nodes and attack nodes with close points. Althunibat et al. (2016) demonstrated the same impact on WSN's overall performance in terms of detection and false alarm rate, both dependent and independent malicious knots. Uddin et al. (2017) suggested the WSN technology model for the detection of power distribution side failure points. The model carries out a process of wireless monitoring, detection, and location of fault nodes using current sensors and wireless protocols. The above literature suggested effective methods for detecting nodes in wireless networks. They did not specify, however, how security flaws are detected nor how the actual data can be safely saved for later traceability (Christidis et al., 2016). The development of Blockchain technology and smart contracts are the fresh able to discover faulty activities on wireless sensor networks. In the event of abnormal conduct or limitation conditions, and all relevant data is formed into data-blocks that can be tracked, monitored, and timed. Smart contracts can automatically and distribution carry out predetermined operational activities. Ellul and Pace (2018) designed a lightweight agreement to detect virtual machines, which, subject to limited conditions, established a connection between both the public blockchain and the Access gateway and encouraged testable blockchain transaction processing automation. Islam et al. (2018) proposed a smart blockchain contract for ensuring domestic and personal privacy protection. Kang et al. (2018) combined payment systems to blockchain technology and established a viable electricity grid to pass out transactions automatically. In the same way, by using an intelligent contract in which they can enforce IoT-based edge device blockchain actions, resources, and accounts, Pan et al. (2019) suggested an IoT-based Edge Chain Framework (Qiu et al., 2018). A smart contract-based architecture was proposed by Zhang et al. (2019) to fix the issue of trustworthy network access and delivery in the IoT. In this paper, a blockchain confidence model is proposed for attacker node identification in WSNs. It offers a more stable, efficient, and reliable solution for the types of fraudulent nodes and the quality control of the WSN control environment. It mostly limits interruption with sensor nodes in standard network operation but also ensures the detection process's transparency and traceability. At the same time, it eliminates the restriction of space to some degree.

SENSOR NODES AUTHENTICATION USING BLOCKCHAIN

It naturally fits with IoT because of the dispersed features of blockchain. The management, control, and safety among the most essential IoT equipment will be expected to take an important role. It introduces additional information security in IoT Application areas, such as safety of the vehicle's network, management of the equipment, and privacy. Blockchain-based module verification is a survey hub for the ongoing investigation. It is impossible to fulfill blockchain deployment circumstances because the restriction of IoT equipment is indeed limited. Hammi et al. (2018) suggested a de-centered blockchain app module verification process to make sure that the verification system is secure mostly on cloud blockchain.

While this approach will essentially satisfy different regulatory criteria, it does not allow cross-domain interaction, and the cloud network requires to be connected, the completion time of authentication is higher, which is not relevant to several settings of WSNs. A blockchain-based security mechanism between IoT services and devices was introduced by (Almadhoun et al., 2019), utilizing a series of fog nodes that can provide IoT devices with localized computing, storage, and networking to improve power constraints. Fog nodes deployed in this scheme near the blockchain. They act as an intermediate to provide blockchain services for the Internet of Things, allowing for shared verification between users and IoT devices. While the scheme does not cover many communication scenarios in the IoT, it is good for scalability and safety. Pan et al. (2019) attaches IoT nodes that cannot use the blockchain apps to the public blockchain utilizing network nodes, handle and authenticate the ethnicity of nodes, and use the idea of "trust" to allocate cloud resources. But they do not clearly state how assets can be allocated via "confidence." Biswas et al. (2019) separated weaker devices from the Internet through local peer-to-peer networks, transaction data is contained on regional frames, and publicly interacted via nearby network layers to handle communication and knowledge accessible to users on Cloud computing. It enhances Artificial intelligence to a great extent. But centralized authentication centers remain necessary in this architecture (Bao et al., 2018). IoT chain, authentication, a blockchain layer, and application-level infrastructure security, are suggested by Cui et al., (2018). The security analysis indicates that perhaps the design carries out verification of identity, access control, protection of privacy, lightweight features, tolerance to regional node failures, denial of elasticity, and storage integrity. This design, even so, will not take the constraints of many of these Smart devices of things fully into account and, using its federated features, provides dispersed network infrastructure for the Internet of things and continues to use an established network center (Kautish et al. 2022)

METHODOLOGY

In this part, in WSNs the system model based on blockchain technology for the avoidance of malicious nodes is proposed. The main elements of this system model are categorized as follows:

System Model

This paper is based on the design of the WSN IoT prototype which is designed for providing solutions to the security issues to validate IoT. This research paper consists of facts and logical theory which assure some of the conditions to propose the scheme for authentication of IoT nodes. The theory is as:

- A unique Ethernet address is provided for every single node (Moorthy et al. 2022)
- Smart contracts can be distributed with the help of cluster head nodes and base station nodes which have the property of storage and calculating abilities.
- The Base station controls all the nodes in an individual network (Sharma et al. 2022)
- Modification of nodes is safe by the base station (Madhu et al. 2022)

Network Prototype

IoT nodes consist of multiple nodes with distinct functions and basically, these nodes are categorized into three types, based on their functions, i.e., sensor nodes, head node, and base station. A network is made of several WSN sub-networks and these sub-networks are comprised of base station nodes, cluster head nodes, and sensing nodes. For the security of the IoT network, the arrangement of these nodes plays a crucial role because authentication is completely dependent on the arrangement of nodes thus the model in this paper is designed to provide the security of the network.

Base Station

The base station collects the data from sensing nodes store the information and then analyzes the data of stored information. To establish a connection with the main network firstly the nodes of sub-networks are initialized by the base station then directly get connected to the public networks and clouds.

Node Cluster Head

Each cluster consists of several ordinary nodes and every cluster is connected with the base station and ordinary nodes, thus the cluster head forwards the sensed data from ordinary nodes to the base station.

Ordinary Node

These nodes are not able to perform the complicated operation and data transformations because their storage capacity and calculating capability are very low. Every individual ordinary node consists of only one cluster head and wireless sensor network just to sense and transfer the simplified information. Camera, sensors, etc., are the ordinary node also known as the variety of IoT networks.

The verified nodes can communicate with each other directly or indirectly (Rajawat et al. 2022). The process of interaction is an important part of the security of IoT networks. In the given prototype, bilateral validation is required for the security of communication channels. The process of validation is applied before the communication takes place between two nodes and when the end-users access the way in the network.

In this research paper we have described four types of information exchanging structure, they are:

- Exchanging of data takes place within a cluster by two ordinary nodes for completing the specific work. These two nodes are ordinarily arranged in a cluster to form this type of structure to provide the security of data in the network.
- The second type of structure is formed by placing two different clusters in a wireless sensor network to perform the safe communication activity by arranging two ordinary nodes in the clusters.
- The next type of structure is formed by connecting two different wireless sensor networks with a safeguard or secured link. And the communication takes place within two similar nodes in different wireless sensor networks with the help of connecting links.
- And lastly when end-user access the right to the way of a node in a network.

This model is the combination of two sections, the local blockchain and the global blockchain as shown in Figure 1. In the local blockchain, identification of nodes is necessary to get connected in the network. The structure is designed as two different wireless sensor networks pertain to different base stations, after the process of validation they can join the local blockchain. While in a global blockchain, nodes are linked with unidentified blockchain and the structure formed is like a dispersed network. This type of network devours more and more time and sources.

Local Blockchain

In this blockchain, the local verification of nodes inside the cluster is done. All information required for verification is retrieved from the local blockchain and validation is performed. Primarily this chain is used to index the verification of ordinary nodes. The local blockchain is formed by arranging cluster heads in the single wireless sensor network. If cluster head node's information is indexed with public blockchain then it is parallel connected with local blockchain.

Figure 1. Hybrid blockchain architecture

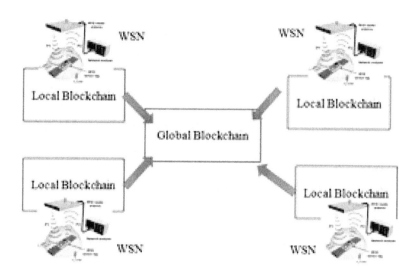

Global Blockchain

The structure formed in the global blockchain is by connecting all base stations and end-users as miners nodes. When Cluster head nodes are validating then it is necessary to equalize the identification of nodes in the global blockchain network and the validate identification of information of the present nodes. These chains index and validate cluster heads for the identified communication between these nodes in the given network.

Secure Authentication

As stated above, the system model proposed requires authentication of nodes which are described in the following steps as shown in Figure 2:

- Initialization: All the security parameters are initialized at the base station.
- Registration: In this step, the identity of each and individual node is stored in local as well as global blockchain.
- Authentication: In this step, all nodes are validated to be authentic nodes according to the hybrid blockchain.
- Exit: In this stage, if any node gets damaged due to energy exhaustion, then it has to exit from the blockchain.

Figure 2. Hybrid blockchain architecture

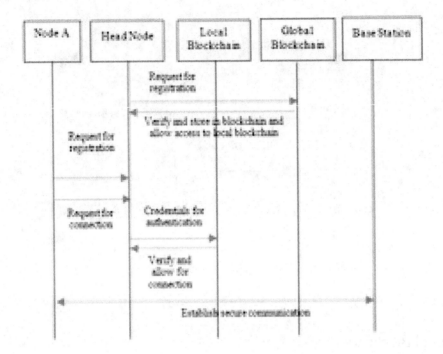

CONCLUSION

WSN is capable to monitor, fetch and transmit data in unconventional conditions. There are lots of risks related to security in this network. In this paper, we gave the solution of the trouble of security of WSN/ IoT network by blockchain concepts. So, a secure authentication model is introduced as a trust model based on blockchain for WSN for communicating with several nodes without having any risks related to security. In the future, we will develop blockchain in any state-of-the-art routing protocol and perform the comparison with the efficiency of the proposed model.

REFERENCES

Zawaideh, F., Salamah, M., & Al-Bahadili, H. (2018). A fair trust-based malicious node detection and isolation scheme for WSNs. *Proceedings of 2nd International Conference on the Applications of Information Technology in Developing Renewable Energy Processes and Systems, IT-DREPS 2017*, 1–6. 10.1109/IT-DREPS.2017.8277813

Zeng, L. G., Yuan, Y., & Wang, H. (2018). Detecting WSN node misbehavior based on the trust mechanism. *J. Zhejiang Normal Univ. Nature and Science, 41*(1), 39–43.

Su, X., Gao, X. F., & Lu, Y. (2018). Credibility based WSN trust model. *Electron. Opt. Control, 25*(3), 32–36.

Ram Prabha, V., & Latha, P. (2017). Fuzzy Trust Protocol for Malicious Node Detection in Wireless Sensor Networks. *Wireless Personal Communications: An International Journal, 94*(4), 2549–2559. doi:10.100711277-016-3666-1

Zhang, W., Zhu, S., Tang, J., & Xiong, N. (2017). A novel trust management scheme based on Dempster–Shafer evidence theory for malicious nodes detection in wireless sensor networks. *The Journal of Supercomputing, 74*(4), 1779–1801. doi:10.1007/s11227-017-2150-3

Anu, P., & Vimala, S. (2019). Reputation based Malicious Node Detection and Elimination in Open Shortest Path First. *Journal of Advanced Research in Dynamic and Control Systems, 11*, 855–860. doi:10.5373/JARDCS/V11SP11/20193107

Das, S., & Das, A. (2015). An algorithm to detect malicious nodes in wireless sensor network using enhanced LEACH protocol. *Conference Proceeding - 2015 International Conference on Advances in Computer Engineering and Applications, ICACEA 2015*, 875–881. 10.1109/ICACEA.2015.7164828

Jaint, B., Indu, S., Pandey, N., & Pahwa, K. (2019). Malicious Node Detection in Wireless Sensor Networks Using Support Vector Machine. *2019 3rd International Conference on Recent Developments in Control, Automation and Power Engineering, RDCAPE 2019*, 247–252. 10.1109/RDCAPE47089.2019.8979125

Chen, Z., Zhang, R., Ju, L., & Wang, W. (2013). Multivalued trust routing based on topology level for wireless sensor networks. *Proceedings - 12th IEEE International Conference on Trust, Security and Privacy in Computing and Communications, TrustCom 2013*, 1516–1521. 10.1109/TrustCom.2013.185

Pinto, E. M. D. L., Lachowski, R., Pellenz, M. E., Penna, M. C., & Souza, R. D. (2018). A machine learning approach for detecting spoofing attacks in wireless sensor networks. *Proceedings - International Conference on Advanced Information Networking and Applications, AINA*, 752–758. 10.1109/AINA.2018.00113

Althunibat, S., Antonopoulos, A., Kartsakli, E., Granelli, F., & Verikoukis, C. (2016). Countering Intelligent-Dependent Malicious Nodes in Target Detection Wireless Sensor Networks. *IEEE Sensors Journal, 16*(23), 8627–8639. doi:10.1109/JSEN.2016.2606759

Uddin, B., Imran, A., & Rahman, M. A. (2017). Detection and locating the point of fault in distribution side of power system using WSN technology. *4th International Conference on Advances in Electrical Engineering, ICAEE 2017,* 570–574. 10.1109/ICAEE.2017.8255421

Christidis, K., & Devetsikiotis, M. (2016). Blockchains and Smart Contracts for the Internet of Things. *IEEE Access: Practical Innovations, Open Solutions*, *4*, 2292–2303. doi:10.1109/ACCESS.2016.2566339

Ellul, J., & Pace, G. J. (2018). AlkylVM: A Virtual Machine for Smart Contract Blockchain Connected Internet of Things. *2018 9th IFIP International Conference on New Technologies, Mobility and Security, NTMS 2018 - Proceedings,* 1–4. 10.1109/NTMS.2018.8328732

Islam, M. N., & Kundu, S. (2018). Poster abstract: Preserving IoT privacy in sharing economy via smart contract. *Proceedings - ACM/IEEE International Conference on Internet of Things Design and Implementation, IoTDI 2018*, 296–297. 10.1109/IoTDI.2018.00047

Kang, E. S., Pee, S. J., Song, J. G., & Jang, J. W. (2018). A Blockchain-Based Energy Trading Platform for Smart Homes in a Microgrid. *2018 3rd International Conference on Computer and Communication Systems, ICCCS 2018*, 291–296. 10.1109/CCOMS.2018.8463317

Pan, J., Wang, J., Hester, A., Alqerm, I., Liu, Y., & Zhao, Y. (2019). EdgeChain: An edge-IoT framework and prototype based on blockchain and smart contracts. *IEEE Internet of Things Journal, 6*(3), 4719–4732. doi:10.1109/JIOT.2018.2878154

Qiu, T., Liu, X., Li, K., Hu, Q., Sangaiah, A. K., & Chen, N. (2018). Community-Aware Data Propagation with Small World Feature for Internet of Vehicles. *IEEE Communications Magazine, 56*(1), 86–91. doi:10.1109/MCOM.2018.1700511

Zhang, Y., Kasahara, S., Shen, Y., Jiang, X., & Wan, J. (2019). Smart contract-based access control for the internet of things. *IEEE Internet of Things Journal*, *6*(2), 1594–1605. doi:10.1109/JIOT.2018.2847705

Hammi, M. T., Hammi, B., Bellot, P., & Serrhouchni, A. (2018). Bubbles of Trust: A decentralized blockchain-based authentication system for IoT. *Computers & Security, 78*, 126–142. doi:10.1016/j.cose.2018.06.004

Almadhoun, R., Kadadha, M., Alhemeiri, M., Alshehhi, M., & Salah, K. (2019). A User Authentication Scheme of IoT Devices using Blockchain-Enabled Fog Nodes. *Proceedings of IEEE/ACS International Conference on Computer Systems and Applications, AICCSA.* 10.1109/AICCSA.2018.8612856

Pan, J., Wang, J., Hester, A., Alqerm, I., Liu, Y., & Zhao, Y. (2019). EdgeChain: An edge-IoT framework and prototype based on blockchain and smart contracts. *IEEE Internet of Things Journal, 6*(3), 4719–4732. doi:10.1109/JIOT.2018.2878154

Biswas, S., Sharif, K., Li, F., Nour, B., & Wang, Y. (2019). A scalable blockchain framework for secure transactions in IoT. *IEEE Internet of Things Journal, 6*(3), 4650–4659. doi:10.1109/JIOT.2018.2874095

Bao, Z., Shi, W., He, D., & Chood, K.-K. R. (2018). *IoTChain: A Three-Tier Blockchain-based IoT Security Architecture.* https://arxiv.org/abs/1806.02008v2

Cui, Z., Xue, F., Cai, X., Cao, Y., Wang, G. G., & Chen, J. (2018). Detection of Malicious Code Variants Based on Deep Learning. *IEEE Transactions on Industrial Informatics, 14*(7), 3187–3196. doi:10.1109/TII.2018.2822680

Madhu, G., Govardhan, A., & Ravi, V. (2022). *DSCN-net: a deep Siamese capsule neural network model for automatic diagnosis of malaria parasites detection. Multimed Tools Appl.* doi:10.100711042-022-13008-6

Moorthy, T. V. K., Budati, A. K., Kautish, S., Goyal, S. B., & Prasad, K. L. (2022). Reduction of satellite images size in 5G networks using Machine learning algorithms. *IET Communications, 16*(5), 584–591. doi:10.1049/cmu2.12354

Kautish, S., Reyana, A., & Vidyarthi, A. (2022). SDMTA: Attack Detection and Mitigation Mechanism for DDoS Vulnerabilities in Hybrid Cloud Environment. *IEEE Transactions on Industrial Informatics.*

Rajawat, A. S., Bedi, P., Goyal, S. B., Kautish, S., Xihua, Z., Aljuaid, H., & Mohamed, A. W. (2022). Dark Web Data Classification Using Neural Network. *Computational Intelligence and Neuroscience.*

Sharma, C., Sharma, S., Kautish, S., Alsallami, S. A., Khalil, E. M., & Mohamed, A. W. (2022). A new median-average round Robin scheduling algorithm: An optimal approach for reducing turnaround and waiting time. *Alexandria Engineering Journal, 61*(12), 10527–10538.

Chapter 6
Smart and Sustainable Economy:
How COVID–19 Has Acted as a Catalyst for China's Digital Transformation

Poshan Yu

 https://orcid.org/0000-0003-1069-3675

*Soochow University, China &
Australian Studies Centre, Shanghai
University, China*

Duo Chen
Independent Researcher, China

Aashrika Ahuja
Independent Researcher, India

ABSTRACT

Digital economy using internet, cloud computing, big data, as well as fintech in order to drive economic activities using digital information as a key factor for production has permeated all aspects of society as a result of unexpected onset of the COVID-19 pandemic. Recently, a white paper titled "The Development and Employment of China's Digital Economy in 2021" was released by The China Academy of Information and Communications Technology (CAICT), analyzing the development pattern of China's digital economy since the onset of COVID-19. This chapter summarizes the development of digital economy, the employment situation in various regions and industries in China, thereby making an in-depth analysis of the digital transformation of traditional industries along with putting forward policy suggestions for promoting further development of China's digital economy. Since the onset of COVID-19, China's digital and smart economy has ushered in creating new opportunities for growth and development as well as simultaneously combatting challenges in the macro environment.

DOI: 10.4018/978-1-6684-4176-3.ch006

INTRODUCTION

Since the 20th century, digitalization has been playing a significant role as a key driver for scientific, economic and social advancement of mankind. Innovation in the digital space has proved to be a great boon for humanity contributing to sustainable use of limited resources and enabling access for a large number of people to places, civilisations, communities, cities, countries which they probably cannot think of visiting in ordinary course of life. Digitalization is a process of transition of information by using 0 and 1 two digit codes. As a result of digitization, digital technology can enable instantaneous access to information, and has by far served as an important innovative tool for promoting economic and political exchange at a global level. As a result of COVID-19 pandemic, one can see how the digital economy has penetrated all aspects of society, including interpersonal interactions, the economic environment, and political decision-making (Gopal et al., 2003, Hindman, 2018).

In 2020, China Academy of Information and Communications Technology (CAICT) issued *China's digital economy development white paper* (2020) wherein it has been categorically emphasized that transition to a digital age in China can be accelerated by integrating the traditional industry and real economy with digitalization of information as the key factors of production. Innovation in digital technology has the potential of becoming the core driving force for a sustainable and smart economy in China.

Using descriptive methods and CiteSpace analysis, this chapter analyzes the development trend of China's digital economy in recent years, and highlights key issues. This chapter aims to help readers understand the development and changes of China's digital economy in more detail.

BACKGROUND

Chinese President Xi Jinping pointed out that "the digital economy is the future direction of global development." Today, China's digital smart economy is booming with continuous innovation and has gradually become an important driving force for high-quality development of the Chinese economy. At the same time, the digital economy is also the focus of many of the world leaders as the global digital economy development competition becomes more fierce with each passing moment.

In *the fifth chapter of China's 14th Five-Year Plan (2021-2025)*, titled "Accelerating Digital Development and Building a Digital China," it is mentioned that the country needs to give full play to the new advantages of the digital economy in order to create a sound digital environment. China aims to develop the digital economy, promote digital industrialization, digitization of industries, deep integration of the digital economy and the real economy, and build digital industry clusters with international competitiveness. All these efforts are bound to strengthen the development of a digital society and a digital government, thereby making public services and social governance more digitized and intelligent. Basic systems, standards and norms, such as data resource property rights, transaction circulation, cross-border transmission and security protection, have been established to promote the development and utilization of data resources. Expanding the access of basic public information and data, and building an open platform for unified sharing of national data have truly become a priority for China. Ensuring the security of national data and strengthen the protection of personal information as well as developing a robust regime for intellectual property (IP) rights in digital space are few of the areas where China is investing and diligently working towards Alongside, a movement for improvement in the digital skills of the entire population in order to increase access as well as fully utilize information services is finding great momentum so as to enable active participation in the formulation of international rules and standards in the digital field.

In the global innovation race, the digital sector has probably been China's strength. The rise of influential Chinese digital giants, including Baidu, Alibaba, Tencent and Xiaomi (known together by the acronym BATX), has proved to the world that China is indeed a global leader in digital innovation (OECD, 2017a). Beyond its domestic market, international statistics clearly point towards China's leading role in exporting digital goods and services. Given that China is densely populated with a fast-growing economy, it is not surprising that China has started to influence the global digital market (Herrero and Xu, 2018).

DEVELOPMENT OF E-COMMERCE IN CHINA

China has also demonstrated great potential and success in the field of development of businesses in online space. By 2019, China's digital economy added value worth 35.8 trillion yuan, and the nominal growth was 14.7%, which proved to be significantly higher than GDP growth in that year. The contribution rate of digital economy to GDP growth reached 67.7 percent, accounting for 36.2% of GDP thereby making it a key driver in China's economic development.

Figure 1. The total size of the digital economy and its proportion in GDP from 2005 to 2019
(Source: CAICT)

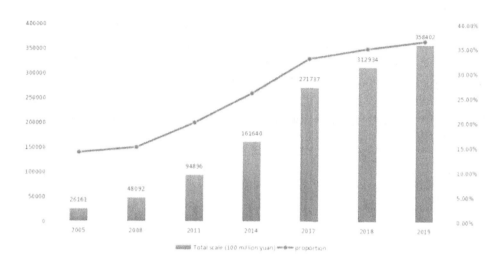

As mentioned above, digital economy has been the driving force of e-commerce development in China. *The China E-commerce Report 2020,* that was released at the Silk Road E-commerce Development Summit between China and Central and Eastern European Countries (CEEC) in Ningbo, Zhejiang Province, China, on June 8, 2021; shows that in 2020, China's e-commerce transaction volume reached 37.21 trillion yuan, an increase of 4.5% as compared to previous years. China's e-commerce platforms have developed rapidly in recent years, and are gradually becoming mature and systematic. Especially during the pandemic and post-pandemic period, China's online payment system has resulted into rapid expansion and growth.

Not only has digital economy contributed to GDP of the economy but has also offered new solutions to China's unemployment concerns. New and innovative methods of employment have emerged. Mobile payment system, has played a major role in alleviating job losses caused by shutdowns during the COVID-19 epidemic. Mobile payment promotes entrepreneurship through three channels: changing individual's risk attitudes, enriching individual's social networks and improving credit availability. The financial universality of mobile payment system has significantly increased the availability of financial services and the possibility for households to obtain formal and informal lending. Due to innovation in information technology, mobile payment system also serves as a new and efficient information communication channel, through which successful experience of entrepreneurship can be spread as well as the potential of risk associated with assets can be minimised (Yin *et al.*, 2019).

Pandemic has resulted into integration and growth of the digital economy and the traditional economy China Internet Network Information Center (CNNIC) has released the 46th *Statistical Report on Internet Development in China* (2020), which shows that as of June 2020, the number of online education users in China reached 381 million, and the number of online food delivery users reached 409 million. Data shows that the number of online food delivery users in China has increased by 11.24 million since March 2020. By December 2020, the number of netizens in China had reached 989 million, an increase of 85.4 million over March 2020, and the Internet penetration rate had reached 70.4 percent.

Figure 2. Digital economy - internet penetration China (percent)
(Source: Statista)

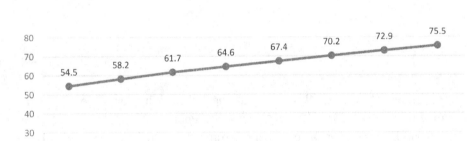

LITERATURE REVIEW

With the rise of a new wave of global technological revolution and industrial change, the digital economy is developing at an unprecedented speed, with a wide ranging impact, becoming a key force in reshaping the global economic structure. Since Xi Jinping has taken charge, great importance has been attached to the development of the digital economy and there has been continuous promotion of the optimization and upgradation of the digital economy governance system.

This chapter examines three aspects of expansion in China's digital economy in the context of the COVID-19 epidemic: The first aspect: the problem itself

The term digital economy or internet economy was used for the first time in the 1990s (Tapscott, 2014). However, it acquired a concrete form in the G20 leaders'

Hangzhou Summit held in September 2016 where world leaders committed themselves towards constructing an inclusive society by addressing the digital divide, affordable access to information for economic growth, digital transformation, e-commerce cooperation along with recognition of constructing a robust and a secure IP rights regime for the purpose of safeguarding people's rights in the digital space. Currently, global economic governance is entering a new era through digital transformation (Paradise, 2019). Resultant business model innovations have fundamentally altered consumers' expectations and behaviours, pressured traditional firms, and disrupted numerous markets (Peter et al., 2021). As a new and emerging branch of economy, digital economy requires building of a scientific knowledge base as well as upgradation in industrial structure. China has already entered a new phase characterized by medium-to-high growth rate focused around comprehensive and sustainable development. Digitalization is definitely in line with this current trend towards qualitative growth in China's economy (Pan et al., 2022).

This chapter quotes the literature on "Digital China Economy" from 2000 to 2021 from Web of Science, and generates the keyword co-occurrence atlas through CiteSpace. As can be seen from the figure, "big data", "innovation", "science and technology" and "digital divide" have become key words in the literature on "Digital China economy" in the past 20 years.

This chapter will review the development of China's digital economy over the past 20 years and introduce the current development of China's digital economy in the wake of COVID-19.

Figure 3. Co-occurrence chart of keywords in literature on "Digital China Economy" from 2000 to 2021
(Source: Web of Science)

Since more than a decade, China's digital economy has maintained rapid growth, with the output of the digital economy increasing from 22.6 trillion yuan in 2016 to 39.2 trillion yuan in 2020. Globally, China's digital economy leads the world, ranking second only to the United States in terms of output size (Jiang and Jin, 2021). The second aspect: antecedent variables

1.   The impact of COVID-19

After the outbreak of COVID-19 in 2019, the digital economy has become a new fulcrum for confidence recovery amid the declining trend in of GDP, and has a profound impact on the efficiency of economic activities. Just take e-commerce, a representative industry in the "platform" economy, as an example. In the "post-COVID-19 era", new retailers have successfully built online shopping platforms through intelligent network systems, closely reviewing transition in consumption habits on account of online transformation, thereby achieving record sales growth directly impacting the economy.

Chinese companies have particularly done exceptionally well in 2020, a year of widespread growth for e-commerce around the world. The latest report from the United Nations Conference on Trade and Development ranks the global B2C e-commerce companies by transaction volume (gross merchandise volume) in 2020. Four of the top 13 e-commerce companies are from China: Alibaba at number one, JD.com at number three, Pinduoduo at number four and Meituan at number seven. Alibaba's gross merchandise volume reached $1,145 billion in 2020, more than double the volume generated by amazon which stood at $575 billion.

2.   The role of government in promoting the digital economy

At the municipal level, China has used data in various forms to drive this movement of digital transformation, including the assignment of color-coded mobile health certificates to indicate an individual's risk level. The economic benefit here is being mentioned in the term of the ability to be more selective in mobility restrictions, thereby reducing the economic impact of the pandemic containment policies. The government approves the use of this form of data in order to make appropriate as well as informed public health decisions (Spence, 2021).

The Chinese government has also been taking a cautious regulatory stance in the digital sector. In the field of livestreaming e-commerce, the State Administration for Market Regulation has recently issued the Guiding Opinions on Strengthening supervision of Online Livestreaming Marketing Activities and other relevant regulations and policies, standardizing the operation process of livestreaming e-commerce and guiding the healthy and orderly development of livestreaming e-commerce.

Third aspect: outcome variables

In the post-COVID-19 era, digital economy has become an important driver of economic recovery and qualitative growth in all countries. The competition worldwide with respect to digital economy is also becoming increasingly complicated. Since there is an unidentified border space in digital environment, even IP regime is unable to display its full potential in terms of addressing any legal anomalies. IP plays a crucial role in protecting companies from misuse of their know-how as well in promoting innovation, creativity and originality. In digital environment, it is often difficult to identify where infringement or violation has taken place and subsequently compensate the owner or creator. Mushrooming of counterfeit portals online as well as digression in quality of products on account of piracy and data theft are few aspects that need to be seriously considered while simultaneously working on digital transformation of economy in China. Be it copyright and related rights, patents, trademarks, industrial designs or geographical indications, China has to invest and explore venues of international cooperation in its expanding digital framework building protective IP framework. In the context of the potential deepening of the "perception gap" caused by the COVID-19, it is particularly important for countries to summarize their development experience and governance guidelines in the digital economy including relevant IP and legal norms by making full use of multilateral dialogue, and seeking global consensus.

In order to analyze the case of China's digital economy and China's digital development, the author analyzed the massive literature in the international database Web of Science and Chinese database in the past 20 years respectively. This study is valuable from the perspective of previous research literature. As the digital economy significantly facilitates social productivity through high-tech innovation and application, including mobile networks, artificial intelligence (AI), blockchain, and cloud computing (Lamberton and Stephen, 2016, Verhoef et al., 2015, Nambisan et al., 2017, Luo et al., 2018).

Due to China's unique national conditions, this chapter analyzes different case scenarios with respect to role of government, state-owned enterprises and SMEs in China's digital economy, the status of China's digital economy during the COVID-19 period as well as the trend of development after the pandemic, putting forward suggestions for the development of China's digital economy in the near future.

The author during research found that the literature on the digital development of China's state-owned enterprises and small and medium-sized enterprises was very limited in international databases such as Web of Science, so the author used CNKI (China National Knowledge Infrastructure) to conduct corresponding literature analysis.

In this chapter, literature on the digital development of State-owned enterprises and SMEs in China from 2000 to 2021 are cited respectively, and keywords co-occurrence maps of the past 20 years have been made through CiteSpace.

Figure 4. Co-occurrence chart of keywords on "digitization of State-owned enterprises (SOEs)" from 2000 to 2021
(Source: CNKI)

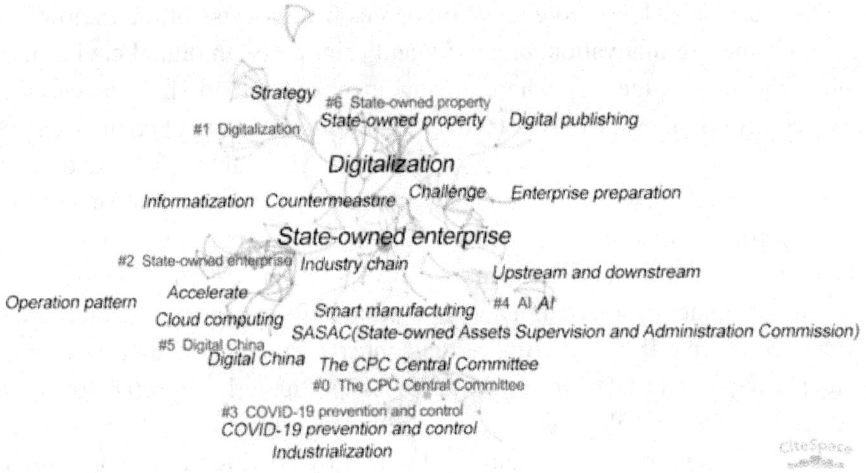

Figure 5. Co-occurrence chart of keywords on "digitization of small and medium-sized enterprises (SMEs)" from 2000 to 2021
(Source: CNKI)

The author based upon research believes that in China, government, state-owned enterprises and SMEs have different characteristics and difficulties in the process leading up to digital transformation. The author has this made suggestions in order to address challenges impacting China's digital economy based on literature available currently.

IMPACT OF COVID-19 ON CHINA'S SMART ECONOMY

Remote working, through the Internet, is being undertaken at an unprecedented scale. Online shopping for groceries, medicines and food from restaurants, became a necessity for many people during the pandemic. Online provision of healthcare services and virtual doctor appointments have now become a common practice. Clearly, the digital economy has played a crucial role in the supply of goods and services during the pandemic, and it will be the driving force for economic growth in the new normal or post pandemic era (Chen, 2020).

Expansion in Opportunities for Growth of Digital Economy, Strengthening of Intellectual Property Rights Regime and Expansion of the Market during the Pandemic

The pandemic has negatively impacted the global economy in every sense be it the scale of economic activity, tourism, hospitality or transport services. All major countries have been suffering an overall contraction in their GDP in 2020, with China as the only exception, where GDP has been expected to grow by 2.6% (Fernandes, 2020).

In the initial days of outbreak of COVID-19 in China, many day-to-day activities unexpectedly came to a halt in many cities, and in a shocking turn of events, even neighborhoods became inaccessible. Everyone had to follow mandates such as "city closures" and "home quarantine" for their own as well as others' safety. In China, a 42% reduction in offline consumption was reported in the year 2020 (year-on-year from 2019), with a smaller but still substantial 20% reduction of online consumption (Chen et al., 2020).

In order to avoid physical contact, many online fresh retail platforms and delivery platforms have gained popularity. One example worth mentioning is when at the beginning of the outbreak of the pandemic in Wuhan, in order to take care of basic survival needs of the city's residents, government established an online store where retail platforms with distribution capabilities in Wuhan, such as Meicai Maimai, Zhongbaidudian, Ele.me, Meituan (takeout + buy food), Hema, Dada-Jingdong Jiajie, Jingdong Youjia Shop, etc., were involved. This gave an opportunity to many delivery platforms to expand and develop their business. This "contactless economy" has brought with itself new opportunities and new models for the development of China's digital smart economy. At the same time, the challenges presented by lack of awareness of protecting and securing one's IP rights too are being widely addresses. Online sales of fake and counterfeit goods resulting into widespread infringement in trademarks, designs and copyright have enabled policy makers, industry as well as common people aware about the need for being vigilant and taking timely action for filing and registering IP.

Digital Economy Has Acted as a Catalyst for Developing a Pattern of Universal Participation as well as Being an Impetus for Leading the Movement towards Sustainability

Before the COVID-19 outbreak, there were still some groups in China that were disconnected from the Internet. But that scenario too has changed during the COVID-19, and the society has been taking a big leap towards inclusiveness in this aspect. Innovation of affordable and sustainable gadgets so that everyone can have access to digital space have now become a norm. There have been significant lifestyle changes as well. By December 2020, the number of non-Internet users in China was 416 million, 80.73 million fewer than in March 2020, and the Internet penetration rate as recorded was 70.4 percent (CNNIC, 2021). This kind of participation by more and more groups in the smart economy in the backdrop of COVID-19, has resulted into providing a broader social base for the transition to the digital economy. Digital economy is also instrumental towards achieving UN Agenda of Sustainable Development Goals towards 2030. Internet of things, big data and digital innovation is leading towards creating a more inclusive society as well as increasing employment opportunities as well. It is having a profound impact across all sectors be it reducing emissions in transport sector, as a result of cutting down on travel cost and energy or be it responsible consumption pattern in terms of reduction in usage of paper and other renewable forms of energy.

Figure 6. Number of mobile internet users in China from 2010 to December 2020 (in millions)
(Source: CNNIC)

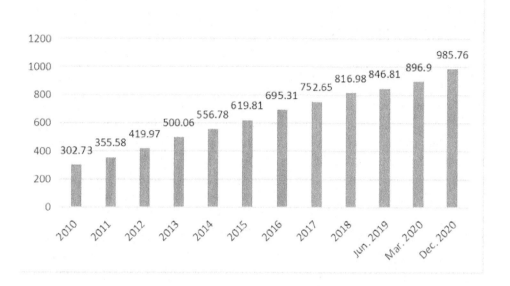

Home isolation has resulted into a significant shift in not only people's way of life, but their education and entertainment as well. In order to contain the spread of virus during pandemic, all schools across the country suspended physical classes and implemented the plans to actively prepare for online education system. In this way, COVID-19 has enabled the digital economy to become a driving force to transform a series of social patterns and lifestyles.

Decline in Economic Vitality and the Deterioration of the Macro Environment

However, there are certain sectors who have even been hit despite a transition to digital mode of working. The online travel industry is a classic example, industry plummeted and many businesses suffered losses. In January 2020, the initial outbreak of the epidemic occurred around the Spring Festival holiday, a traditional Chinese holiday, which is usually a golden time for national tourism since many years. After the lockdown in various provinces and cities, flights and high-speed rail and other modes of transportation were largely canceled. Many large online travel companies in China, such as Ctrip, Qunar, Feizhu and Hornet's Nest, have been facing the risk of paying huge sums of money in advance or breaking their funds, with losses amounting to hundreds of millions of yuan.

The film industry has also been significantly affected. According to China's State Film Administration, the annual box office loss is estimated at more than 30 billion renminbi, or about $3 billion, on account of a nationwide cinema shutdown and a virtual halt to production.

Role of Smart Cities

Development of Smart cities has played an important role in the development of digital economy in urban management and livelihood services too. Another area where digital economy came to rescue for large number of people during pandemic was when there was persisting shortage of personal protection equipment (PPE). Leading e-commerce, logistics and delivery companies developed PPE supply chain management platforms and coordinated with health authorities in Hubei to source and procure PPE from a global network of suppliers. Big data technology was used to forecast and automate matchmaking. One business-to-business (B2B) e-commerce company launched a digital supply chain management system (29 January 2020) with more than 3000 suppliers and delivery services, securing essential volume of PPE early in the outbreak (Chen et al., 2020).

However, there are certain shortcomings that need to be addressed as well. Some smart cities with relatively complete and mature construction have made use of digital technologies such as cloud computing, big data and the Internet of Things to alleviate governance problems and play an active role in fighting the epidemic. However, the construction of some smart cities is still in a state of paralysis. Problems such as lack of smart city infrastructure, reasonable use of data acquisition method and insufficient coordination among various departments are common. It can be seen that COVID-19 has tested the effectiveness of smart city construction in China, which is a good opportunity to strengthen public governance capacity.

THE ROLE OF GOVERNMENT IN PROMOTING SMART ECONOMY'S DIGITALIZATION

In the digital economic reform, the government is not only the core subject and object, but also the key actor driving the digital technology to transform social set up and people's way of life. Without government management and policy protection, the transformation of digital economy is bound to get out of control. The following are the policies and relevant contents promulgated by the Chinese government in the development of digital economy in the past ten years:

Table 1. In the past decade, the Chinese government has issued some policies and related contents on the development of digital economy

Time	Name of policy/meeting	Related content
Nov. 2015	*Outline of the 13th Five-Year Plan for National Economic and Social Development of the People's Republic of China*	Implementation of the national big data strategy, promotion of open sharing of data resources.
Dec. 2017	The Political Bureau of the CPC Central Committee studied for the second time	Promotion of the implementation of the national big data strategy, acceleration in the improvement of digital infrastructure, promotion of the integration and open sharing of data resources, ensuring data security, and acceleration of the building of a digital China.
Dec. 2017	The Political Bureau of the CPC Central Committee studied for the second time	Promotion of the implementation of the national big data strategy, acceleration in the improvement of digital infrastructure, promotion of the integration and open sharing of data resources, ensuring data security, and acceleration in the building of a digital China.
Nov. 2019	The Fourth Plenary Session of the 19th CPC Central Committee	Advancement in construction of a digital government, strengthening the system of data sharing, and protection of personal information in accordance with the law.
Nov. 2019	*Implementation Plan of National Digital Economy Innovation and Development Pilot Zone*	In Hebei Province (Xiongan New Area), Zhejiang Province, Fujian Province, Guangdong Province, Chongqing City, Sichuan Province and other provinces, assisting the creation of national digital economy innovation and development pilot zone, after a 3-year exploration plan. So far, digital industrialization and industrial mathematics has achieved remarkable results.
Apr. 2020	*Implementation Plan on Promoting the Action of "Endowing Intelligence with Number on Cloud" and Fostering New Economy Development*	Vigorously fostering new forms of businesses in the digital economy, focusing on promotion of the digital transformation of enterprises, and creating a data adaptation chain. Data flow leading to the flow of materials, talent, technology and capital, so as to form a digital ecosystem integrating the upstream and downstream of the industrial chain
Jul. 2020	*Opinions on Supporting the Healthy Development of New Forms and Models of Business and Activating the Consumer Market to Expand Employment*	Actively exploring new models of online service to activate new consumption markets. Acceleration of the digital transformation in industries and strengthening new drivers of the real economy. Encouraging the development of a new individual economy and opening up new space for consumption and employment.

Since China has come up with the national Big Data Strategy in 2015, policies to promote the development of digital economy and digital transformation are being implemented at a great pace. Since 2017, the digital economy has been included in the government work report for four consecutive years. In the report on the work of the Government in 2020, it was made clear that the government will continue to introduce supportive policies to comprehensively promote the Internet Plus initiative and forge new alliances to explore potential advantages of the digital economy.

By the end of 2020, more than 60 digital-economy-related policies had been proposed and the number of digital-economy-related policies promulgated by local governments in 2020 accounted for a maximum of 37 percent. Among these 60 policies related to the digital economy, about 49 percent of the policies are action plans and 37 percent are industrial plans.

Figure 7. Map of the administrative region of the People's Republic of China
(Source: Baidu)

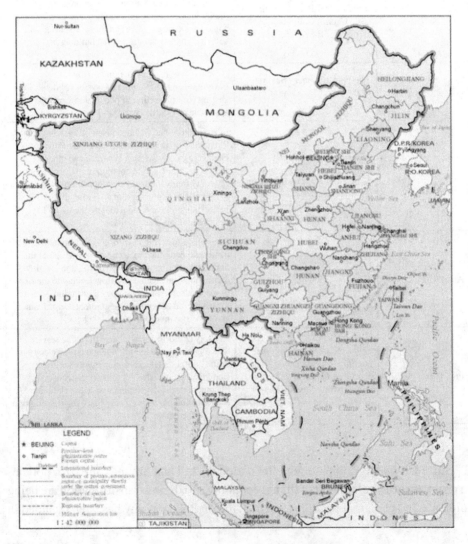

Table 2. Recently, some provinces in China issued policies and related contents to promote the development of local digital economy

Province	Policy name	Related content
Beijing Province	*Beijing Action Report on Promoting Innovative Development of Digital Economy (2020-2022) Implementation Plan of Beijing to Build Digital Trade Experimental Zone (Sep. 2020)*	In terms of industrial digitalization, the pace of digital transformation of Beijing's primary, secondary and tertiary industries has been accelerating. Rural revitalization efforts have been strengthened in order to strategically plan, transition of digital agriculture and rural areas step by step. Furthermore, the level of digitalization in agriculture has significantly increased. Success in 4 districts namely Shunyi, Haidian, Chaoyang, Shijingshan has been included in the new national industrialization industry demonstration base. Along with this, the ground identification of industrial Internet infrastructure, such as large data center, to make a national plan for industrial development of the Internet highlands, has further resulted into increase in the digitalization level of the service industry. For example, in the field of consumer digital space, Beijing has become is a place for consumer Internet unicorns to come together at a common platform. In terms of digital governance, Beijing takes data sharing services as the key to improve governance capacity, and actively promotes data sharing and the integration of public service systems into the cloud throughout the city, providing strong support for data convergence and sharing, resource development and utilization, thereby resulting in improvement of business environment as a whole.
Shanghai Province	*Action Plan for Promoting the Digital Transformation of Shanghai daily Life and enabling construction of qualitative Digital environment(2021-2023) (Jul. 2021)*	With cities, enterprises and citizens playing the main role, we should strive to create a new vision of digital life in which demand is precisely catered to, services benefit in a balanced way, potential is effectively utilized, and value is fully realized. The goal is to significantly enhance the digital literacy and ability of citizens by 2023, and continuously improve digital services to improve quality of life, build at least 50 innovative policies for the digital transformation of environment, thus promoting Shanghai to become a model of global, innovation pilot zone, and emerge as city of intelligence in the near future.
Jiangsu Province	*Nanjing Digital Economy Development Three-Year Action Plan (2020-2022) (Apr. 2021)*	By 2022, the added value of the city's digital economy is expected to reach 1 trillion yuan, accounting for more than 56% of its GDP, actively striving to create a national pilot zone for digital economy innovation and development and a national pilot zone for new generation AI innovation and development. Nanjing will be built into an innovation highland of key core technologies of digital economy, a development highland of high-end industries of digital economy, an innovation demonstration highland of urban digital governance, and a gathering highland of highly talented professionals of digital economy.
Fujian Province	*Working Plan of the National Digital Economy Innovation and Development Pilot Zone (Fujian) (Mar. 2021)*	Further integrating next-generation information technology with government services, speeding up the building of an intensive and integrated digital government, further improving governance and service efficiency, and making government decision-making more scientific, social governance more targeted, and public services more efficient.
Guangdong Province	*Shenzhen Digital Economy Industry Innovation and Development Implementation Plan (Draft for Comments) (Jun. 2020)*	By 2022, the digital economy industry is expected to become one of the core engine to promote the development of our city's economic and social life, effective transformation and upgradation of industry, with focus on efforts to build, a world -class digital economy industry leading cities everywhere

Continued on following page

Table 2. Continued

Province	Policy name	Related content
Hunan Province	*Digital Economy Development Plan of Hunan Province* (2020-2025) (Feb. 2020)	By 2025, the scale of the digital economy will be among top 10 in China, exceeding RMB 2.5 trillion with an average annual compound growth rate of over 15.8%. The proportion of the digital economy in GDP will reach 45%, of which the total volume of digital industrialization will exceed RMB 750 billion and the total volume of industrial digitalization will exceed RMB 1.75 trillion. The main focus will be to vigorously develop digital industrialization, accelerate industrial digitalization, strive to break through the key core technologies, build digital economy infrastructure, innovate the governance model of digital economy, strengthen the information security of digital economy, and build digital economy ecosystem.

Chinese government at all levels has actively responded to the call of the state and formulated some policies to promote the digital economy as suitable to the local conditions prevailing in the economy and current situation. Beijing and Shanghai are among China's first-tier cities, Jiangsu and Fujian provinces are developed coastal areas in southeast China, and Hunan province is in central China with inland rivers.

The share and proportion of China's digital economy is increasing year by year, but there are still obvious differences among provinces, which are divided into four echelon. The first tier includes Guangdong, Jiangsu, Shandong, Zhejiang, Shanghai and Beijing, each with a digital economy of more than 1 trillion yuan. The second tier includes Fujian, Hubei, Hebei and Tianjin, with a digital economy scale between 600 billion yuan and 1 trillion yuan. The third tier includes Shaanxi, Jilin, Guangxi, Heilongjiang, Guizhou, Inner Mongolia, Shanxi and Xinjiang, with a digital economy scale of 200 billion to 600 billion yuan. The fourth tier includes three provinces, Gansu, Ningxia and Qinghai, with a digital economy of less than 200 billion yuan (Chen, 2018).

The development of China's digital economy presents typical spatial disequilibrium characteristics. Although the overall regional gap in the development of digital economy shows a significant downward trend, there is still a relatively obvious regional gap in the development of Digital economy in China. The top three in Gini coefficient among the five urban agglomerations are the Beijing-Tianjin-Hebei urban agglomeration, the Chengdu-Chongqing urban agglomeration and the Yangtze River Delta urban agglomeration (Liu, 2020).

IMPORTANT CASE STUDIES RELATED TO CHINA

Government Driven Digital Platforms in the COVID-19 Era

Central Government: National Government Service Platform and Itinerary Code

During the outbreak of the pandemic in February 2020, under the guidance of the E-Government Office of The General Office of the State Council, Tencent actively participated in promoting the construction of health information code on the national integrated government service platform for epidemic prevention and control.

In order to speed up epidemic prevention and control across the country and resume work and production as soon as possible, the National Government Affairs Service Platform WeChat mini program officially launched the new epidemic prevention and control project in February 2020, providing for a database of number of infections and risk areas, close contact personnel check list, local outbreak service window and treatment guidelines, etc. Residents were able to keep abreast with the latest situation of the epidemic and the latest data on the number of infected people in order to take better measures to protect themselves and their loved ones. Up till now nucleic acid and antibody test results query and national nucleic acid testing institutions query, peer close contact with the self-examination and other items too have been added on the platform.

On 29 February 2020, the National Government Affairs Service Platform officially launched the Health Code for Epidemic Prevention. Residents could apply for a Health Code by verifying their real names and reporting health status through the Epidemic Prevention Information Code in the WeChat mini program of the National Government Affairs Service Platform. Residents could use this Health Code to get in and out of neighborhoods, supermarkets and other places. At the same time, considering the situation of children and the elderly, the National Government Affairs Service Platform opened a "Health Code for the elderly and the young" function, where relatives, friends or others could help the elderly over 60 years old and children under 16 years old to check their health status. To protect privacy, the phone of the person helping with the query did not store any cached information or data.

In addition, as China's epidemic control situation gradually started to improve, many provinces across the country who began to resume work, colleges and universities have planned to reopen, Communication Big Data Travel Cards which will provide important health information records and certificates for people returning from all over the country. The big data travel card is provided to 1.6 billion mobile phone users in China by China Academy of Information And Communications Technology

(CAICT) and three basic telecom enterprises (China Telecom, China Mobile and China Unicom) to receive data through mobile phones and provide free query services through the base station location of the users' phones.

In the Mini program of The Chinese State Council on WeChat, users can enter their mobile phone number and verification code to check the cities in China where they have stayed for more than four hours within 14 days, as well as foreign countries or regions they have visited. This operation requires no ID number, home address, or other personal information to be collected. It is more convenient and secure, and fully protects user privacy. Communication Big Data Travel Cards make operation more convenient for users to in case of any query as well as to prove their epidemic prevention and health status. After obtaining the trip code, the trip card will display colors according to the user's recent trip. There are four colors: green card, yellow card, orange card and red card. The new card rules are: the red card indicates a confirmed or suspected COVID-19 patient; the orange card indicates that the user is a close contact of a confirmed or suspected COVID-19 patient; Yellow card refers to the overseas countries and regions through which the user travels; a green card means a user comes to a low-risk area, it's safe. The color card only serves as a reminder of the place to visit, not related to health status.

Compared with the Health Code, the Communication Big Data Travel Card focuses more on the user's travel path. To control the spread of the virus nationwide, where the basic function is to trace the source, which has nothing to do with the personal qualities of users or residents. It is important to ensure that people in circulation are healthy and that the areas they pass through are risk-free. Otherwise, we need to trace the infection to its source.

Provinces: Health Code

In the early days of the outbreak, the Health Codes introduced by Chinese provinces helped provincial prevention and control efforts. However, there are as many as 100 species in China. Due to inconsistent standards, data sharing and lack of mutual recognition mechanism, it has been very difficult for residents to move across provinces and regions.

In order to facilitate inter-provincial and inter-regional epidemic service connectivity among 34 provinces, the Health Code of the National Government Affairs Service Platform is being gradually connected with the Health Code of Guangdong, Shanghai and other places according to the Health Code interface standard. On the basis of the data and information code sharing services provided by the National Government Affairs Service Platform, local governments are responsible for providing local Health Code related management and services thereby gradually increasing mutual trust and recognition of health information codes among regions.

On 10 December 2020, the National Health Commission of The People's Republic of China, China National Health Insurance Administration and The National Administration of Traditional Chinese Medicine jointly issued the Notice on Further Promoting the Action of "Internet + Medical And Health" and "Five one" Services, which clearly proposed to promote the integration of one code and universal access service, break down the information barrier that multiple codes bring along which are not common to each other, and effectively facilitate people's travel and inter-provincial mobility. Now, the national Health Code exchange has become the norm, the epidemic prevention "health code" has unified policy, unified standards, mutual recognition with one-code access.

State-Owned Enterprises

From a macroscopic point of view, the operating environment of central enterprises has changed. Technology is changing rapidly. Traditional business models are finding it difficult to adapt to new changes. The digital economy has, become a core element of economic growth and a key area for business competition in the post-epidemic era. At the same time, state-owned enterprises are an important force leading and driving high-quality economic development. Accelerating the digital transformation of central government enterprises will accelerate new technological innovation, enable enterprises to be more widely and deeply integrated into the global supply system thereby contributing to overall improvement in the global supply system, and propel China's industries to climb upwards in the global value chain. In this era of digital transformation, central enterprises should follow the trend of the times accelerating the pace of digital transformation.

From the microscopic perspective, digital transformation is an important cornerstone in order for central enterprises to achieve qualitative growth. Accelerating digital transformation is conducive to fully utilizing the innovation potential of state-owned enterprises and improving their core competitiveness and risk resistance ability.

China Mobile International (CMI) × AWS

China Mobile International Co., Ltd. (CMI) is a wholly owned subsidiary of China Mobile, headquartered in Hong Kong. Its main responsibility is to run China Mobile's international business professionally. In the process of Chinese enterprises "going out" and foreign enterprises "coming in", enterprises' demand for multi-cloud services and cross-border communication network services is growing rapidly. AWS, Amazon Web Services, is Amazon's LaaS and PaaS platform Services for cloud computing. Amazon Web Services (AWS) is a comprehensive, evolving cloud computing platform provided by Amazon that includes a mixture of infrastructure, platform, and packaged software offerings. It provides a highly reliable, scalable, low-cost infrastructure platform in the cloud that powers multitude of businesses in 190 countries around the world (Maurya et al., 2021).

In order to provide customers with convenient, stable and secure cross-regional communication services worldwide, CMI has made use of the efficient and agile digital tools provided by AWS to launch Cloud Connect, which is combined with AWS Direct Connect, enabling CMI and AWS customers to connect with the AWS global region and AWS China region in just a few minutes, thus significantly reducing the business opening time. It has realized the rapid transformation of its own products, accelerated the opening process of customers and broadened its own customer acquisition channels.

SANY Group × China Enterprise Power and China Enterprise Ultimate (CE ULTIMZTE)

Sany Group is a world-renowned engineering equipment manufacturer. During the epidemic, the Group sought for a breakthrough in traditional sales model and carried out digital transformation. The first model being that of brand digitization, an Omni-channel digital transformation service provider. China Enterprise Ultimate in collaboration with Sany Group International Exhibition fulfills the requirements for international exhibitions and online digital marketing, thereby helping it to build a "one-stop" comprehensive digital marketing platform. Based on the internationalization strategy of SANY Group, CE ULTIMATE have carried out a new visual design for the official website of SANY Group, so as to create an international brand image by improving the user experience.

The second is to use the new digital technology to open a new marketing model. Due to the outbreak, many customers were unable to attend the Shanghai BMW Expo in 2020. The digital marketing management platform designed for the companies enables customers to participate in the online WeChat, official website and other channels to display various links, and the data is there after fed back to the sales staff.

In the 2020 Shanghai BMW Expo, SANY Group reported a breakthrough success. The 72-hour uninterrupted multi-language and multi-platform live broadcast program provided by CE ULTIMZTE for SANY Group achieved a deposit of more than 100 million yuan in 8 minutes and a turnover of more than 23.489 billion yuan in 2 hours.

1.   Challenges of China's State-Owned Enterprises' digital transformation:

Most of China's state-owned enterprises have begun digital transformation, and some leading enterprises in the industry rely on their position as well as the industrial chain, to empower the upstream and downstream towards digital transformation.

However, most state-owned enterprises are still in the initial stage of transformation. The obstacles and stagnation in achieving breakthroughs have resulted in the status quo in digital transformation for the majority of state-owned enterprises. Only a small percentage of digital transformation has been carried out smoothly and achieved significant results.

Although State-owned enterprises (SOEs) have an absolute advantage over Non-state-owned enterprises (NSOEs) in terms of size, social credibility, and government support, their innovation is more vulnerable to epidemic. First of all, SOEs need to undertake macro-political functions and have characteristics of heavy-asset operation mode, which make it difficult to adjust flexibly and timely in the face of epidemic (Ghazvini et al., 2015). Second, as an integral part of national finance, SOEs have mandatory social responsibilities, and the government directly instructs SOEs to implement various measures to support other enterprises, which further increases the financial pressure on SOEs (Hu, 2020).

For the digital transformation of state-owned enterprises, the biggest challenge is not come the lack of leadership support or financial support, but the main difficulties include inability to find the entry point for the integration of digital technology and the company's business; lack of equipped manpower; the cognitive differences of digital transformation within enterprises, and the difficulty of breaking the original departmental boundaries and interest walls within organizations base.

2.   Views on the digital Transformation of State-owned enterprises:

    a.   Management guidance:

Relevant government departments need to strengthen guidance and support for the digital transformation of State-Owned enterprises, carry out pilot work, create demonstrated examples of digital transformation, and conduct classified guidance according to different industries of enterprises, especially manufacturing, energy, construction, service and other industries with strong demand. It not only provides the application scenario of the integration of digital technology and enterprise transformation, but also points out the entry point of digital transformation for state-owned enterprises. At the same time, it is suggested to further improve the performance appraisal mechanism for state-owned enterprises that promote digital transformation and give them enough time and space to promote digital transformation, so as to lay a good foundation for the high-quality development of enterprises in the future.

    b.   Talent pool:

With the increasing popularity of digital technology, the gap on account of lack of professional manpower in enterprises is expanding day by day. Professionals who have only mastered information technology can no longer meet the needs of digital development. Nowadays, there has been observed real scarcity of professionals who not only understand digital technology, but also are good at business and management.

In addition, there is also a need to focus on improving the ability of the existing staff. It is necessary to improve the incentive mechanism and management system for employees in the digital environment, so that employees can actively embrace digitalization and become professionals familiar with both technology and business and management. Trained manpower can support in providing a strong impetus for the digital transformation of enterprises at a faster pace.

c. Digital processing power:

Big data security governance is not only related to enterprise development, but also to national security. To this end, enterprises should strengthen the governance capacity of big data, solve the problems of big data sharing and converged application, clarify the ownership and user rights of data, clarify the boundaries of rights and responsibilities, as well as effectively protect user privacy and security.

Small and Medium-Sized Enterprises (SMEs)

Governments across the globe are issuing policies and implementing action plans including restrictions (i.e. lockdowns of countries, temporary closure of physical operations of businesses) to prevent further spread of Covid-19. Those restrictions have implications for sustainable operations of businesses including reduction of business activities, HR issues related to staffing and supply chain disruptions. Those restrictions have more severe effects on small and medium-sized enterprises (SMEs) than on larger and global firms. In fact, SMEs are most vulnerable since they tend to have a lower capital reserve, fewer assets, and lower levels of productivity than larger firms (OECD, 2020).

Digitization can lessen SMEs concerns about economic survival, allowing them to meet their various social and environmental obligations (Zhanna and Yana, 2020).

Environment Business Group × Partner Cloud

For small and medium-sized enterprises, there has been a consistent lack of supporting service institutions for digital transformation. Investment in almost all supporting domains, such as design, testing, verification etc. need to be carried out by the enterprises themselves, and the cost for the same is quite high. However, Partner

Cloud indeed provides a relatively perfect digital transformation supporting platform and scheme for small and medium-sized enterprises, which solves the problems for most small and medium-sized enterprises.

Since 2016, Environment Business Group, with the aid of digital tools - Partner Cloud has been gradually providing necessary tools for digital management to all sectors of the Environment Business Group which is slowly breaking past the original state of affairs brought about by incompetent management, thus transforming data as the core as well as contributing to better operation and scientific development of real estate enterprises. Partner Cloud is not only suitable for medium-sized enterprises such as environmental business group, but also for other small and micro enterprises. As a result of its flexible mechanism for customization (without writing code), one can configure one's own applications to meet complex and personalized needs, thus covering more than 90% of the user scenarios of small, medium and micro enterprises.

1.   China's small and medium-sized enterprises digital transformation pain points

    a.   Trial and error cost concerns, insufficient resources

Most small and medium-sized enterprises have low profits and limited investment capacity in digital transformation. It takes millions of yuan for system transformation and tens of thousands of yuan of industrial software so in this case-scenario, small and medium-sized enterprises are majorly struggling.

b.   Transfer efficiency gains

The actual benefits brought by the industrial Internet are hard to see in the short term. Many enterprises make huge investments but no returns in the long run, and that is what fuels lack of willingness on their part to continue to invest in the venture to transform. At the beginning of 2020, due to the impact of COVID-19, market expectations were unstable, demand was weak with orders falling, production declining and resulting in small and medium-sized enterprises' lack of confidence in capacity for investment. According to the Development Index of small and Medium-sized Enterprises released by China Association of Small and Medium-sized Enterprises, the investment index of small and medium-sized enterprises in the first quarter of 2020 was 56.2, with an average decrease of nearly 20 points in the fourth quarter of 2019.

c.   The personnel training mechanism is not sound

Small and medium-sized enterprises are short of professional manpower as compared to large enterprises or state-owned enterprises. Most SMEs do not have a training program for skill and capacity building in digital technology for their staff.

2.   Views on digital Transformation of Chinese SMEs

   a.   Industrial Internet platform

In the case of small and medium-sized enterprises, as a result of availability of sufficient funds, it is difficult to provide a low cost, fast and reliable industrial Internet platform. At this stage, it is crucial that small and medium-sized enterprises choose a platform suitable to their needs. At present, there are many small industrial Internet platforms in China, suitable for the initial construction of small and medium-sized enterprises, which can be updated and developed as and when the need arises; such as Jiyun, Yunzhiyi, iNeuOS, QingCloud and so on.

With a dynamic market environment, increasing competition, need for product improvement as well as production process optimization changes, industrial Internet platform needs to constantly upgrade and improve itself.

   b.   Government subsidies and support

To help SMEs from emerging markets find innovative solutions for COVID-related problems, significant and timely support (e.g., financial and institutional) from the government is essential (Markovic et al., 2021).

The digital transformation of SMEs requires the joint efforts of government and enterprises (Räisänen and Tuovinen, 2020). First, the government plays a role in promoting the digital processing of SMEs. Government interference involves determining how digital transformation is strengthened by the existing legal and regulatory system. For SMEs digital transformation, the government can play a prominent role by raising digital transformation awareness, increasing labor-power competence, providing technical and financial support, and strengthening data communication infrastructure (Mukaila Ayanda and Sidikat Laraba, 2011).

OPPORTUNITIES AND CHALLENGES FOR CHINESE COMPANIES WHILE INTEGRATING DIGITALIZATION STRATEGIES INTO THEIR BUSINESS OPERATIONS

Opportunities

1. Integrating the digital economy with the real economy

Restructuring the value chain using digital means to enable mass customization.

The digital transformation of industries has enabled the in-depth integration of the digital economy and the real economy, and has enabled the rapid development of digital education, digital cultural industry, "Internet + retail" and "Internet + tourism". In terms of digital governance, steady progress has been made in joint prevention and control of digital public security, standardized management of digital government affairs, intelligent upgrading of urban facilities, and promoted competition in the digital market.

2. Digital economy promotes the emergence of new industries and new structures

With the arrival of 5G era, digital technologies such as AI and blockchain can create new industries and new points of consumption. In terms of digital industrialization, information technology has played a positive role and the development of the big data industry and the Internet of Things industry has received lot of attention. In addition, the development of AI is also accelerating. In August 2020, China's Standardization Administration and five other departments released *the Guidelines for the Construction of a National New Generation of Artificial Intelligence Standard System*.

3. Improving digital infrastructure

China has reportedly added 580,000 5G base stations in 2020, bringing the total number of 5G base stations completed to 718,000. In March 2020, the Ministry of Industry and Information Technology of China issued *the Notice on Accelerating the Development of 5G*, with a view to vigorously promote the construction, application and promotion, technology development and security of 5G networks.

According to *the Smart Winter Olympics 2020 and Sustainable Development Report*, 5G construction will be integrated with the construction of venues and parks for the upcoming Beijing 2022 Winter Olympics, for the participants and spectators. China Unicom, the official communication service partner of the 2022 Beijing Winter Olympic Games, will use digital technologies such as cloud computing, big data and the Internet of Things to achieve medical monitoring for athletes and spectator watching experience.

4.   New progress in international digital cooperation

With international digitalization and informatization now entering an innovation- and information-driven era due to cross-border innovation and accelerated development, the digital economy truly has become a new engine of economic growth (Curran, 2018, Gomber et al., 2018, Brynjolfsson and Collis, 2019). In April 2020, the G20 Digital Economy Ministers' Special Meeting reached a consensus on using digital technology to accelerate research on Novel Coronavirus, enhance the flexibility of business activities and create job opportunities. In June, Singapore, New Zealand and Chile signed a digital economy partnership agreement. South Korea and Singapore also announced the launch of a Digital Partnership Agreement (KSDPA); In August, Singapore signed a digital economy agreement with Australia; In November, China, ASEAN, Japan, the Republic of Korea and Australia signed the RCEP, which covers telecommunications services and e-commerce.

Challenges

1.   Lack of core technology support for digital economy

Compared with some core components, core materials and key technologies of developed economies, China lacks certain competitiveness. For example, operating systems, basic software and other products are still highly dependent on the outside world. Under the circumstance that the technological foundation is not stable enough, the development of digital economy may encounter certain difficulties on account of technical support.

At the same time, there is also a shortage of expert manpower, leading to practical difficulties in the upgradation of traditional industries. Problems such as excess capacity, lack of core technologies and lack of innovation capacity are common problems in China's traditional manufacturing industry. Transformation of the traditional industry and upgradation of the management and maintenance, needs skilled manpower and the lack of same is becoming one of the obstacles affecting the competitiveness in the industry and the stability of the industrial chain (Lv and Ma, 2021).

2.   Need for improvement in digitalization in industry and government

In recent years, the general trend China's digital economy has got better, but there is still a gap between China and developed countries. According to *the White Paper on the Development of China's Digital Economy*, the digital economy penetration rate in China's primary, secondary and tertiary industries reached 8.9%, 21.0% and 40.7% respectively in 2020. However, the digital economy penetration rates of agriculture, industry and service industries in developed countries reached 13.3%, 33.0% and 46.7% in 2019, which were all higher than that of China even after one year of rapid development.

Figure 8. China's digital economy growth rate and three industries growth rate comparison (in trillions RMB)
(Source: CAICT)

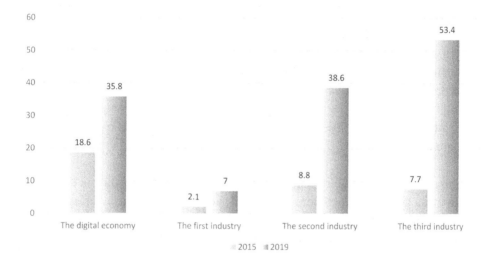

There has also been observed a huge gap between domestic industries and regions. In the primary, secondary and tertiary industries, the tertiary industry is larger than the secondary industry, and the secondary industry is larger than the primary industry. Industrial digitization is exploding in service sector (CAICT, 2021). The digital transformation of service industry is stronger than that of any industry, and the digital transformation of industry is obviously stronger than that in agriculture.

3.   Follow up with respect to relevant laws

With the development of China's digital smart economy, digital tools such as big data and cloud computing are widely in use However, users' privacy and data security cannot be guaranteed if relevant regulations fail to be implemented.

At present, China's laws and regulations on the construction of digital government are mainly administrative regulations, departmental regulations or local laws and regulations. For example, *the Guidance on Accelerating the Work of "Internet + Government Services"* issued by the State Council's Legal Affairs in September 2016, *the Action Program for Promoting the Development of Big Data* released by the State Council in January 2018, and the revision of *the Regulations of the People's Republic of China on Government Information Disclosing* in April 2019. There are still huge gaps in formulation of a basic legislation, and a complete and mature legal framework of digital government has not been completely established.

SOLUTIONS AND RECOMMENDATIONS

In order to realize full potential of China's digital smart economy, it can be strengthened based on following aspects:

1. Enhancing research development and innovation capabilities in key digital areas

China's basic scientific research level and international influence in the digital field are at a good level, but there are serious shortcomings in basic research in the field of mathematics and insufficient investment in basic research. Lack of basic software, basic materials, key parts have made autonomous controllability quite weak (Liu, 2020).

First of all, we should strengthen the research and development of core technologies as well as new digital technologies, increase investment, and make up for the lack of key technologies and weaknesses in core technologies in key industries of the digital economy, such as cloud computing, big data, Internet of Things, AI, and blockchain as soon as possible. Secondly, we need to develop cutting-edge technologies such as quantum computing and quantum communication in a forward-looking way, and strive to seize the commanding heights of future digital industry development. Thirdly, we need to strengthen cross-innovation between the new generation of information technology and advanced technologies in life sciences, materials, energy and other fields, drive technological breakthroughs in multiple fields, in a systematic and collective way, and lay the foundation for the continuous emergence of new industries, new products, new forms of business and new models (Luan, 2021).

Simultaneously working on protecting the IP in associated with these products and processes too needs to handle with utmost caution and care.

2. Acceleration of the industry digitalization and the construction of digital government

During the pandemic, many enterprises assisted the government to break through ways through online mode to support the government with prevention and control activities. At the same time, in order to updated information in a timely manner during the pandemic, as well as take correct facts and credible news to the public at large, digitalization played a great role maintaining and stabilizing social order.

Networking platforms to be used by the government and by private citizens need to be developed with utmost caution as network for the government might involve privacy and security concerns. Technological research in this aspect needs to be started as soon as possible. At present, block chain construction has been put on an important agenda and this can provide an opportunity and revamping a smart platform for the government in a record time.

3. Establishing a legal system and institutional system that is suitable for the development of digital economy at the present stage

After entering the era of steady development of digital economy, the legal supervision system needs to make corresponding adjustments. The COVID-19 outbreak has become a booster for the industry to make a transition to a digital society.

The expeditious ascendency of China's E-commerce market to its global hegemony is nourished by carefully designed public policies. To implement these policies, also to redress information asymmetries and other pertinacious market failures, a tailored regulatory paradigm is being developed by China's policy makers. The new regulatory paradigm manifests a polycentric, participatory, and collaborative governance model that strives to strike a balance between interests of various stakeholders. The dynamic relationship exemplified in China's E-commerce market would provide a valuable lesson for transformation in other sectors of economy, not only in China but also across other jurisdictions that openly embrace commercial innovations in the context of information technological transformation (You, 2020).

In the era of digital economy, data collection, utilization, sharing, flow, transaction, and profit distribution mechanism are particularly important. The Civil Code defines data as the subject matter of contract, thus laying a legal foundation for the transaction and market-oriented utilization of data production factors (Yang, 2020).

4. China's digital economy development strategy needs to seek international recognition

Strengthening international cooperation in science and technology is the only way to address the major challenges facing mankind. In recent years, the development of China's information technology and Internet has been suppressed by some countries and regions. China needs to promote digital industrialization and industrial digitization, as well as integration of digital economy and real economy.

With a large domestic market as an advantage, China can provide a platform for global digital economy cooperation, become a driving force for strengthening international exchange and cooperation in 5G, big data, AI, industrial Internet and other fields, so that digital technology can better serve the sustainable development of the global economy. Its Digital Silk Road (DSR), part of the broader Belt and Road Initiative, aims at promoting and facilitating the digital economy, including cross-border e-commerce and digital payment systems, in developing countries and emerging economies (Majcherczyk and Shuqiang, 2019).

At the same time, China needs to actively integrate itself into the global innovation network and explore models and mechanisms for scientific and technological cooperation under the new circumstances.

FUTURE RESEARCH DIRECTIONS

In the post-epidemic era, China's digital technology innovation, application and development will be more extensive, and the quality will be more optimized. To tap the potential of China's digital economy, we will move forward in the direction of accelerating the innovation of data circulation services, deepening the integration of the digital economy and the real economy, advancing digital infrastructure, maturing new business forms and models, becoming more pragmatic in digital governance, and further improving the level of digital trade.

First, the dividends of the digital economy driven by technological innovation will be further released to promote the economic development of all industries, increase the research on core technology, and consolidate the digital foundation of software, chips, core components and so on. The superposition of data enabling effect and technology multiplier effect will promote the innovation of application scenarios centered on element integration, resource sharing and value co-creation to deepen, accelerate the fission, integration and reconstruction of industrial elements, and create new growth points for the digital economy.

Second, the data element market competition will be increasingly fierce. At present, the market-oriented development of China's data factors still faces many problems and challenges. First of all, the asset status of data has not been established at the legal level, and data has no legal asset identity, which restricts the development of the data factor market. Second, a unified standard and platform needs to be established to promote data sharing. To realize data sharing and establish a unified standard system is the key. Therefore, it is necessary to strengthen the top-level design of data standardization, gradually unify the digital infrastructure, underlying technology, platform tools, industrial application, management and security data standard system, unify the standard resources of different departments and fields, and establish and constantly improve the cross-department and cross-industry data standard system.

Third, the integration of the digital economy and the real economy will continue to expand. The real economy after being assigned a platform, will promote the relationship between the enterprises thus amplifying economic efficiency through constant fission.

Fourth, digital infrastructure will be accelerated in an effort to achieve national and regional balance. "Digital infrastructure" represented by 5G, industrial Internet, big data center and AI has become the core of China's "new infrastructure". In the regional integration strategy guidance, Guizhou, Ningxia western provinces and, the less developed areas also want to seize the development opportunity, advance planning new digital infrastructure, in order to promote economic and social transformation as well as upgradation, to build internationally competitive digital infrastructure cluster.

Fifth, the service supply and digital consumption will adopt the idea named "two ends of power". New business forms and new models will become mature, and AI application will become the leading field. As digital technology such as AI, big data, 5 g, the Internet of things mature, unmanned, online service in the industry (CCID, 2021).

Sixth, digital governance needs to be combined with smart cities to improve the government's digital governance capacity and smart city construction level. Digital reform is an important tool to promote a more scientific and rational allocation of government leadership which will be more efficient in operation and management, thus promoting a more scientific, precise and coordinated level of governance. Solid achievements of smart city construction can provide comprehensive insight into city data and make it fast and real from bottom to top, so as to provide support for government management and decision making. Among the various industry models of the digital economy, e-commerce has developed in ways that enable people to gain fairer and more equal access to information and government services, to overcome the prevailing digital divide between "Internet haves and have-nots," and to provide a backbone architecture to aid in the alleviation of poverty in areas that need help the most. The digital economy will ensure that no place is remote or inaccessible anymore (Li et al., 2020).

Seventh, digital trade will become an important part of international trade and become the accelerator of building domestic and international economy. Digital trade has a broader scope than e-commerce, though the two terms are often viewed by many as synonyms. China is being increasingly recognized as the global leader in digital trade, with its national economy benefiting from an estimated productivity-led gain of up to RMB 37 trillion (USD 5.5 trillion) by 2030 (Yang, 2019). There has also been a broad agreement that digital trade will be the dominant mode for international and domestic exchange in the coming years, as digital economy transaction models spread around the world (Akhtar and Morrison, 2017).

Wang Bingnan, Vice Minister of Commerce of PRC, has remarked that the world is experiencing a broader and deeper scientific and technological revolution and industrial transformation. On one hand, digital trade can enhance the sharing of knowledge and technological elements among various industries through data flow, lead the collaborative integration of various industries, drive the digital transformation of traditional industries and extend to the high-end of the global value chain. On the other hand, digital technology has brought disruptive innovation, spawned a large number of new business forms and models of trade, and greatly enhanced the global value chain (People's Daily Overseas Edition, 2020). Therefore, it is conducive to the formation of a new pattern of development in which the domestic cycle is the main body and the domestic and international double cycles promote each other.

CONCLUSION

According to the above analysis, four characteristics of China's digital smart economy can be highlighted at the present stage:

1. Development of digital industrialization is steady

Digital industrialization, namely information and communication industry, is the forerunner industry of the development of digital economy. It provides technology, products, services and solutions for the development of digital economy, including electronic information manufacturing industry, telecommunications industry, software and information technology service industry, Internet industry and so on. According to the China Academy of Information and Communications Technology, the structure of China's digital industry has changed from electronic information in 2012 to software in 2019. In 2019, the proportion of digitalization in China's software industry rose to about 55%, while the proportion of telecommunications industry in digitalization industry dropped to about 28% (CAICT, 2021).

2.   The process of industrial digitalization is accelerated

"In 2020, China's digital industrialization accounted for 19.1% of the digital economy, and industrial digitalization accounted for 80.9% of the digital economy, providing a strong driving force for the sustainable and healthy development of the digital economy."(CAICT, 2021) In the China's digital economy development white paper, Wang Zhiqin, vice president of the China Academy of Communications and Information Technology, remarked that the digitization of industries is the main direction for the development of digital economy in various regions. In the context of the COVID-19 outbreak in 2020, more domestic enterprises in China have carried out strategic digital transformation, accelerating the process of industrial digitalization.

3.   The government's digital governance capacity has improved

Digital governance is an important driving force and strategic support for the modernization of China's national governance system and governance capacity, and an important part of Digital China. The number of government websites nationwide has increased from 84,000 in 2015 to 14,500 by the beginning of December 2019, increasing the efficiency of online government work. At the same time, local governments have promoted the cross-platform sharing and integration of government data, which has improved the working capacity of Internet government services.

Figure 9. China e-government development index from 2003 to 2020
(*Source: Report of the UN E-Government Survey 2020*)

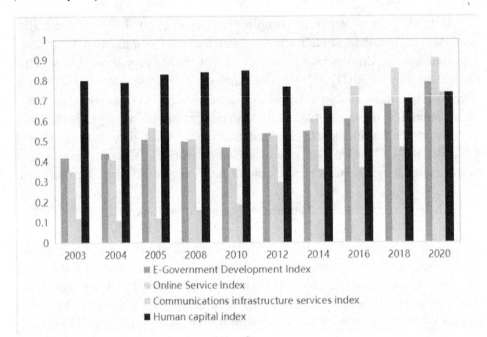

4.   Deep integration of the whole value chain

As can be seen from the examples of Chinese cases in part IV, the digital transformation of Chinese enterprises is not only a simple demonstration of technology, but also a deep integration of technology and all aspects of enterprise operation. Such digital development promotes gives the enterprises a new vitality.

ACKNOWLEDGMENT

The authors extend sincere gratitude to:
    • Our colleagues from Soochow University, the Australian Studies Centre of Shanghai University and Krirk University as well as the independent research colleagues who provided insight and expertise that greatly assisted the research, although they may not agree with all of the interpretations/conclusions of this chapter.
    • China Knowledge for supporting our research.
    • The Editor and the International Editorial Advisory Board (IEAB) of this book who initially desk reviewed, arranged a rigorous double/triple blind review process

and conducted a thorough, minute and critical final review before accepting the chapter for publication.

• All anonymous reviewers who provided very constructive feedbacks for thorough revision, improvement, extension and fine tuning of the chapter.

REFERENCES

Akhtar, S. I., & Morrison, W. M. (2017). *Digital trade and U.S. trade policy.* Report R44565, Congressional Research Service, U.S. Government.

Aremu, A. M., & Adeyemi, L. S. (2011). Small and medium scale enterprises as a survival strategy for employment generation in Nigeria. *CiteSeerX, 4*(1), 200–206. doi:10.5539/jsd.v4n1p200

Brynjolfsson, E., & Collis, A. (2019). How should we measure the digital economy? *Harvard Business Review Home, 97*(6), 140–146.

Chen, H., Qian, W., & Wen, Q. (2020). *The impact of the COVID-19 pandemic on consumption: Learning from high frequency transaction data. SSRN* preprint no. 3568574.

Chen, M., Xu, S., Husain, L., & Galea, G. (2021). Digital health interventions for COVID-19 in China: a retrospective analysis. *Intelligent Medicine, 1*(1), 29-36. doi:10.1016/j.imed.2021.03.001

Chen, X. (2018). The development of China's digital economy shows obvious provincial differences. *International Finance, 2018*(4), 80.

Chen, Y. (2020). Improving market performance in the digital economy. *China Economic Review, 62.*

China's digital economy development white paper. (2021). *China Academy of Information and Communications Technology.* Retrieved from http://cnnic.cn/gywm/xwzx/rdxw/20172017_7084/202102/t20210203 _71364.htm

Curran, D. (2018). Risk, innovation, and democracy in the digital economy. *European Journal of Social Theory, 21*(2), 207–226. doi:10.1177/1368431017710907

Elder-Vass, D. (2016). *Profit and Gift in the Digital Economy.* Cambridge Univ. doi:10.1017/CBO9781316536421

Fernandes, N. (2020). *Economic effects of coronavirus outbreak (COVID-19) on the world economy. SSRN* Preprint no. 3557504.

Ghazvini, M. A. F., Faria, P., Ramos, S., Morais, H., & Vale, Z. (2015). Incentive-based demand response programs designed by asset-light retail electricity providers for the day-ahead market. *Science Direct, 2015*(82), 786–799.

Gomber, P., Kauffman, R. J., Parker, C., & Weber, B. W. (2018). On the fintech revolution: Interpreting the forces of innovation, disruption and transformation in financial services. *Journal of Management Information Systems, 35*(1), 220–265. doi:10.1080/07421222.2018.1440766

Gopal, R. D., Ramesh, R., & Whinston, A. B. (2003). Microproducts in a digital economy: Trading small, gaining large. *International Journal of Electronic Commerce, 8*(2), 9–30. doi:10.1080/10864415.2003.11044292

Herrero, A. G., & Xu, J. (2018). *How Big IS China's Digital Economy?* www.jstor.org/stable/resrep28511

Hindman, M. (2018). *The Internet Trap: How the Digital Economy Builds Monopolies and Undermines Democracy.* Princeton University Press.

Hu, Y. (2020). The Nature and Function of State-Owned Enterprises from the COVID-19 Prevention and Control. China State-Owned Enterprise Management.

Jiang, X., & Jin, J. (2021). Review and prospect of China's digital economy. *Journal of the Party School of the CPC Central Committee (National School of Governance),* 1-15. . doi:10.14119/j.cnki.zgxb.20211204.001

Jin, X., Zhang, M., Sun, G., & Cui, L. (2021). The impact of COVID-19 on firm innovation: Evidence from Chinese listed companies. *Finance Research Letters.*

Lamberton, C., & Stephen, A. T. (2016). A thematic exploration of digital, social media, and mobile marketing: Research evolution from 2000 to 2015 and an agenda for future inquiry. *Journal of Marketing, 80*(6), 146–172. doi:10.1509/jm.15.0415

Li, K., Kim, J. D., Lang, R. K., Kauffman, J. R., & Naldi, M. (2020). How should we understand the digital economy in Asia? Critical assessment and research agenda. *Electronic Commerce Research and Applications, 44.* doi:10.1016/j.elerap.2020.101004

Liu, C., Yin, X., & Wang, L. (2020). Regional differences and distribution of China's digital economy development dynamic evolution. *China Science and Technology Forum, 2020*(3), 97-109.

Liu, X. (2020). Various efforts were made to consolidate the foundation for the development of the digital economy. *Economic Daily.*

Luan, Q. (2021). *The Trinity: Create new competitive advantages in the digital economy.* China Public Research Network. Retrieved from http://www.zgzcinfo.cn/expertsbbs/show-32267.html

Luo, X., Zhang, W., Li, H., Bose, R., & Chung, Q. B. (2018). Cloud computing capability: Its technological root and business impact. *Journal of Organizational Computing and Electronic Commerce, 28*(3), 193–213. doi:10.1080/10919392.2018.1480926

Lv, M., & Ma, L. (2021). Promoting the upgrading of traditional industries by digitization. *Economic Daily.*

Majcherczyk, M., & Shuqiang, B. (2019). Digital Silk Road - The Role of Cross-Border E-commerce in Facilitating Trade. *Journal of WTO and China, 9*(2), 106–128. https://heinonline.org/HOL/Page?handle=hein.journals/jwtoch9&id=234&div=&collection=

Markovic, S., Koporcic, N., Arslanagic-Kalajdzic, M., Kadic-Maglajlic, S., Bagherzadeh, M., & Islam, N. (2021). Business-to-business open innovation: COVID-19 lessons for small and medium-sized enterprises from emerging markets. *Technological Forecasting and Social Change, 170.*

Maurya, S., Lakhera, S., Srivastava, K. A., & Kumar, M. (2021). Cost analysis of amazon web services–From an eye of architect and developer. *Materials Today: Proceedings, 46*(20), 10757-10760.

Nambisan, S., Lyytinen, K., Majchrzak, A., & Song, M. (2017). Digital innovation management: Reinventing innovation management research in a digital world. *Management Information Systems Quarterly, 41*(1), 223–238. doi:10.25300/MISQ/2017/41:1.03

National Development and Reform Commission. (2021). *China E-commerce Report 2020 was released in Ningbo.* National Development and Reform Commission. Retrieved from https://www.ndrc.gov.cn/fggz/qykf/xxjc/202107/t20210701_1285221.html

OECD. (2017a). *The Next Production Revolution: Implications for Governments and Business.* doi:10.1787/9789264271036-en

OECD. (2020). *Coronavirus (COVID-19). SME policy responses.* Retrieved from https://read.oecd-ilibrary.org/view/?ref=119_119680-di6h3qgi4x&title=Covid-19_SME_Policy_Responses

Pan, W., Xie, T., Wang, Z., & Ma, M. (2021). Digital economy: An innovation driver for total factor productivity. *Journal of Business Research, 139*, 303-311. doi:10.1016/j.jbusres.2021.09.061

Papadopoulos, T., Baltas, N. K., & Balta, E. M. (2020). The use of digital technologies by small and medium enterprises during COVID-19: Implications for theory and practice. *International Journal of Information Management, 55*. doi:10.1016/j.ijinfomgt.2020.102192

Paradise, J. F. (2019). China's Quest for Global Economic Governance Reform Journal of Chinese Political Science. *Springer Link, 24*(3), 471–493.

People's Daily Overseas Edition. (2020). *Digital trade will be the accelerator of a "double cycle"*. Available at: http://www.gov.cn/xinwen/2020-09/08/content_5541389.htm

Räisänen, J., & Tuovinen, T. (2018). Digital innovations in rural micro-enterprises. *Science Direct, 73*, 56–67. doi:10.1016/j.jrurstud.2019.09.010

Research Group of Digital Economy Situation Analysis of CCID Think Tank. (2021). Digital economy: The enabling effect on the real economy will be further released. *Network Security and Informatization, 4*(3), 4-6.

Spence, M. (2021). Government and economics in the digital economy. *Journal of Government and Economics, 3*. doi:10.1016/j.jge.2021.100020

Sun, Y., Zeng, X., Cui, X., Zhang, G., & Bie, R. (2019). An active and dynamic credit reporting system for SMEs in China. *Personal and Ubiquitous Computing*. Advance online publication. doi:10.100700779-019-01275-4

Tapscott, D. (2014). *The Digital Economy Anniversary Edition: Rethinking Promise and Peril in the Age of Networked Intelligence* (2nd ed.). Amazon.

Verhoef, C. P., Broekhuizen, T., Bart, Y., Bhattacharya, A., Dong, Q. J., Fabian, N., & Haenlein, M. (2021). Digital transformation: A multidisciplinary reflection and research agenda. *Journal of Business Research, 122*, 889–901. doi:10.1016/j.jbusres.2019.09.022

Verhoef, P. C., Kannan, P. K., & Inman, J. (2015). From multi-channel retailing to omni-channel retailing: Introduction to the special issue on multi-channel retailing. *Journal of Retailing, 91*(2), 174–181. doi:10.1016/j.jretai.2015.02.005

Yang, D. (2020). Civil Code Opens a New Era of Building Digital Economy Legal System. *Procuratorial Daily*.

Yang, Y. (2019, Mar. 4). Report: China becoming digital trade leader. *China Daily*.

Yin, Z., Gong, X., Guo, P., & Wu, T. (2019). What Drives Entrepreneurship in Digital Economy? Evidence from China. *Economic Modelling, 82*, 66-73.

You, C. (2020). Law and policy of platform economy in China. *Computer Law & Security Review, 39*. doi:10.1016/j.clsr.2020.105493

Yuan, G. X., & Wang, H. (2019). The general dynamic risk assessment for the enterprise by the hologram approach in financial technology. *International Journal of Financial Engineering, 06*(01), 1950001. doi:10.1142/S2424786319500014

KEY TERMS AND DEFINITIONS

Digital Economy: There is currently no authoritative definition of the "digital economy". Based on existing research, the digital economy refers to an economic system that widely uses Information and Communications Technology (ICT), including infrastructure (high-speed internet access, computing power and security services), e-commerce (the business model making significant use of ICT at the front end and back end) and application of B2B, B2C and C2C transaction modes of ICT.

Digital Innovation: Digital innovation refers to the innovative combination of various physical transactions and digital components to realize new products or technologies.

Digital Platforms: Digital platforms are a way to develop information technology infrastructure, including social media, mobile computing, and e-commerce platforms. They help companies break down barriers to creating smoother processes through digital technology. Digital platforms have a wide range of applications, including payments, accommodation, and healthcare, many of which have related applications.

Digital Technology: Digital technology refers to the use of advanced information and communication technology to collect, store, analyze and share physical information and market information in each link of the product value chain, providing important technical support for innovation in various fields.

Digital Transformation: Digital transformation is the development of digital technologies and supporting capabilities to create a dynamic digital business model. Digital transformation can be described as an organizational shift to big data, analytics, the cloud, mobile communication technologies, and social media platforms to provide goods and services.

Intellectual Property: Intellectual property rights refer to the exclusive rights that people enjoy according to law with respect to their intellectual achievements, usually the exclusive right granted by the state to creators for a certain period of time. Intellectual property is essentially an intangible property right. Its object is intellectual achievements or intellectual products.

State-Owned Enterprises (SOEs): The main function of a Chinese state-owned enterprise is to maximize social welfare, and profit is not its focus. State owned enterprises are an important part of China's economy. Although state-owned enterprises are generally considered inefficient, China's economy, which depends significantly upon state-owned enterprises, has made great achievements in the past four decades.

Chapter 7
Assessment of Service Quality of Payment Wallet Services in India Using the Servqual Model

Pranav Saraswat
Nirma University, Ahmedabad, India

Vineet Chouhan
Rajasthan Vidyut Utpadan Nigam Ltd., India

ABSTRACT

In India, 40 companies are currently providing the electronic wallet service for approximately 500 million mobile internet users, and this number is constantly growing. For the payment wallets, the key strategy for the success and survival of any business depends on the service quality it provides to its customers. Thus, with such a huge number of consumers using these services, it is essential to study how effective and consumer friendly these new age payment instruments are. The payment wallets being a new concept in the financial market may not be easily accepted by the consumers. Consumers above the age of 40 may not feel comfortable in using the electronic modes of payments, especially where the payment wallet market is majorly dominated by private players. The data collected from 1000 respondents has been interpreted with the help of the SERVQUAL model for the payment wallets. The Paired t test for all payment wallets revealed an expected and perception gap, and the level of satisfaction is measured with ANOVA analysis revealing that PayTm has better perception.

DOI: 10.4018/978-1-6684-4176-3.ch007

INTRODUCTION

The liberalization of markets has led to intense competition across all sectors prevalent in the market (Poultonet.al.,2004). The financial sector of a country is one of the critical sectors responsible for the growth of its economy (Lentneret.al., 2015). Further, with the constant technological developments in every sphere of the modern world, and India's strong inclination towards adopting digitization across all sectors, it is it is only a matter of time that financial services would become completely electronic or web based (Gomberet.al., 2018). One of the significant developments in this regime is the emergence of electronic wallets providing pre-paid payment options to consumers (Wilson, 2012). The Government of India has immensely influenced the growth of such wallets with its programs like 'Cashless India' (Cashless India, n.d.). It can be thus expected that the reliability quotient of the service would be substantially low among users (Qi et.al., 2018). The quality of services provided to and the expectation of service quality by users of such payment wallets (Talwaret.al., 2020). As per the information provided by the Ministry of Electronics and Information Technology, Government of India, there are presently 40 (forty) companies existing in India proving the electronic wallet service. India has approximately 500 million mobile internet users, and this number is constantly growing. In February 207, PayTm, one of the leaders in the electronic wallet market, declared that it had reached a customer base of 200 Million. The key strategy for the success and survival of any business depends on the service quality it provides to its customers (Parasuramanet.al., 1985). Thus, with such huge number of consumers using these services it is essential to study how effective and consumers friendly are these new age payment instruments (Kautish et al. 2022).

PAYMENT WALLETS

Evolution of Payment Wallets

Payment banks are a new model of banks which have been established by the Reserve Bank of India (RBI) (Pramani&Iyer, 2022). On January 7, 2014, the Committee on Comprehensive Financial Services for Small Businesses and Low-Income Households, chaired by Mr. Nachiket More, recommended, among other things, that a new type of banks called payment banks be formed (RBI, 2014). On November 27, 2014, RBI released the Guidelines for Licensing of Payment Banks. As per these guidelines, payment banks can accept a deposit of up to Rupees One Lakh per customer. These entities are not allowed to issue loans or credit cards (Reddy, 2018). Further, payment banks require a minimum capital of Rupees One Hundred

Crore, and most importantly they have to compulsorily invest 75% of their assets in government securities (Veluvali, 2019).

On July 01, 2015, (updated on July 01, 206) RBI published the Circular Master on Policy Guidelines for Issuing and Operating Prepaid Payment Instruments in India. This was a milestone for the entire online wallet service providers like Airtel Money and PayTm who were earlier conducting their businesses as payment banks in India (Moorthy et al. 2022)

Requirement of Payment Wallets

After the "Payment and Settlement Systems Act, 2007" came into force, banks and non-banking entities had started to conduct the business of providing pre-paid payment instrument, mostly in a web based platform (Esoimeme, 2018). RBI had been providing approvals to these entities under the guidelines of the Master Circular on Issuance and Operation of PPIs issued on April 2009 (Roy, 2021). Thus, taking into account the rapid digitization within India and development made in their respective field by PPI issuers, it became important to have a consolidated document prescribing the guidelines.

Mechanism of Payment Wallets

The Payment Wallet Mechanism (Sharma et al. 2022) begins with a 'Holder' who acquires pre-paid payment instruments for the purchase of goods or services. The Holder can be an individual or an organization. The pre-paid payment instruments are issued to the Holder by the Issuer (Shamraev, 2019). The Issuers collect the money from the Holder and make payment to the merchants through a settlement mechanism (Vijai, 2019). Pre-paid payment Instruments (Madhu et al. 2022) have certain value stored in them and can be issued in various forms including internet accounts, internet wallets, mobile accounts, mobile wallets or magnetic stripe cards, smart cards etc (Almuhammadi, 2020, Ali &Gopalan, 2018). These instruments can then be used to access the pre-paid amount purchased by the Holder.

TYPES OF PRE-PAID PAYMENT INSTRUMENTS

There are primarily three types of prepaid instruments in India:

1. **Closed System Payment Instruments**: In order to facilitate the purchase of goods and services from him, these instruments are issued by individuals and

cannot be withdrawn or redeemed for cash. Third-party services cannot be paid for or settled using these instruments.

2. **Semi-Closed System Payment Instruments**: This kind of payment instrument is used to buy products and services, as well as financial services, from a group of merchants that have agreed to accept the payment instruments under a particular contract. There is no way for the owner of these instruments to get any cash.

3. **Open System Payment Instruments**: This Equipment may be used to buy products and services, as well as financial services such as money transfer, at any merchant location that accepts cards, and they can also be used to withdraw cash from ATMs.

All three kinds of instruments may be issued by banks that meet the RBI's eligibility conditions. Only closed and semi-closed system payment instruments can be issued by non-banking financial institutions (NBFIs).

Transaction Limits

The maximum value of any pre-paid payment instruments shall not exceed Rs 50,000/-. (Rupees fifty thousand). On conducting proper Customer Due Diligence and abiding to KYC norms, the following types of semi-closed pre-paid payment instruments can be issued:

1. If the customer's outstanding balance does not exceed Rs.10,000/- and the total value of reloads within a given month does not exceed Rs.10,000/-, he or she may use the service for up to Rs.10,000/-. These can only be distributed electronically;

2. Any "officially legitimate document" as specified in Rule 2(d) of the PML Rules 2005, as modified from time to time, may be accepted for up to Rs.50,000/-. PPIs of this kind can only be issued electronically and should not be reloadable;

3. With complete KYC and the ability to be reloaded, you may get up to Rs.1,00,000/-. At no time shall the PPI balance surpass Rs.1,00,000/-.

BHARAT INTERFACE FOR MONEY (BHIM) AND UNIFIED PAYMENT INTERFACE (UPI)

The Government of India launched the BHIM Mobile App on December 30, 2016. It is based on the UPI developed by the National Payments Corporation of India (NPCI). Consumers with UPI enabled bank accounts will be able to use the BHIM app to carry out electronic transactions. The BHIM app has been developed by the NPCI enables users to send and receive money from both UPI supported as well as non-supported banks (using IFSC Code), check account balance, and create custom payment addresses for receiving payments. There is presently a transaction limit of maximum Rs. 10,000 (ten thousand) per transaction and Rs. 20,000 (twenty thousand) within 24 hours. The app is a clear indication that the Government of India is aggressively trying to promote and make users adopt cashless payment methods (Kumar, Kishore & Prakash, 2020, Anjali & Suresh, 2019).

TYPES OF WALLET

PayTm: PayTm was launched in 2010, by Mr. Vijay Shekhar. PayTm is the first company to be funded by Alibaba. As per DQ India PayTm has a user base of more than 200 million (DQIndia, 2017). It has operational relations or tie ups with various companies. PayTm can also be used to make e-commerce transactions, make payments of bills, transfer money, various services from the tie ups such as movie tickets, cab rides wallet link etc. can also be availed from the mobile wallet. The loading of money in the app and paying from the wallet has been kept simple for the consumers to understand.

As per the DMR report (DMR, 2022) PayTm has developed in the following manner

1. It has total 200 million users
2. There are 80 million active users
3. There was total transaction of INR 1 billion in 2016
4. Also there were 2 billion sessions conducted in 2016
5. Average 5 million daily transactions
6. It was recorded in March, 2017 there are 2.1 million PayTm merchants (Mishra, 2016)

Post demonetization there was a 300 percentage raise in use PayTm.13 PayTm has also launched PayTm Payment Banks, under which now the consumer gets an option to save his money in form of savings account in the app, entitling him to earn interest on the same (Rajawat et al. 2022)

PayTm Mall: PayTm after its success with the Mobile Wallet App as now also entered into the e-commerce market and has created a PayTm Mall, where 1.4 million sellers (Yadav, 2017) are on board to sell products in electronics, fashion, home furnishing, durables etc. Currently it is only available to Android users. The mall would be a unique combination of high end FMCG product and also will have a Bazaar touch by selling products of small vendors (Niu, et.al., 2021).

Oxigen Wallet: Oxigen Services (India) Pvt Ltd, one of India's major payment solution providers, has introduced this wallet. Therefore the consumer can be assured their money is in a safe place. Further the wallet secures its transaction by using a six digit One Time Password received on the registered number. Oxigen has approvals from RBI and is integrated with NPCI so that there is immediate money transferring to any banks from the wallet and by using the Immediate Payment Service money can be transferred from bank to wallet.

MobiKwik: MobiKwik is a major independent mobile payment network that has more than thiry million users and over one lakh retail tie ups. The wallet is accessible from both desktop mobile site or through app on the phone. More than 30 million customers have access to this mobile wallet, which links them to over 100,000 shops. MobiKwik has Prepaid Payment Instrument license from RBI (Startup Talky, n.d.)

Vodafone M-Pesa: Vodafone M-Pesa has been authorized by The Reserve Bank of India and is also associated with ICICI bank, thus making the mobile transaction secure. Further it is also convenient for the consumers and leads to fast transactions.

Freecharge: With 20 million registered customers, FreeCharge is one of the most popular mobile wallets. It was established in 2010. Freecharge facilitates payments for DTH, prepaid, postpaid, utility bills, and metro recharges for a variety of service providers. It also has retail partnerships with Cinepolis, Hypercity, McDonald's, and Shoppers Drug Mart. Stop making it easy for customers to pay at such stores. (Khan, 2015)

State Bank Buddy: The State Bank of India has released this mobile wallet. The wallet helps in transferring money to other bank accounts easily. Also one can book tickets, book hotel or entertainment tickets with the help of Sate Bank Buddy. The key feature of State Bank Buddy is that it provides its services to non-SBI consumers that too in thirteen different languages. Also the app helps set reminders for dues and money transfers. (State Bank Buddy, n.d.)

Citi Master Pass: Master Card and Citi Bank India have introduced a digital wallet. It is India's first worldwide wallet, and it offers services to make online buying more convenient and safe. All of your shipping, credit, debit, prepaid, loyalty card, and payment information is securely stored in one place via the app. Citi Master Pass helps the consumer to checkout while shopping and other services faster and are easy to follow.

Jio Money: JioMoney is a digital wallet app that was introduced by Reliance in 2016. It was launched after demonetization thus in mere time it has gained popularity. Payment for any Reliance Jio connection shall be made by Jio Money as it is the cheapest form for doing the same. It provides with services such as online payments, pay utility bills. It has collaborated with The State Bank of India and provides its customers with an option to open a Digital Bank Account.

MARKET BASED ASPECTS OF MOBILE WALLET

With the understanding, awareness and huge availability of mobile devices due to fall in prices of internet data charges lead to popularity of mobile wallets amongst consumers and it being cost efficient with no large investment in installing them the vendors too adopted the means of mobile wallets.

India is a country, which largely depends upon cash transactions. However now the economy is changing and there has been a significant raise in mobile based transactions along with usage of cards. The Government of India and the regulators have in recent years through various means promoted India to go cash-less and become a cashless society; however the impact of the same hasn't been satisfactory. India continues to use cash in transaction of small, medium and large magnitude. Thus, making India one of the top developing economies using physical form of currency. (Raj, 2016)

The idea that it is too costly for small businesses, as well as the high cost of card payment technology and the absence of underwriting data for credit card issue and merchant onboarding. As a result, few shops are willing to accept online payment methods. Mobile phones provide a low-cost technique of gaining banking access and making payments. It may either use business correspondents (BCs) or directly approach end users to offer financial services to the final mile. Improvements in telecommunications infrastructure, internet connectivity, and low-cost smartphones will reduce the requirement for fixed-line-based devices. (ePaisa Content Team, 2016)

Protecting customers against fraud is crucial to ensuring the continuing acceptance of digital payments, particularly in a growing economy like India. Fraudsters have gotten more sophisticated, thus future payment systems must be capable of dealing with such threats. While chip-and-PIN-based payments provide an extra degree of protection above less secure mag-stripe cards, mobile-based payments may also provide a comparable level of security. Mobile phones may safeguard customer information using tokens, device ID, and biometric authentication in addition to the secure element built in phones, which is equivalent to the chip on cards.

Challenges

1. Many times while making mobile payments the transaction fails or the session expires because the Internet and data plans show poor connectivity in many areas in India.

2. When it comes to finances, Indian consumers have a habit of using cash and to change such mode of transaction poses as a challenge.

3. Service providers of such online portals shall simplify their technology, as the consumer base in India is still not comfortable with using technology.

4. While travelling most Indians prefer travelling with cash as it ensures them more safety.

5. Additional tracking and logging are required on mobile transfers because of regulatory demand.

6. Due to rigorous regulatory framework and future compliances with KYC norms to prevent terrorist activities and money laundering the cost of installing such mode of payments shall become more expensive for the merchant or vendor (EY, n.d.).

The number of mobile wallet users has been steadily growing, and has reached about 150 Million, because of offers such as cashbacks and discounts. PayTm, the biggest mobile wallet in the market, has over 100 million wallet users and it registers approximately 75 million transactions every month. According to RBI data, in 2014-15, more than 255 Million transactions were registered, with a combined value of transactions of approximately Rs.8,184 crore. This is a 137 per cent increase from 107.61 Million transactions during 2013-14.

Customer Expectation

1. Help customers with not just completing a transaction but also help completing daily activities such as payment of bills, transfer money from one account to another etc.

2. Should not be limited only to online transaction but should be available everywhere including any retail store.

3. Shall have multiple layers of securities and not just username and password protection.

4. Provides with certain reward points or cashbacks.

5. The user expects a simple experience while transacting money; therefore the wallet shall be kept simple.

SERVQUAL MODEL

Evolution

Parasuraman et al. (1985) had identified 97 attributes that were found to make an impact on the service quality. The said 97 attributes were the parameters important for assessment of customers' expectations and perceptions on the delivered service. Further, these attributes were reorganised and categorised into 10 dimensions, namely: tangibles, reliability, credibility, security, competence, responsiveness, communication, knowing, customers, courtesy, understanding, and access. Later on the dimensions were reduced to 5, namely, reliability, responsiveness, tangibility, assurance and empathy. These 5 dimensions are subject to 22 statements. However, any new dimension or statement may be added as per the requirement of the service whose quality is intended to be assessed (Kulašin & Santos, 2005)
The five dimensions are categorised as follows:

1. Reliability: The capacity to deliver on a promise with accuracy and consistency.
2. Tangibility: Personnel appearance, equipment, and physical facilities.
3. Responsiveness: refers to the ability to provide quick service and a readiness to assist consumers.
4. Empathy: Customers are cared for and given personalised attention.
5. Assurance: Employees' politeness and expertise, as well as their capacity to instil confidence and trust in clients.

Functioning

Servqual Model measures service quality as the difference between customers' expectations for services offered and customers' perceptions of service received. The customers are required to answer the questions based on 22 statements developed by Parasuraman based on both, their expectations and perceptions.

A questionnaire is prepared based on the 22 statements with necessary changers, if required based on the nature of service. Data is collected of customers' expectations and perceptions on each statement.

Average score of each dimension is calculated using simple average or weighted average method for both, expectations and perceptions. The difference/gap between the average of expectations and perceptions for each dimension is calculated. Overall gap between expectations and perceptions is also calculated (Daniel & Berinyuy, 2010).

Criticism

Servqual model is widely used for assessment of service quality of services in different categories. However, the model is subjected to various theoretical and operational criticisms that are as follows:

Theoretical Criticisms

Paradigmatic Objections: SERVQUAL'S model is based on a disconfirming paradigm instead of an attitudinal paradigm, which means it doesn't follow established statistical, economic, or psychological theory.

People Who Work in the Same Way: Servqual is a model that focuses on the process of service delivery rather than the outcome of the service

Gap Model: There is no surety that the customers assess the service quality in terms of expectations and perceptions. Customers intend to lack clarity between their expectations and perceptions.

Dimensionality: The five dimensions of servqual model are not universal in nature. Some of the items are too contextual in nature and may not be required to assess a particular type of service. For example, for assessment of service quality of payment wallet, the dress-up of personnel is of no importance. Additionally, there is high correlation between the 5 dimensions leading to confusion in minds of the customers while they answer the questionnaire since some of the statements appear to be similar (Buttle, 1996).

Operational Criticisms

Item Composition: 4 or 5 statements/items may be less for evaluating a particular dimension. Also, some dimensions may require lesser statement for evaluation. For example, dimension of tangibility in case of service by payment wallet does not require 4-5 statements.

Expectations: The term expectation has different meanings and customers have varied standards rather than expectations for evaluating service quality. The model fails in measurement of absolute service quality expectations.

Moments of Truth: Customers' assessment of service quality depends on different moments of truth. The evaluation of expectations and perceptions largely depend on recent experiences. One bad experience will have a strong impact on their evaluation of expectations as well as perceptions.

Two Administrations: Assessment of 22 instruments/statements for both expectations and perceptions makes the entire process lengthy and often leads to boredom for customers. Lengthy questionnaire often leads to unwillingness of customers to fill the questionnaire. It often causes confusion in the minds of the customers since some of the statements appear to be similar and they are unable to assess differently, their expectations and perceptions (Ladhari, 2009).

LITERATURE REVIEW

The SERVQUAL model to figure out how good the service was and how satisfied the customers were. The most important concepts that a company shall take into consideration are service quality and customer satisfaction. Both these concepts are subjective and a company must know how to measure the quality of their services. The SERVQUAL model was developed by Parsuraman, to assess the quality of services provided by the companies to its customer base. The model basically interprets the discrepancy between customer expectations and the services actually provided to them. It is based on five criteria's, which include Tangibility, Reliability, Responsiveness, Assurance and Empathy thereby helping the company to assess its services on fixed criteria.

Digital Payment- Step by Step Instruction for various modes of Payment 2 E-wallets are electronic pre-paid system, which allows its user to do online transactions such as buying things online. The customer has to create an account and link this wallet account with individuals account in order to load money in the same. Mostly all banks have their own wallets and many private companies are now involved in the business. Post de-monetisation and the Government of India's agenda of making India cashless has also helped in promoting e-wallets. PayTm is the leading payment wallet in India with over 200 million users. Also, most of the e-wallets have tie-ups with retailers providing a platform for merchants to showcase their products. The payment banks have also put sincere efforts in providing utmost security for their customers.

METHODOLOGY

This empirical research was conducted on a sample of 1000 randomly selected payment wallet users ranging between the ages of 16 to 60 years with the average age of 32.92 years of the subjects residing in Ahmedabad, India. A questionnaire was designed comprising of questions relating to use of payment wallets, awareness of UPI, 22 statements/instruments for assessment of service quality of payment wallet based on reliability, responsiveness, tangibility, empathy and assurance based on customers' expectations and perceptions.

Tool Used for Analysis

The SERVQUAL Model has been developed in the pretext of assessment of service quality of services such as banking, insurance, hospitality, hotels and retail stores. All of these services have a physical platform for interaction between customers and service providers; thereby the five criteria (Reliability, Tangibility, Responsiveness, Empathy, and Assurance) are developed accordingly. Since, payment wallet is an online platform for interaction between customers and service providers, the instruments falling under each criterion have been modified to assess service quality of payment wallets in the best manner possible. For example, empathy requires lesser instruments for assessment for payment wallets as there is minimum direct interaction between the customers and the employees of the company.

The payment wallets that are used by the subjects are shown in Table 1 as follows:

Table 1. Respondents of Various Payment Wallets

SR. NO.	PAYMENT WALLET	NO. OF USERS
1.	PayTm	600
2.	Airtel	100
3.	MobiKwik	80
4.	Jio Wallet	80
5.	Vodafone	60
6.	PhonePe	60
7.	Freecharge	20

Note: Some of the subjects use more than one payment wallets.

The following table provides average score of customers' expectations and perceptions on service quality of payment wallets based on criteria of tangibility, reliability, responsiveness, assurance and empathy. The detailed table showing average score for each of the 22 statements/instruments under the criteria is shown in table-1.

Testing of H₁

H₁(alternative)**:** The levels of satisfaction of Customers with the quality of services rendered weresignificant from select Banks.

The result of the hypothesis test is presented in Table 2 and Table 3 as under:

Table 2. Average score of customers' expectations and perceptions

S. NO.	Criteria	Average score of Customers' Expectations	Average score of Customers' Perceptions
1.	Tangibility	5.3075	5.4375
2.	Reliability	5.192	5.142
3.	Responsiveness	5.136667	5.228333
4.	Assurance	5.166	5.292
5.	Empathy	5.15	5.161122
	Total	**5.190433**	**5.252191**

Table 3. Paired t test for all payment wallets

Attributes	Expectation		Perception		Gap (E-P)		T	DF	Sig.
	Mean	SD	Mean	SD	Mean	SD			
Tangibility	5.307	0.924	5.437	1.242	-0.13	1.083	5.399	999	0.000
Reliability	5.192	0.898	5.142	1.028	0.05	0.963	5.889	999	0.000
Responsiveness	5.136	0.841	5.228	0.894	-0.091	0.868	4.426	999	0.000
Assurance	5.166	0.879	5.292	1.038	-0.126	0.959	5.119	999	0.000
Empathy	5.15	0.826	5.161	1.118	-0.011	0.972	4.503	999	0.000

Using a seven-point Likert Scale, a questionnaire was made to see if this was true. It asked people to answer questions about how SERVQUAL dimensions fit into their expectations and perceptions of certain hypermarkets. The hypothesis looks at how big of a difference there is between the general expectations of the payment wallet's customers and the perceptions they have when they see some of the payment wallet's features.which included Paytm, Airtel, Mobi-Kwik, Jio Wallet, Vodafone, PhonePe and Free charge. The outputs produced are shown in table-3, 4, and 5. Because the disparity is considerable, the first table, marked paired sample test for Tangibility, indicates an iota of satisfaction for the qualities ($t_{tangibility}$ = 5.399, p = 0.000>0.05 ; $t_{Reliability}$ = 5.889, p = 0.000>0.05 ; $r_{esponsiveness}$ = 4.426, p = 0.000>.05 ; $t_{assurance}$ = 5.199, p = 0.000>0.05 and $t_{Empathy}$ = 4.503, p = 0.000>0.05). However, for the attribute Reliability the Gap is positive explaining SERVQUAL, the customers' demonstrated their dissatisfaction as the expectation and perception gap is positively significant.

Testing of Hypothesis H$_2$

H$_{2(alternative)}$: The levels of satisfaction remains significantly improvedamong the chosen Payment wallets for study

The result of the hypothesis test is presented in Table 4and Table 5as under:

Table 4. Descriptive statistics- level of satisfaction

Hypermarkets	N	Mean	Std. Deviation	Std. Error	95% Confidence Interval for Mean	
					Low Bound	Up Bound
PayTm	600	5.486	1.097	.09814	4.938	6.035
Airtel	100	4.321	1.080	.07030	3.781	4.861
MobiKwik	80	5.377	0.896	0.518	4.929	5.825
Jio Wallet	80	5.182	1.036	0.638	4.664	5.700
Vodafone	60	5.106	1.277	0.442	4.468	5.745
Phonepe	60	5.306	0.884	0.502	4.864	5.748
Freecharge	20	5.015	1.003	0.549	4.514	5.517

Table 5. ANOVA- level of satisfaction

	SS	Df	MS	F	Sig.
Between Groups	125.482	6	20.91358	64.7751	.000
Within Groups	320.605	993	0.322865		
Total	446.086	999			

The outcome were collected on a seven-point Likert scale to test this hypothesis. The respondents were asked to express their level of agreement or dissatisfaction with the amount of satisfaction they received from each hypermarket. The ANOVA test was used to see whether the mean satisfaction level remained consistent throughout the categories defined on the Payment Wallets under investigation. Table 5 shows that there is a significant difference in satisfaction levels across the categories (F= 64.7751, p = 0.0000.05) at the 5% level of significance. As seen in table 4, respondents agreed on the degree of satisfaction for PayTm (mean = 5.486) when compared to the other respondents.

KEY OBSERVATIONS

The 93.8% of the respondents uses payment wallets while the 72.9% of the respondents are aware of UPI.PayTm has gained increased customer base and market share due to various facilities mentioned earlier in the paper such as PayTm Banks and PayTm Malls. It has tie up with top brands such as cashback offer on shopping from PayTm Mall with every bottle of Coca-Cola. There is extensive advertising on social media, television, print media. To create brand awareness, PayTm sponsors various events such as International Cricket matches.

Tangibility: The score of customers' perceptions is marginally greater than customers' expectations. Since payment wallet is comparatively a newer concept evolved and online platform is yet to unfold in all phases, the customers tend to have lower expectations since they are not completely aware of the ideal structure of website/mobile application.

Reliability: The score of customers' perceptions is lower than customers' expectations indicating that service providers fail to meet the customers' expectations with respect to reliability on payment wallets. There are two primary reasons for the fallout that are as follows:

1. The key reason for inability to meet the expectations of reliability due to the high expectation of error free records. One error in credit of account creates a negative perception in the minds of the customers and they tend to mark the service providers lower on the error free record aspect while making assessment based on their perceptions.

2. The service providers often fail to fulfil the promises that are made. They provide offers with terms and conditions that the customers are not aware on the face of it which creates a sense of deceive in the minds of the customers. Often, the service providers fail to adhere to the offers provided to the customers.

Responsiveness: The score of customers' perceptions is higher than customers' expectations indicating that service providers provide prompt services, the customers feel safe in transacting with payment wallets and the employees of service providers are always willing to help thecustomers. Expectations of the customers is marked relatively lower since there is minimal interaction of customers with employees of service providers and with contracts having extensive clauses on security of customer information, the customers tend to feel safer while doing transactions through payment wallets.

Assurance: The score of customers' perceptions is higher than customers' expectations indicating that the service providers have made relevant disclosures on the website/mobile application, the policies are implemented as promised and the employees are courteous as well as knowledgeable enough to address the queries of the customers. With strict regulations relating to disclosure of information and display of the terms of use of website, the customers are assured that there is no hiding of any relevant information. The employees are trained and well informed before they deal with the customers as the customer is the king in modern times and it is important that the customers are assured of the quality of service provided by payment wallets.

Empathy: The score of customers' perceptions is higher than customers' expectations indicating that the service providers focus on fulfilling the interests of the customers and the employees of the service providers understand the specific needs of the customers.

Overall, the average score of customers' perceptions cumulatively in all the aspects is higher than customers' expectations indicating that the customers are by and large satisfied with the services relating to payment wallets provided by service providers. The primary reason is that the concept of payment wallet is still at a developing stage and hence, the customers are unable to differentiate clearly between their expectations and reality. The customers tend to have average expectations and are more or less satisfied with the services provided to them since they are unaware of the quality of services that are usually required to be provided otherwise.

SUGGESTIONS

The primary focus of the service provider is to develop a user-friendly website/ mobile application and ensure that the layout is attractive and visually appealing thereby meeting the expectations of the customers regarding criteria of tangibility. There shall be a short yet apt user guidelines on the website/mobile application. The customers shall be able to easily locate customer support and contact details.

In order to match up to the expectations of customers relating to criteria of reliability, the service providers shall improve their back-end work to ensure that there are error free records and minimum errors in the transactions. The service providers shall clearly state the offer and stick to the offers that are provided to the customers. In order to maintain the clientele, it is necessary that the service providers fulfil the expectations of the customers relating to reliability.

Responsiveness is one of the most important tools for measuring the service quality of payment wallets. The service providers shall take extra steps to ensure that the customers feel safe while transacting through payment wallets. There shall not be any violation of privacy and the information of the customers shall be kept safe. The major interaction between employees of service providers and customers is through customer care support. The employees are required to showcase willingness to help the customers and be cordial and professional with the customers. Single instance of unsatisfactory response from customer care support is sufficient to shake the customers' willingness to continue with the service provider. Employees' attitudes while dealing with customers plays in a key role in maintaining good customer relations and instil confidence in the minds of the customers.

In order to match up to the expectations of customers relating to criteria of assurance, the service providers shall ensure that the employees are well trained and informed to address the queries raised by the customers and deal with them in courteous manner. As mentioned above, customer satisfaction and customer assurance is the key to maintain clientele.There shall be proper grievance mechanism against the unsatisfactory or unprofessional response from the employees of the service provider. The customers shall be aware of the transaction cost and other extra charges right at the beginning stage of the transactions and not the last stage of payment. The service providers shall strictly adhere to the offers and other policies such as refund policy as informed to the customers. In case of faulty credit, the refund shall be provided as per the refundpolicy. By such ways, the customers shall be assured of the services provided by the service providers.Service providers shall empathise towards the customers and formulate policies and terms of use and come up with offers keeping in mind the interest of the customers. The objectives of service providers can be achieved only by fulfilling the interest of the customers.

The service providers shall keep in mind that the customers tend to quickly switch to other service providers on account of better offer, better customer redressal or ease of transactions. The service providers shall not only satisfy the customers based on tangibility, reliability, responsiveness, assurance and empathy of existing services, but expand their horizon and introduce more services. Payment wallets might have been developed to ease payment of various bills such as mobile bills, electricity bills, etc., but it has increased its reach to food joints, cab services, booking of movie tickets, flight tickets and other services. The service providers shall ensure that the have tie-ups with other service providers to ease the payment for customers. Lessons shall be learnt from PayTm as to how they have link ups with Zomato for food services, with Uber for cab services, PayTm Banks for deposits with interests, tie-up with Coca-Cola for cashback and PayTm Malls. In order to capitalise on markets and increase customer base, the service providers shall provider more services and better-quality services.

RESEARCH INSTRUMENT

The instruments measuring the criteria for assessment of service quality of payment wallets are as follows:

Tangibility: Equipment, physical facilities and appearance of the personnel

1. Payment wallet has modern looking website/mobile application.
2. The facilities at payment wallet website/mobile application are visually appealing.
3. The website/mobile application is user-friendly.
4. Materials associated with the service (such as pamphlets or statements) are visually appealing on the website/mobile application.

Reliability: Ability to perform promised service accurately and dependably

1. When the company promises to do something by a certain time, it does so.
2. When you have a problem, the company shows a sincere interest in solving it.
3. The company performs the service right the first time.
4. The company provides its service at the time it promises to do so.
5. The company insists on error free records.

Responsiveness: Providing prompt service and willingness to help customers

1. Company tells you exactly when the services will be performed.
2. Company gives prompt service to you.
3. Employees in the company are always willing to help you.
4. Employees in the company are never too busy to respond to your request.
5. The behaviour of employees in the company instils confidence in you.
6. You feel safe in your transactions with the company.

Assurance: Caring and individualised attention to customers

1. Employees in the company are consistently courteous with you.
2. Employees in the company have the knowledge to answer your questions.
3. All the policies (such as refund policy) and offers (such as cashback offers) are honoured as promised in a convenient manner.
4. The company has operating hours convenient to all its customers.
5. The company makes relevant disclosures on the website/mobile application such as transaction cost and terms of service.

Empathy: Courtesy and knowledge of employees and ability to inspire confidence and trust among customers

1. The company has your best interests at heart.

2.   The employees of the company understand your specific needs".

REFERENCES

Ali, J. M., & Gopalan, L. V. (2018). E-Wallet Payment: Swot Analysis from Customer Perception. *International Journal of Recent Research Aspects,* 155-158.

Almuhammadi, A. (2020). An overview of mobile payments, fintech, and digital wallet in Saudi Arabia. In *2020 7th International Conference on Computing for Sustainable Global Development (INDIACom)* (pp. 271-278). IEEE.

Ananda, S., Kumar, R. P., & Singh, D. (2022). A mediation analysis of perceived service quality, customer satisfaction and customer engagement in the banking sector. *Journal of Financial Services Marketing*, 1–15.

Anjali, R., & Suresh, A. (2019). A Study on Customer Satisfaction of Bharat Interface for Money (BHIM). *International Journal of Innovative Technology and Exploring Engineering*.

Buttle, F. (1996). *SERVQUAL Model: Review, critique and research agenda.* Available at: https://pdfs.semanticscholar.org/2311/5dc190a4d045bc0e6ec08bb0e 80485 e2c872.pdf

Cashless India. (n.d.). *Digital Payment Methods, Mobile Wallets.* Ministry of Electronics and Information Technology, Government of India. http://cashlessindia. gov.in/mobile_wallets.html

Chaudhary, N., & Anand, S. (2022). Effectiveness of Online Payment System during COVID-19. *Education, 109,* 54–50.

Daniel & Berinyuy. (2010). *Using the SERVQUAL Model to assess Service Quality and Customer Satisfaction. An Empirical study of grocery stores in Umea.* http:// www.diva-portal.org/smash/get/diva2:327600/fulltext01

DMR. (2022). *PayTm Statistics and Facts.* Available at https://expandedramblings. com/index.php /PayTm-statistics-facts/

DQIndia Online. (2017). *Paytm crosses milestone of 200 Mn Wallet users Dataquest.* Available at: https://www.dqindia.com/paytm-crosses-milestone-of-200-mn-wallet-users/

ePaisa Content Team. (2016). *Payment Trends in India 2017.* https://www.epaisa. com/payment-trends-india-2017/

Esoimeme, E. E. (2018). A comparative analysis of the prepaid card laws/regulations in Nigeria, the UK, the USA and India. *Journal of Money Laundering Control*.

EY. (n.d.). *Case for mobile payments in India*. http://www.ey.com/Publication / vwLUAssets/EY-the-case-for-mobile-payments-in-india/%24FILE/EY-the-case-for-mobile-payments-in-india.PDF

Fainusa, A. F., Nurcahyo, R., & Dachyar, M. (2019, December). Conceptual Framework for Digital Wallet User Satisfaction. In *2019 IEEE 6th International Conference on Engineering Technologies and Applied Sciences (ICETAS)* (pp. 1-4). IEEE.

Fainusa, A. F., Nurcahyo, R., & Dachyar, M. (2019, December). Conceptual Framework for Digital Wallet User Satisfaction. In *2019 IEEE 6th International Conference on Engineering Technologies and Applied Sciences (ICETAS)* (pp. 1-4). IEEE.

Gomber, P., Kauffman, R. J., Parker, C., & Weber, B. W. (2018). On the fintech revolution: Interpreting the forces of innovation, disruption, and transformation in financial services. *Journal of Management Information Systems*, *35*(1), 220–265. doi:10.1080/07421222.2018.1440766

Halvadia, N. B., Halvadia, S., & Purohit, R. (2022). *Using Text Mining to Identify Key Dimensions of Service Quality for the Indian Public Sector Banks' Mobile Banking Apps*. Academic Press.

Kautish, S., Reyana, A., & Vidyarthi, A. (2022). SDMTA: Attack Detection and Mitigation Mechanism for DDoS Vulnerabilities in Hybrid Cloud Environment. *IEEE Transactions on Industrial Informatics*.

Khan, T. (2015). Snapdeal stands to gain big from Freecharge acquisition. *Business Today.IN*. Retrieved from https://www.businesstoday.in/current/corporate/snapdeal-stands-to-gain-big-from-freecharge-acquisition/story/216909.html

Koay, K. Y., Cheah, C. W., & Chang, Y. X. (2022). A model of online food delivery service quality, customer satisfaction and customer loyalty: A combination of PLS-SEM and NCA approaches. *British Food Journal*.

Kulašin & Fortuny-Santos. (2005). *Review of the Servqual Concept*. Available at: http://www.quality.unze.ba/zbornici/QUALITY%202005/021-Q05-005.pdf

Kumar, R., Kishore, S., Lu, H., & Prakash, A. (2020).Security analysis of unified payments interface and payment apps in India. In *29th USENIX Security Symposium (USENIX Security 20)* (pp. 1499-1516). USENIX.

Ladhari, R. (2009). *A review of twenty years of SERVQUAL research*. Available at: http://www.emeraldinsight.com/doi/abs/10.1108/17566690910971445?src=recsys&journalCode=ijqss

Lentner, C., Szegedi, K., & Tatay, T. (2015). Corporate social responsibility in the banking sector. *PénzügyiSzemle. Public Finance Quarterly*, *60*(1), 95–103.

Lim, W. M., Gupta, G., Biswas, B., & Gupta, R. (2021). Collaborative consumption continuance: A mixed-methods analysis of the service quality-loyalty relationship in ride-sharing services. *Electronic Markets*, 1–22.

Madhu, G., Govardhan, A., & Ravi, V. (2022). DSCN-net: a deep Siamese capsule neural network model for automatic diagnosis of malaria parasites detection. *Multimed Tools Appl.* doi:10.1007/s11042-022-13008-6

Mir, R. A., Rameez, R., & Tahir, N. (2022). Measuring Internet banking service quality: An empirical evidence. *The TQM Journal*.

Mishra, L. (2016). *E-wallet customer base surges*. Available at http://www.thehindu.com/business/E-wallet-firms'-customer-base-surges/article16695644.ece

Moorthy, T. V. K., Budati, A. K., Kautish, S., Goyal, S. B., & Prasad, K. L. (2022). Reduction of satellite images size in 5G networks using Machinelearning algorithms. *IET Communications*, *16*, 584–591. https://doi.org/10.1049/cmu2.12354

Niu, B., Mu, Z., Cao, B., & Gao, J. (2021). Should multinational firms implement blockchain to provide quality verification? *Transportation Research Part E, Logistics and Transportation Review*, *145*, 102121.

Parasuraman, A., Zeithaml, V. A., & Berry, L. L. (1985). A conceptual model of service quality and its implications for future research. *Journal of Marketing*, *49*(4), 41–50. doi:10.1177/002224298504900403

Poulton, C., Gibbon, P., Hanyani-Mlambo, B., Kydd, J., Maro, W., Larsen, M. N., Osorio, A., Tschirley, D., & Zulu, B. (2004). Competition and coordination in liberalized African cotton market systems. *World Development*, *32*(3), 519–536. doi:10.1016/j.worlddev.2003.10.003

Pramani, R., & Iyer, S. V. (2022). Adoption of payments banks: A grounded theory approach. *Journal of Financial Services Marketing*, 1–15. doi:10.105741264-021-00133-w

Qi, L., Zhang, X., Dou, W., Hu, C., Yang, C., & Chen, J. (2018). A two-stage locality-sensitive hashing based approach for privacy-preserving mobile service recommendation in cross-platform edge environment. *Future Generation Computer Systems*, *88*, 636–643. doi:10.1016/j.future.2018.02.050

Raj, R. (2016). *Are mobile wallets still to stay, or is cash still the king.* Available at https://inc42.com/resources/mobile-wallet-scenario-india/

Rajawat, A. S., Bedi, P., Goyal, S. B., Kautish, S., Xihua, Z., Aljuaid, H., & Mohamed, A. W. (2022). Dark Web Data Classification Using Neural Network. *Computational Intelligence and Neuroscience*.

Ray, N., & Ghosh, D. (2017). Online Banking Service: A Boon or Bane? *Asian Journal of Research in Banking and Finance*, *7*(5), 179–194.

RBI. (2014). *Report of the Committee on Comprehensive Financial Services for Small Business and Low Income Households.* The Reserve Bank of India. https://rbi.org.in/scripts/BS_PressReleaseDisplay.aspx?prid=30353

Reddy, S. (2018). Announcement of payment banks and stock performance of commercial banks in India. *Journal of Internet Banking and Commerce*, *23*(1), 1–12.

Roy, P. M. (2021). Anatomy of the Digital Payment Ecosystem in India. *Bimaquest*, *21*(3), 40–61.

Shamraev, A. (2019). Legal and regulatory framework of the payment and e-money services in the BRiCS countries. *BRICS Law Journal*, *6*(2), 60–81.

Sharma, C., Sharma, S., Kautish, S., Alsallami, S. A., Khalil, E. M., & Mohamed, A. W. (2022). A new median-average round Robin scheduling algorithm: An optimal approach for reducing turnaround and waiting time. *Alexandria Engineering Journal*, *61*(12), 10527–10538.

State Bank Buddy-Mobility. (n.d.). Retrieved from: https://mobility.onlinesbi.com/sbf_buddy.html

Talky, S. (n.d.). *Indian Startup success story: MobiKwik*. http://www.startuptalky.com/ startup/mobikwik/

Talwar, S., Dhir, A., Khalil, A., Mohan, G., & Islam, A. N. (2020). Point of adoption and beyond. Initial trust and mobile-payment continuation intention. *Journal of Retailing and Consumer Services*, *55*, 102086. doi:10.1016/j.jretconser.2020.102086

Twum, K. K., Kosiba, J. P. B., Hinson, R. E., Gabrah, A. Y. B., & Assabil, E. N. (2022). Determining mobile money service customer satisfaction and continuance usage through service quality. *Journal of Financial Services Marketing*, 1–13.

Veluvali, P. (2019). Legal Framework and Governing Design for IPOs in India. In *Retail Investor in Focus* (pp. 33–58). Springer. doi:10.1007/978-3-030-12756-5_3

Vijai, C. (2019). Mobile wallet and its future in India. *Journal of Emerging Technologies and Innovative Research*, *6*(5), 574–580.

Wilson, T. A. (2012). Supporting social enterprises to support vulnerable consumers: The example of community development finance institutions and financial exclusion. *Journal of Consumer Policy*, *35*(2), 197–213. doi:10.100710603-011-9182-5

Wong. (2020). *Constructing a Survey Questionnaire to Collect Data on Service Quality of Business Academics*. http://eprints.utar.edu.my/860/1/6343.pdf

Yadav, N. (2017). *PayTm launches e-commerce platform PayTm Mall*. https://www.bgr.in/news/PayTm-launches-new-e-commerce-platform-PayTm-mall/

Chapter 8
Role of Technological Readiness on the Adoption of Artificial Intelligence in the Accounting Profession:
Evidence From a Developing Economy

Ratan Ghosh

(iD) https://orcid.org/0000-0002-2506-8357
Bangaladesh University of Professionals, Bangladesh

Asia Khatun
University of Dhaka, Bangladesh

ABSTRACT

The internet of things (IoT) is changing the paradigm in every aspect of human life. IoT embedded with big data is sparking the adoption of artificial intelligence (AI) in the business field. Subsequently, this study investigates the role of technological readiness in adopting artificial intelligence (AI) in the accounting profession of Bangladesh. To analytically assess the impact of technological readiness on the adoption of AI, four dimensions of technological readiness (TR) have been measured: TR optimism, TR innovativeness, TR discomfort, and TR insecurity. A self-administered closed-ended questionnaire is developed and distributed among the students studying accounting in various public universities in Bangladesh. Six hundred eight responses are recorded and used to test this study's hypothetical relationships. Findings reveal that TR optimism and TR innovativeness have a positive and significant relationship with AI adoption. TR insecurity and TR discomfort have a negative and significant relationship with AI adoption.

DOI: 10.4018/978-1-6684-4176-3.ch008

INTRODUCTION

The use of technology is extended to every part of human life. Artificial intelligence (AI) is a new addition to this technologically advanced context. AI is a branch of science by which machine intelligence is activated, and those can behave, think, and make decisions like humans according to the logic program in their memory. Accounting and auditing will not be an area where AI cannot be used. According to the World Economic Forum (2015), by 2025, AI will perform 30% of corporate audits. AI has the key potential to change any business environment and performance by using technological advancement. Ucoglu (2020) concluded that new technologies like machine learning and AI make it possible to ease the different tasks that will affect the accountancy and audit profession. AI will act as a connection between transforming traditional information into intelligent systems, which will enhance the computerization and optimization of information systems (Damerji and Salimi, 2021). Data security, bug-free information systems, and automation are AI's main applications and advantages.

AI allows the corporation to use a systematic information system that accelerates the strategic decision-making process (Turluev and Hadjieva, 2021). However, information will play a vital role in uncovering opportunities and challenges for a corporation. By effectively analyzing the stated information, the company can increase its business performance. Moreover, the acceptability of AI is confined to accounting and auditing and marketing strategy planning, financial decision-making, production planning, and many more (Yawalkar, 2019). In human resource management, hiring, recruiting, and managing staff training are repetitive and tedious. It can be easily sorted out by implementing AI in the human resource department (Yawalkar, 2019)

The job environment is the external environment that shapes an area of continuous change as employers demand. As this era is for technological advancement, employers expect this advanced and updated knowledge of technology and technological skills to be available among the students (Cory and Pruske, 2012; Stoner, 2009). To cope with this technological advancement, universities should take some initiatives to adopt AI and machine learning in their curricula. As different accounting firms invest more in AI and machine learning (Kokina & Davenport, 2017; Ucoglu, 2020), students need to update themselves with this technological skill to optimize their future career goals. However, the existing accounting curricula lack this AI-related knowledge, resulting in lower technological knowledge and skills among the accounting students (Damerji and Salimi, 2021).

The job environment will not be the same after 20 or 30 years for accounting students as the work criteria of accounting firms are mainly based on AI, which is repetitive and clerical (Ucoglu, 2020). So, the students need to prepare themselves by adopting new technology. According to Azjen and Fishbein (1975), the adoption of new technology by accounting students and technological readiness (TR) has a causal relationship, and this can be explained with the use of the technology adoption model (TAM) developed by Davis back in 1986. Davis (1986) took the theory of reasoned action (TRA) (Azjen and Fishbein, 1975) as the root for initiating TAM. This study planned to determine the impact or role of technology readiness on the adoption of AI in the accounting profession from accounting students' perspectives. The need for work in this part from the viewpoint of a developing country is necessary as the future development of a developing country depends on a smart workforce. Accounting students will be the future of many accounting firms and firms changing their work variety by implementing AI. With the help of the TR concept, TRA, and TAM, it is possible to measure the opinion of accounting students about embracing new technological knowledge and skill. Moreover, the universities should also include this AI and machine learning in their curricula, and then it is possible to measure the behavioral intention of their students to accept those. With the result of this analysis, it is possible to find out the strategies to uncover the problems for accepting new technology and initiating policies to uphold its possibilities, as TR deals with the technological discomfort, insecurity, optimism, and innovativeness of AI adoption.

LITERATURE REVIEW

Theoretical Framework

A set of connected concepts that evolved from one or more theories to comply with research findings is a theoretical framework. A valid theoretical framework is needed to justify any research work's importance, especially quantitative ones. This study explores the rapport between technological readiness and the adoption of artificial intelligence if any. Research design is developed here emphasizing on following two theories, namely (i) Diffusion of innovation theory (DIT) by Rogers (1976, 1995, 2003) and (ii) theory of reasoned action (TRA) by Ajzen and Fishbein (1975, 2010).

DIT tries to conclude how innovation is interconnected through certain networks over time among the followers of a community (Roger, 2003). The failure and success of innovation can be measured by following five steps over time: knowledge, persuasion, decision, implementation, and confirmation (Ong *et al.,* 2008). Persuasion is the toughest step as acceptance or declination of technological innovation is determined here. According to Roger (2003), comparative advantage, compatibility, complexity, trialability, and observation ability will be the main factors for any innovation adoption decision. TRA can explain the motive of accepting new technology, accentuating users' behavioral intentions. According to TRA, a person's behavioral intention (an extent of the level of one's intention to execute an identified behavior) is conjointly affected by the person's attitude (an individual's optimistic or adverse emotional state about performing the target behavior) towards the behavior and subjective norm (the person's insight that most people who are vital to him think he should or should not execute the behavior on demand) (Ajzen and Fishbein, 1975). TRA is expertise in many settings to envisage human behavior (Ajzen and Fishbein, 1980).

In recent times, many Business corporations and public accounting firms have been interested in adopting new technology like AI in their operation. These firms will be the future employers of different graduates. Moreover, students of accounting and other subjects mainly depend on their universities' fixed curricula to develop themselves for future endeavors. Consequently, university education directly connects to preparing students with new technology skills for their upcoming careers. However, the firms' adoption degree of new technology and knowledge acquired by the students from the university regarding technology are not the same. As a result, the expectation gap between employers and students will emerge. On that note, DIT and TRA will play a vital role in the study mentioned above.

AI, IoT, and Technological Readiness

Digitalization of economics and production will be the main characteristic of every industrial development sector soon, and this is the goal of the fourth industrial revolution. This revolution requires the interconnection of different types of machines horizontally. Boston Consultancy Group (BCG) includes the industrial Internet of Things (IIoT) and big data & analytics (this is the combination of AI and machine learning) as the two important elements at the time of describing the nine technological pillars for the advancement of industry 4.0 (Ślusarczyk, B at el., 2020). The Internet of Things (IoT) is a network that connects anything to the Internet using pre-determined protocols and information sensing equipment to perform data exchange and communications to achieve smart recognition, locating, tracking, monitoring, and administration. Moreover, the Internet of Things (IoT) offers solutions that combine information technology (hardware and software used to preserve, retrieve, and process data) with communications technology (electronic systems used to communicate between individuals or organizations. Smart devices like smartwatches, glasses or health monitoring systems, smart home locks, sensors for temperature, and drones these all examples of modern IoT domain used technology. However, IoT devices interchange information among millions of users worldwide, and in most cases, this has happened with some illegal intention (Stoyanova et al., 2020). Financial technologies, IoT, and AI incorporation and alliance in many sectors will generate more precise and rapid jobs and reduce costs by monitoring production, maintenance, logistics, and many other business utilities. Finance and accounting, which are the two main functions of businesses, will be changed forever with the help of IoT. Yilmaz and Hazar (2019) concluded a positive association among all the technology acceptance model variables among the students of accounting and finance for IoT through a survey analysis. Though IoT has some negative aspects (Stoyanova et al., 2020), it is a fundamental part of the fourth industrial revolution. Along with this IoT, AI can change the behavior of the users of new technology and their intention to prepare them for this automated job field.

Adoption of AI in Accounting and Auditing

Artificial intelligence has the potential that will transform our daily life dramatically. Zemankova (2019) concluded that in accounting and audit, AI helps to concentrate on the complex and value-added works rather than tedious, time-consuming, and rules-based work, as AI can bring higher efficiency to some routine works. Whistleblowing enables the customer, employee, and general public to report the wrongdoing to the organization confidential from AI applications. In Malaysia, this practice will create more strength in the internal control system to reduce the amount of fraud and corruption and increase transparency and accountability in the public sector (Noor and Mansor, 2019). AI and machine learning will alter the traditional work structure of financial audits and some work of accounting records.

Moreover, students need to prepare themselves to cope with this technological paradigm shift, and universities must prepare future generations to take this challenge. The accounting cycle is a collection of interconnected processes. This process can be integrated through big data, artificial intelligence, blockchain, electronic billing, digital signature, and XBRL languages (Faccia *et al.,* 2019). Moreover, this mentioned integrated process would benefit the public, stakeholders of a firm, government people, and policymakers and will revolutionize big data management. Works related to a huge amount of data like accounting and auditing can use AI to reduce the time with a high level of effectiveness (Gusai, 2019). Universities should include this technological advancement in their accounting curricula; otherwise, their graduates will fail to comply with the requirements of this accounting and auditing firm as they are more prominent to include AI, big data, blockchain in their operational policy (Qasim and Kharbat, 2020).

Additionally, this inclusion will balance the accounting firm's needs and accounting graduates' knowledge. Al-Sayyed et al. (2021) emphasized the effectiveness of the AI in collecting audit evidence as it saved time and error from the perspective of Jordan. Consequently, implementing AI in auditing will increase audit quality, and it is empirically tested with the perception of certified auditors in Jordan (Albawwat and Frijat, 2021). Fukas et al., (2021) proposed an "Auditing Artificial Intelligence Maturity Model (A-AIMM), which contains eight different dimensions and five different maturity models that accelerates the audit firms to become AI-Enabled organization. Additionally, this A-AIMM model will act as a threshold point for strategic audit management and enable AI to integrate long-term and targeted audit plans.

Above is the empirical evidence that AI will reshape accounting and auditing activities. Universities and other concerns related to this will take their position to improve or prepare their accounting students or graduates to cope with this technological change. Over the year, "Big 4" multinational accounting firms have taken initiatives and invested money in technological advancement in their organization (Kokina and Davenport, 2017). Since some repetitive work in accounting firms like accounts receivable and payables management, risk assessment, asset assessment can be done easily with the help of machine learning.

Ernst and Young (EY) initiated "Canvas" and "Helix" as machine learning techniques to analyze and extract data from unstructured data to gain further audit evidence, and material misstatement will also be detected to avoid fraud by this process. However, "Canvas" is an online platform that creates a connection between the auditors and their clients for audit engagement and management for any size and distance. In the changing regulatory environment, "Canvas" can provide audit service and quick customization of audit service is possible here. Next, "Helix" enables high-quality audits rather than giving time to data collection as this platform helps analyze journal entries, expense and revenue, receivables and payables collection, asset assessment, risk analysis, and many more. Moreover, "Blockchain Analyzer" supports ensuring transparency in the audit process. Pricewaterhouse Coopers (PwC) introduced "GL.ai," "Cash.ai," and "Halo" as their machine learning outcome. GL.ai is a robot that uses machine learning algorithms to process AI into accounting practices. Doing cash audits by inspecting cash balances, bank reconciliation, and confirmation letters Cash.ai involves AI with machine learning. Using graphical visualization, "Halo" can differentiate high-risk transactions, and in the case of auditing, it provides a risk assessment service for a huge volume of data.

Deloitte commenced "Argus", "Cortex", "Omnia DNAV", "Optix", "Signal", "Reveal", "Sonar", "GRAPA", "HR Agent Edgy", "DocQMiner", "Egle Eye", and "BrainSpace" for introducing AI and machine learning for their audit activities. Except "HR Agent Edgy," "DocQMiner," "Egle Eye," and "BrainSpace," others are used for the advancement of audit service. Such as, Argus was the first audit application used by Deloitte to extract useful data from the electronic database. Cortex was initiated for tax clients and audits, and now it also provides some risk and financial advisory services. HR Agent Edgy can provide consultancy services, and it is a chatbot that can interact with employees and clients. DocQMiner and Egle Eye launched a risk advisory service attached with AI and machine learning. Lastly, BrainSpace does financial advisory services for some legal issues. It uses cluster information and machine data to support clients in legal disputes. Klynveld Peat Marwick Goerdeler (KPMG) partners with Microsoft to offer clients combined modernization services such as Intelligent Underwriting Engine, Sales Intelligence Engine, Sales Cycle Optimization Tool, Strategic Profitability Insights etc. KPMG also initiated "Clara," the latest artificial intelligence platform, to easily perform audit work with huge amounts of data. It is an advanced K-analyzer for tax service, and thousands of transaction is inspected within a very limited time as it uses RPA technology.

AI implementation in accounting and auditing will enable the accounting profession to automated versions. It has a tremendous effect on auditing activities, making them speedier and freer from errors and mistakes. Moreover, AI also enables the auditors to have time for value-added work rather than routine and tedious workload. Consequently, accounting students need to be motivated to acquire this new technological knowledge and skill to prepare themselves for future career prospects.

Technological Readiness (TR)

People's tendency to accept and use new technologies for achieving aims at work and home is defined as technological readiness (Parasuraman, 2000). New technologies can be viewed as an overall state of mind resulting from a gestalt of mental enablers and inhibitors that jointly define a person's susceptibility (Parasuraman, 2000). Effective management of technology readiness will act as a vital factor for the firm's business procedure and accelerate the firm's business performance. The concept of technology readiness is the combination of positive and negative features of any stated new technology, which will affect the adoption of new technology. It is concluded that the positive sides of new technology will help people accept that, and the negative aspects will demotivate them from doing that action (Parasuraman and Colby, 2015). In 2000, Parasuraman developed a 36-item scale to measure the person's intention to accept new technology and again, in 2015, Parasuraman and Colby reduced the items to 16 to measure the level of affirmation towards the new technology. Both the index (Parasuraman, 2000; Parasuraman and Colby, 2015) divided the beliefs and intentions of people into four different dimensions: optimism, innovativeness, discomfort, and insecurity to measure the degree of acceptance of new technology. Optimism and innovativeness will be treated as positive measurements, while discomfort and insecurity are objectionable.

Technology Adoption

The technology adoption model (TAM) was first established by Davis (1986) and used in many studies related to technology acceptance. This model was initiated to discover the individual's attitude toward embracing and using a given technology system. Davis (1986) developed this model as the extended version of Ajzen and Fishbein's (1975) theory of reasoned action, and it enlightened the affiliation of attitudes-intention-behavior. Individual attitudes and subjective norms directly influence the behavioral intention to perform certain behavior (Davis, 1986).

The TAM comprises five variables: perceived ease of use, usefulness, behavioral intention to use, attitude toward use, and actual use. The two most influential aspects in the model are perceived ease of use (PEOU), which refers to the confidence that exertion will not be required for accepting any new technology and perceived usefulness (PU), which defines the certainty that the technology enriches job enactment. These explained two variables jointly combined with attitude toward use encompassing the core variables of TAM.

Outcome variables comprise behavioral intention to use and actual use. Notably, while the behavioral intention is predictive of use, such a relationship may also exist in the opposite direction as positive user experience can determine behavioral intentions. Lastly, peripheral variables consist of subjective norms, computer self-efficacy, and facilitating conditions. According to Davis (1989), PEOU and PU are the two important and significant variables that help determine the attitude toward accepting new technology. PEOU is demarcated as the level to which a person is confident that using a particular system would be without exertion. PU is defined as the degree of belief that a person thinks using a certain technology or system will enhance their job enactment (Davis, 1989). Moreover, PU has an uninterrupted influence on the intention to use while PEOU impacts the intention to use secondarily use attitude as a medium. The TAM and its two variables, PU & PEOU, have proven valid and reliable over various systems (Li, 2003; Ma and Liu, 2004; Alfadda and Mahdi, 2021; Salloum *et al.,* 2019).

Hypotheses Development

From the previous empirical literature, it can be concluded that AI and machine learning implementation will shape the future accounting profession. Different accounting firms will convert their operational activities from traditional to automated with AI's help. Moreover, they need some technologically sound accounting graduates who are easily acquainted with their changing workplace environment. If the accounting students are not prepared for this technological advancement, they will hire more IT graduates than accounting graduates. However, technology readiness and new technology adoption will impact the accounting students' future career choices and career improvement. So, it is proposed that there may be a relation between readiness and acceptance as both are related to AI technologies. The main intention of this study is to figure out the role of this stated technological readiness in the adoption of new technology like AI in the future accounting profession. The following research question will have emerged for this study.

- What is the opinion of the accounting students towards technology readiness?
- What is the opinion of the accounting students towards technology adoption of AI in accounting and auditing?
- What is the impact of use opinion on the relationship between technology readiness and technology adoption of AI in the accounting profession?

Now the alternate hypotheses depicted from the previous research question are as follows:

H_1: *Technology readiness (TR) optimism positively influences accounting graduates' AI adoption.*

H_2: *Technology readiness (TR) innovativeness positively influences accounting graduates' AI adoption.*

H_3: *Technology readiness (TR) discomfort negatively influences accounting graduates' AI adoption.*

H_4: *Technology readiness (TR) insecurity negatively influences accounting graduates' AI adoption.*

RESEARCH METHODS

Research Design

The study aims at analyzing the role of technological readiness on the adoption of artificial intelligence in the accounting profession. A self-administered survey questionnaire is developed and distributed to university students of Bangladesh who major in accounting or graduate in accounting. Cross-sectional data analysis has been applied to relevant data collected from respondents to test the hypothetical relationships of the study. (Copper and Schindler, 2006; Sekaran and Bougie, 2016).

SAMPLE TECHNIQUE

The judgment sampling method has been used for collecting responses for the study. A purposive sampling strategy is frequently used to select respondents best suited to answering research questions. As the study focuses on technological readiness and AI adoption in the accounting profession, university students studying accounting are selected accordingly.

Measures of Constructs

Technological readiness (TR) to adopt AI is measured by four variables: TR Optimism, TR Innovativeness, TR Discomfort, and TR Insecurity. Four items of each variable (16-item scale) have been adapted from Parasuraman and Colby (2015). Two items have been adapted from Damerji and Salimi (2021) to assess the adoption of AI in the accounting profession.

FINDINGS AND INTERPRETATION OF RESULTS

Respondents Profile

1200 questionnaires were distributed to the students at various reputed public universities in Bangladesh using their email. The email survey method has been used in this study as this method helps reach the respondents faster in this COVID-19 pandemic. However, 618 respondents were documented, and 608 were complete and usable. This represents a response rate of 50.67%. Table 1 represents the respondents' profiles. 59.04% of respondents are male, whereas 40.96% are female. Most of the responses have been obtained from the undergraduate students as it is 90.30%, and graduate students' presence is 9.70%.

Table 1. Profile of the respondents (Source: Author's Calculation)

Demographic Profile	Number of Respondents (=608)	Percentage
Gender		
Male	359	59.04%
Female	249	40.96%
Education		
1st Year of Bachelor	60	9.90%
2nd Year of Bachelor	242	39.80%
3rd Year of Bachelor	99	16.30%
4th Year of Bachelor	147	24.20%
Masters	59	9.70%
Institution		
University of Dhaka	236	38.82%
Bangladesh University of Professionals	80	13.16%
Jahangirnagar University	88	14.47%
University of Barishal	202	33.55%

Source: Data Analysis

Measurement Model

The result of measurement models can substantiate the estimated model. This study has employed convergent validity and discriminant validity as the measurement models. Convergent validity is measured by factor loading of items, composite reliability (CR), and average variance extracted (AVE). Hair et al. (2019) recommended that the value of average variance extracted (AVE) and the composite reliability (CR) should be 0.50 and 0.70, respectively. Chin (2010) recommended that the cut-off value to measure the factor loading of each item can be 0.50. Accordingly, the study has taken this cut-off value (0.50) of factor loading as a standard value to assess the validity of each item. **Table 2** shows the value of measurement models under convergent validity. In this study, all the items of studied variables have a factor loading of more than 0.50.

Figure 1. Outer loadings of all the measurement items

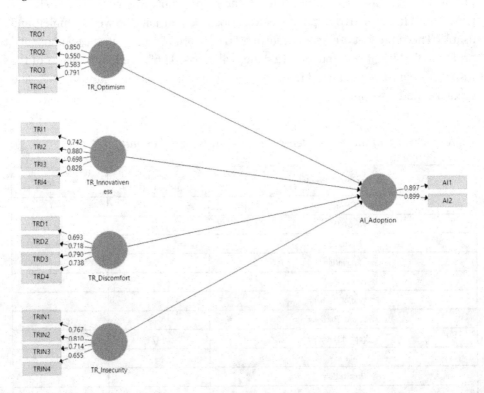

Table 2. Result of measurement model (Source: Author's Calculation)

Factor/Construct	Items	Loading	AVE	CR	Cronbach's Alpha	rho_A
AI Adoption	AI1	0.896	0.807	0.893	0.760	0.760
	AI2	0.899				
TR Discomfort (TRD)	TRD1	0.693	0.541	0.825	0.719	0.720
	TRD2	0.718				
	TRD3	0.790				
	TRD4	0.738				
TR Innovativeness (TRI)	TRI1	0.742	0.624	0.868	0.799	0.827
	TRI2	0.880				
	TRI3	0.698				
	TRI4	0.828				
TR Insecurity (TRIS)	TRIN1	0.767	0.546	0.827	0.725	0.723
	TRIN2	0.810				
	TRIN3	0.714				
	TRIN4	0.655				
TR Optimism (TRO)	TRO1	0.850	0.510	0.793	0.725	0.774
	TRO2	0.550				
	TRO3	0.583				
	TRO4	0.791				

Source: Data Analysis

Note: AVE (Average Variance Extracted), CR (Composite Reliability)

Heterotrait-Monotrait Ratio (HTMT Ratio)

Hair et al., (2019) recommended that the threshold of HTMT ratio should be less than 0.85. Table 3 reports the HTMT ratio of the constructs employed in this study. As documented in table 3, all the diagonal values are within the value threshold as recommended by Hair et al., (2019).

Table 3. Discriminant validity (Source: Author's Calculation)

	AI_Adoption	TRD	TRI	TRIS	TRO
AI_Adoption					
TRD	0.420				
TRI	0.583	0.228			
TRIS	0.389	0.452	0.171		
TRO	0.327	0.350	0.356	0.214	

Source: Data Analysis

Structural Model

Structural equation modeling (SEM) helps identify the hypothetical relationships between dependent and independent variables. A total of 5000 resamplings have been taken to verify the statistical significance of the model through bootstrapping technique. Model goodness-of-fit is confirmed by the coefficient of determination (R^2) and the coefficient of the path model (b) (Hair et al., 2017). The value of R^2, as suggested by Hair et al., (2019), are 0.75, 0.50, and 0.25, considered substantial, moderate, and weak, respectively. The value of the R^2 is 33.60% in this study, meaning the goodness-of-fit is moderately weak. TR Optimism (TRO) has a positive and significant relationship with AI Adoption with the value of ($\beta = 0.140, p < 0.082$) at a 90% significance level, *and* this result supports *H1*. TR Innovativeness (TRI) has a positive and significant relationship with the adoption of AI ($\beta = 0.386, p < 0.000$) at a 1% significance level, and this result supports *H2*. Moreover, TR Discomfort (TRD) and TR Insecurity (TRIS) Discomfort have a negative and significant relationship with AI Adoption with the value ($\beta = -0.141, p < 0.046$) and ($\beta = -0.220, p < 0.005$), respectively. These findings support the acceptance of *H3* and *H4*.

Table 4. Path analysis (Source: Author's Calculation)

H	Relations	Beta	Std. Dev.	T-stat	P-value	BCL LL	BCL UL	Decision
H1	TRO → AI Adoption	0.140	0.100	1.395	0.082*	-0.050	0.276	Supported
H2	TRI → AI Adoption	0.386	0.085	4.538	0.000***	0.236	0.518	Supported
H3	TRD → AI Adoption	-0.141	0.084	1.684	0.046**	-0.260	0.018	Supported
H4	TRIS → AI Adoption	-0.220	0.086	5.545	0.005**	-0.345	-0.065	Supported

Note: ***p<0.01, **p<0.05, *p<0.10 (based on one-tailed test with 5000 bootstrapping)

DISCUSSION

This study investigates the role of technological readiness in adopting artificial intelligence (AI) in the accounting profession of Bangladesh. Therefore, perceptions of accounting graduates of reputed public universities in Bangladesh have been taken and analyzed to test the hypothetical models of this study. Technological Readiness (TR) has been measured by four variables, namely- TR Optimism (TRO), TR Insecurity (TRIS), TR Innovativeness (TRI), and TR Discomfort (TRD).

TRO and TRIS have a positive and significant relationship with AI Adoption. In contrast, TRD and TRIS have a negative and significant relationship with AI Adoption. This asserts a significant relationship between technological readiness and the adoption of AI in the accounting profession. The value of the R^2 is 33.60% which denotes 33.60% of the variability of the adoption of AI can be explained by four variables used in this study.

The vision of Digital Bangladesh has made it possible to advance the country in the field of information and technology over the last decade. However, there are plenty of sectors where more and more developments can be made with the help of information technology. Business and education sectors are a few of them. Sophisticated business environment, transaction volume, and complexities in recording business transactions have called for adopting Artificial Intelligence (AI) in accounting. Many domestic and multinational companies in Bangladesh have started adopting AI in the accounting division on a small scale. Before adopting AI in a full-fledged structure, professional accountants commonly doubt the readiness of upcoming accounting graduates to work with the latest technology like AI and machine learning. While conducting this study, it is found that graduates or currently accounting studying students feel the importance of technological skills before entering the job market. To prepare future graduates as per the market requirement, universities of Bangladesh should focus more on developing the technological readiness of accounting graduates to adopt AI-based accounting processes.

Figure 2. Structural path model

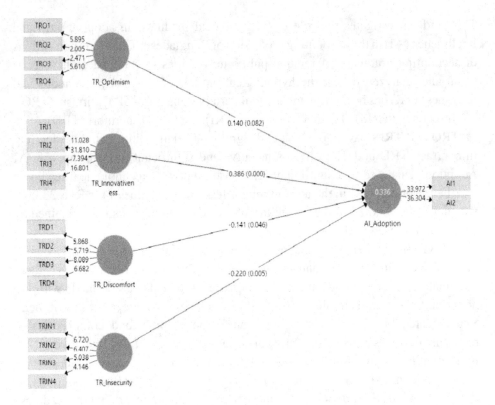

CONCLUSION

The study aims at investigating the role of technological readiness of accounting graduates on the adoption of AI in the accounting profession. The study has adapted four variables of technological readiness (TR) from Parasuraman and Colby (2015) to investigate their impact on AI adoption. Findings reveal that TR Optimism, TR Innovativeness, TR Discomfort, and TR Insecurity are positively related to the adoption of AI in the accounting profession. This also asserts that accounting students studying at different reputed public universities in Bangladesh recognize the importance of different dimensions of technological readiness required for their future employment. As business complexities have increased, corporates are now shifting to adopting AI in their accounting-related works. All the relevant stakeholders should develop a well-connected policy to make future graduates technologically adept. From academia, the universities of Bangladesh should focus more on accepting new knowledge of AI or accounting analytics in the curriculum and provide the students with the latest knowledge of accounting and AI in the classroom. Corporates should also work more on implementing AI in a full-fledged structure in the firm. Afroze and Aulad (2020) pointed out that huge investment in IT and impoverished digital infrastructure can hinder the implementation of AI in Bangladesh's auditing industry. The policymakers can facilitate both the universities and corporates by guiding them with financial incentives, a technical workforce, and a competitive environment to promote AI-based learning for the accounting students to contribute to the country's development. This study has only focused on AI's technological readiness and adoption in accounting. Future studies can be done from the employer's perspective, where the recruiter's priority of various dimensions of technological readiness can be analyzed.

REFERENCES

Afroze, D., & Aulad, A. (2020). Perception of professional accountants about the application of artificial intelligence (AI) in auditing industry of Bangladesh. *Journal of Social Economics Research, 7*(2), 51–61. doi:10.18488/journal.35.2020.72.51.61

Ajzen, I., & Fishbein, M. (1975). A Bayesian analysis of attribution processes. *Psychological Bulletin, 82*(2), 261–277. doi:10.1037/h0076477

Ajzen, I., & Fishbein, M. (1980). *Understanding attitudes and predicting social behaviour.* Prentice-Hall.

Al-Sayyed, S., Al-Aroud, S., & Zayed, L. (2021). The effect of artificial intelligence technologies on audit evidence. *Accounting, 7*(2), 281–288. doi:10.5267/j.ac.2020.12.003

Albawwat, I., & Frijat, Y. (2021). An analysis of auditors' perceptions towards artificial intelligence and its contribution to audit quality. *Accounting, 7*(4), 755–762. doi:10.5267/j.ac.2021.2.009

Alfadda, H. A., & Mahdi, H. S. (2021). Measuring students' use of zoom application in language course based on the technology acceptance model (tam). *Journal of Psycholinguistic Research, 50*(4), 883–900. doi:10.100710936-020-09752-1 PMID:33398606

Chin, W. W. (2010). How to write up and report PLS analyses. In *Handbook of partial least squares* (pp. 655–690). Springer. doi:10.1007/978-3-540-32827-8_29

Cooper, D. R., Schindler, P. S., & Sun, J. (2006). *Business research methods* (Vol. 9). McGraw-Hill.

Cory, S. N., & Pruske, K. A. (2012). A factor analysis of the skills necessary in accounting graduates. *Journal of Business and Accounting, 5*(1), 121–128.

Damerji, H., & Salimi, A. (2021). Mediating effect of user perceptions on technology readiness and adoption of artificial intelligence in accounting. *Accounting Education, 30*(2), 107–130. doi:10.1080/09639284.2021.1872035

Davis, F. D. (1986). *A technology acceptance model for empirically testing new end-user information systems: Theory and results* (Doctoral dissertation). ProQuest Dissertations and Theses database. (UMI No. 0374529)

Davis, F. D. (1989). Perceived usefulness, perceived ease of use, and user acceptance. *Management Information Systems Quarterly, 13*(3), 319–340. doi:10.2307/249008

Faccia, A., Al Naqbi, M. Y. K., & Lootah, S. A. (2019, August). Integrated cloud financial accounting cycle: how artificial intelligence, blockchain, and XBRL will change the accounting, fiscal and auditing practices. In *Proceedings of the 2019 3rd International Conference on Cloud and Big Data Computing* (pp. 31-37). 10.1145/3358505.3358507

Fukas, P., Rebstadt, J., Remark, F., & Thomas, O. (2021). Developing an Artificial Intelligence Maturity Model for Auditing. *29th European Conference on Information Systems Research Papers*. https://aisel.aisnet.org/ecis2021_rp/133

Gusai, O. P. (2019). Robot human interaction: Role of artificial intelligence in accounting and auditing. *Indian Journal of Accounting, 51*(1), 59–62.

Hair, J. F., Hult, G. T. M., Ringle, C. M., Sarstedt, M., & Thiele, K. O. (2017). Mirror, mirror on the wall: A comparative evaluation of composite-based structural equation modeling methods. *Journal of the Academy of Marketing Science, 45*(5), 616–632. doi:10.100711747-017-0517-x

Hair, J. F., Risher, J. J., Sarstedt, M., & Ringle, C. M. (2019). When to use and how to report the results of PLS-SEM. *European Business Review, 31*(1), 2–24. doi:10.1108/EBR-11-2018-0203

Kokina, J., & Davenport, T. H. (2017). The Emergence of Artificial Intelligence: How Automation is Changing Auditing. *Journal of Emerging Technologies in Accounting, 14*(1), 115–122. doi:10.2308/jeta-51730

Noor, N. R. A. M., & Mansor, N. (2019). Exploring the adaptation of artificial intelligence in whistleblowing practice of the internal auditors in Malaysia. *Procedia Computer Science, 163*, 434–439. doi:10.1016/j.procs.2019.12.126

Ong, J. W., Poong, Y. S., & Ng, T. H. (2008). 3G services adoption among university students: Diffusion of innovation theory. *Communications of the IBIMA, 3*(16), 114–121.

Parasuraman, A. (2000). Technology Readiness Index (TRI) a multiple-item scale to measure readiness to embrace new technologies. *Journal of Service Research, 2*(4), 307–320. doi:10.1177/109467050024001

Parasuraman, A., & Colby, C. L. (2015). An updated and streamlined technology readiness index: TRI 2.0. *Journal of Service Research, 18*(1), 59–74. doi:10.1177/1094670514539730

Qasim, A., & Kharbat, F. F. (2020). Blockchain technology, business data analytics, and artificial intelligence: Use in the accounting profession and ideas for inclusion into the accounting curriculum. *Journal of Emerging Technologies in Accounting, 17*(1), 107–117. doi:10.2308/jeta-52649

Rogers, E. M. (1976). New product adoption and diffusion. *The Journal of Consumer Research, 2*(4), 290–301. doi:10.1086/208642

Rogers, E. M. (2003). *Diffusion of innovations* (5th ed.). Free Press.

Rogers, E. M. (2004). A prospective and retrospective look at the Diffusion Model. *Journal of Health Communication, 9*(sup1), 13–19. doi:10.1080/10810730490271449 PMID:14960401

Salloum, S. A., Alhamad, A. Q. M., Al-Emran, M., Monem, A. A., & Shaalan, K. (2019). Exploring students' acceptance of e-learning through developing a comprehensive technology acceptance model. *IEEE Access: Practical Innovations, Open Solutions, 7*, 128445–128462. doi:10.1109/ACCESS.2019.2939467

Sekaran, U., & Bougie, R. (2016). *Research methods for business: A skill building approach*. john Wiley & Sons.

Stoner, G. (2009). Accounting students' IT application skills over a 10-year period. *Accounting Education, 18*(1), 7–31. doi:10.1080/09639280802532224

Turluev, R., & Hadjieva, L. (2021). Artificial Intelligence in Corporate Governance Systems. In *SHS Web of Conferences* (Vol. 93, p. 03015). EDP Sciences. 10.1051hsconf/20219303015

Ucoglu, D. (2020). Current Machine Learning Applications in Accounting and Auditing. *PressAcademia Procedia, 12*(1), 1–7. doi:10.17261/Pressacademia.2020.1337

Yawalkar, M. V. V. (2019). A Study of Artificial Intelligence and its role in Human Resource Management. *International Journal of Research and Analytical Reviews*, *6*(1), 20–24.

Zemankova, A. (2019, December). Artificial Intelligence in Audit and Accounting: Development, Current Trends, Opportunities and Threats-Literature Review. In *2019 International Conference on Control, Artificial Intelligence, Robotics & Optimization (ICCAIRO)* (pp. 148-154). IEEE. 10.1109/ICCAIRO47923.2019.00031

ADDITIONAL READING

Baskerville, R. F., & Hay, D. (2010). The impact of globalization on professional accounting firms: Evidence from New Zealand. *Accounting History*, *15*(3), 285–308. doi:10.1177/1032373210367669

Clarke, M. (2018). Rethinking graduate employability: The role of capital, individual attributes and context. *Studies in Higher Education*, *43*(11), 1923–1937. doi:10.1 080/03075079.2017.1294152

Hassan, H., Hsbollah, H. M., & Ali, R. H. R. M. (2021). Accounting Software Application: Understanding Behavioural Intention to Use and the Moderating Role of Gender. *International Business Education Journal*, *14*(2), 48–60.

Jackson, D., Michelson, G., & Munir, R. (2022). New technology and desired skills of early career accountants", Pacific Accounting Review. doi:10.1108/PAR-04-2021-0045

Jackson, D., Michelson, G., & Munir, R. (2022). Developing accountants for the future: New technology, skills, and the role of stakeholders. *Accounting Education*, 1–28. doi:10.1080/09639284.2022.2057195

Kotb, A., Abdel-Kader, M. G., Allam, A., Halabi, H., & Franklin, E. (2019). Information technology in the British and Irish undergraduate accounting degrees. *Accounting Education*, *28*(5), 445–464. doi:10.1080/09639284.2019.1588135

Maali, B., & Al-Attar, A. M. (2020). Accounting curricula in universities and market needs: The Jordanian case. *SAGE Open*, *10*(1). Advance online publication. doi:10.1177/2158244019899463

Phan, D., Yapa, P., & Nguyen, H. T. (2020). Accounting graduate readiness for work: A case study of South East Asia. *Education + Training*, *63*(3), 392–416. doi:10.1108/ET-02-2019-0036

Prikshat, V., Kumar, S., & Nankervis, A. (2019). Work-readiness integrated competence model conceptualisation and scale development. *Education + Training*, *61*(5), 568–589. doi:10.1108/ET-05-2018-0114

Setyaningrum, D., Muktiyanto, A., & Hermawan, A. A. (2015). How Indonesian accounting education providers meet the demand of the industry. *International Research Journal of Business Studies, 8*(1), 1-11.

Chapter 9

How AI–Enabled Agile Internet of Things Can Enhance the Business Efficiency of China's FinTech Ecosystem

Poshan Yu
(iD) https://orcid.org/0000-0003-1069-3675
Soochow University, China &
Australian Studies Centre, Shanghai
University, China

Michael Sampat
Independent Researcher, Canada

Ruixuan Li
Independent Researcher, China

Shengyuan Lu
(iD) https://orcid.org/0000-0002-9847-4604
Independent Researcher, China

Aashrika Ahuja
Independent Researcher, India

ABSTRACT

According to the 2020-2021 evaluation report on the development of human intelligence computing power in China released by the global market analysis agency IDC, the scale of China's artificial intelligence infrastructure market reached $3.93 billion, a year-on-year increase of 26.8%. For the traditional financial industry, artificial intelligence will be an important step in improving its business efficiency and innovation. AI is an essential technology for traditional risk management and financial supervision. China's FinTech ecosystem will gradually move towards a new ecosystem of "AI + Finance." This chapter aims to study how AI-enabled agile internet of things can enhance the business efficiency of China's FinTech ecosystem. This chapter will investigate the characteristics of China's AI-enabled agile internet of things. Case studies will be used for discussion. In addition, scientometrics analysis through CiteSpace will be conducted. Finally, this chapter will provide suggestions for policymakers to build a sustainable FinTech ecosystem for enterprises.

DOI: 10.4018/978-1-6684-4176-3.ch009

INTRODUCTION

The key to FinTech is the integration of finance and technology, and technological breakthroughs are the driving force of FinTech development. Therefore, considering the promotion of information technology to finance, the development of FinTech can be divided into the following three stages in China (Forbeschina, 2021):

The first stage is 2005-2010—the Internet era. The Internet accelerated the interconnection of the world, leading to the rapid development of Internet commerce and some changes in the financial industry. Specifically, financial network connection, simple traditional financial business online, through the application of IT technology to realize the electronic automation of office and business, to improve business efficiency.

The second stage is the period from 2011 to 2015 which is the era of Mobile Internet. The popularity of smartphones makes it possible for people to communicate anytime and anywhere, which greatly improves the efficiency of network utilization. In this stage, traditional financial institutions build online business platforms, transform traditional financial channels, and realize information sharing and business integration. The explosive growth of China's mobile Internet has driven the rapid development of Internet finance (Ding et al., 2022). At this time, the penetration rate of the Internet in the financial industry is gradually increasing, but it does not change the nature of traditional finance.

The third stage is the strong combination of finance and technology. In the era of artificial intelligence (AI) since 2016, technologies such as cloud computing, big data, blockchain and artificial intelligence have become increasingly mature and become an important driving force for financial innovation. At this stage, the financial industry will change the traditional sources of financial information collection, risk pricing models, transaction decision-making processes and the role of credit intermediaries through new technologies, greatly improving the efficiency and solving the pain points of traditional finance, such as digital currency, big data credit investigation, intelligent investment, and supply chain finance (Chen et al., 2022). At this point, the combination of finance and science and technology has revolutionized traditional finance.

At present, the new generation of artificial intelligence is booming all over the world. The AI-enabled agile Internet of Things (IoT) has also injected new momentum into economic and social development, profoundly changing people's production and lifestyle. According to the 2020-2021 evaluation report on the development of human intelligence computing power in China released by the global market analysis agency IDC (2020), the scale of China's artificial intelligence infrastructure market reached $3.93 billion, a year-on-year increase of 26.8%. At the same time, FinTech represented by artificial intelligence has also ushered in a new stage of transformation and upgrading. For the traditional financial industry, artificial intelligence will be an important step in improving its business efficiency and innovation. AI is an essential technology for traditional risk management and financial supervision. China's FinTech ecosystem will gradually move towards a new ecosystem of "AI + Finance". The development of BSN blockchain (a global public infrastructure network for deploying and running blockchain applications with cross-cloud services, cross-portal and cross-underlying framework) and Robo-advisor (a digital platform for automated, algorithmically driven financial planning services) are both the evidence that artificial intelligence enhancing the Chinese financial market.

This paper aims to study how AI-enabled agile Internet of Things can enhance the business efficiency of China's FinTech ecosystem. This chapter will investigate the characteristics of China's AI-enabled agile Internet of Things. Case studies will be used for discussion. In addition, scientometrics analysis through CiteSpace will be conducted. Finally, this chapter will provide suggestions for policymakers to build a sustainable FinTech ecosystem for enterprises in emerging economies. Since the AI-enabled agile Internet of Things in China's FinTech ecosystem is in its early stages of development, research in this field is scarce. This paper to a certain extent fills the research gap in this field, especially by doing three specific case studies of the Chinese application of AI-enabled agile Internet of Things in the business sector. The paper will give a general and systematic framework of AI-enabled agile Internet of Things in the financial sector to the students, researchers, financial institutions, or some venture capital enterprises. In addition, through the analysis of the Chinese successful case study, this paper also sheds some light on the related companies and research subjects.

For this purpose, this paper proceeds with the following sections. In Section 2, we do the literature reviews of AI-enabled agile Internet of Things in the financial sector. Then the paper introduces and analyzes the characteristics of AI-enabled agile Internet Internet of Things in the Chinese FinTech ecosystem in Section 3. In Section 4, we introduce the methodology and data collection of our bibliometric analysis with CiteSpace. AI-enabled agile Internet of Things research by using the keyword clustering atlas and keyword co-occurrence map analysis through China National Knowledge Infrastructure (CNKI) and Web of Science (WOS) will be analyzed with the methods and data collection in Section 4. While 5 presents the sustainable FinTech ecosystems through integrated AI-enabled agile Internet of Things innovation management, which includes the transformation of financial institutions and innovation in financial technology. In Section 6, we do the three typical case studies of current AI-enabled agile IoTs practice in China's financial sectors from the side of agile Internet of Things applications and its impact on the business sector in the region. Finally, in Section 7 we present the conclusions and outlooks of the development status of the FinTech ecosystem and some FinTech regulatory issues, then give some solutions.

LITERATURE REVIEW

Through the study of some literature, this section first reviews the literature on the performance of financial technology products and commercial banks. The rise of FinTech companies has had a significant impact on the traditional business of commercial banks (Petraliaetal et al., 2019). The study (Chen et al., 2021) shows that digital innovation and FTPs (such as ATM, VTM and mobile banking) promote inclusive financial services, providing new impetus for the banking industry to improve its competitiveness in many aspects. Yang et al. (2021) believe that FinTech products are conducive to commercial banks to reduce bank operating costs, improve service efficiency, enhance risk control ability, and then form a customer-oriented business model based on upgrading the traditional business model, to improve their comprehensive competitiveness. However, the level of these utilities depends on the level of banks using technological innovation.

Secondly, in terms of financial innovation, according to Yang et al. (2009), FinTech is one of the important elements and tools to shape and develop financial innovation. Financial innovation has certain risks, but its value is obvious both theoretically and empirically (Gomber et al., 2018; Ng and Kwok, 2017; Wang et al., 2020; Woicik and Ioannou, 2020). Examples of innovations that are central to FinTech today include various applications of blockchain technologies, new digital advisory and trading systems, artificial intelligence and machine learning, as well as peer-to-peer lending.

Crowdfunding, and mobile payment systems (Philippon, 2015; Darolles, 2016). For example, the innovation in FinTech enables many people in the world without bank deposits to access digital financial services through mobile devices. It also broadens the direction of the upgrading and transformation of traditional financial institutions. Senyo (2020) said the actual use of FinTech innovation will lead to a deepening of financial inclusion. Such innovations can impact existing industry structures, change how existing firms create and deliver products and services, blur industry boundaries, facilitate strategic disintermediation, and provide new gateways for entrepreneurship (Admati and Hellwig, 2013; Philippon, 2016).

In addition, in terms of financial regulation, Degerli (2019) proposed that regulators usually have three different ways to regulate FinTech: ignore, imitate or regulate. Wall (2018) believes regulators are supposed to take into account the opportunities to improve compliance and security created by the AI-enabled agile Internet of things in the emerging FinTech ecosystem and be aware of the problem that AI development is not fully compatible with existing regulatory goals. Ideally, the development of AI is not just a challenge to whether regulators can keep up with the industry transition, it will also create more effective opportunities and channels for regulators to deploy their resources to meet regulatory goals. However, with the increasing growth rate of FinTech innovation and the emergence of new financial patterns, financial companies will face new types of risks, such as network security risks and third-party supplier risks. At the same time, regulators are also facing the impact of system risks and changing financial stability, which requires the use of new tools to address risks faced by the digital FinTech ecosystem (Jagtiani, 2018).

Finally, on the issue of financing channels for SMEs, Bollaert et al. (2020) found that FinTech loans (such as P2P loans) are regarded as the main alternative financial technology solutions for enterprises and entrepreneurs. FinTech companies have opened digital financing channels through new information technology and innovation solutions. It has improved the investment and financing efficiency of SMEs. The research model of Abbasi et al. (2021) suggests that P2P lending FinTech increases access to financing for SMEs. SME managers can meet their needs of corporate liquidity by using P2P lending FinTech. It has been suggested that, when making decisions to lend, P2P lending FinTech incorporates factors that conventional banks may not consider (Lee and Shin, 2018). This makes up for the small scale and weak operational capacity of SMEs to some extent. In addition, Abbasi et al. (2021) found that better institutional quality has a positive regulatory impact on the association between P2P lending FinTech and the financing of SMEs, which provide a more adequate platform for entrepreneurs to establish P2P loan funds.

CHARACTERISTICS OF AI-ENABLED AGILE INTERNET OF THINGS FOR FINTECH ECOSYSTEMS IN CHINA

What is AI? Even today, many people still think that artificial intelligence is a robot with its own ideas. However, artificial intelligence is not human intelligence. It is a scientific and technological product produced by artificial intelligence and will be a container of human intelligence. It can simulate the information process of human consciousness and thinking. Therefore, AI-enabled agile Internet of Things combines AI and IoTs, uses various intelligent technologies to extend and expand based on the Internet, analyzes and processes the perceived and transmitted data and information, and realizes the intelligence of monitoring and control.

China's AI-enabled agile Internet of Things has three characteristics: real-time, digital and intelligent. In terms of real-time, the Internet of things has the characteristics of real-time. It interconnects the physical object and the virtual world in an embedded way, uses the senior to obtain information parameters and transmit them to the control center, which strengthens the control of the physical object and the speed of character interaction, and realizes the real-time control of each production node (Keegan et al., 2022). In the case of large network coverage, the Internet of Things can monitor and regulate the network interconnection of different media states by connecting to the wireless network system (Kolagar et al., 2020). At the same time, the nodes in a large regional range are monitored in real-time to the greatest extent possible, which has a wide area of coverage.

The digital and intelligent characteristics of AI-enabled agile Internet of Things are interrelated. The data layer is the core of the whole Internet of Things system. It is mainly composed of a real-time database, neural network, historical database, model base and knowledge base. Each module has its specific function and strengthens the intelligent level of the Internet of things under the common operation. In the application of the Internet of things, intelligent control is its key core system function. Technicians can use artificial intelligence technology to solve the intelligent control problem in the Internet of things, which maximizes the use function of the Internet of things and meets the needs of more users (Knieps & Bauer, 2022). To some extent, it also improves the operation and work efficiency of the overall FinTech ecosystem in China. In addition, AI-enabled agile Internet of Things brings a higher degree of automation, which can help control risks and improve the speed and accuracy of decision-making (Rejeb et al., 2022). Financial institutions use computer vision, natural language processing, speech recognition, knowledge map, machine learning, robot process automation and other new-generation artificial intelligence technologies to improve the digital level of financial institutions. New technologies such as blockchain, cloud computing and big data accelerate digital transformation and reshape a new digital pattern.

CITESPACE ANALYSIS

Firstly, by studying the literature on AI-enabled agile Internet of Things in CNKI through CiteSpace (Chen, 2017), selecting a keyword as the node type of CiteSpace operation interface for visual analysis of the scientific map, we can get the keyword co-occurrence map in Figure 1 below. The keywords in the atlas are clustered and summarized according to relevant algorithms to obtain the keyword clustering atlas as shown in Figure 2 below. The clustering atlas focuses on reflecting the structural characteristics among clusters, highlighting key nodes and important connections. Large-scale keywords such as AI, IoT and AIoT appear In Figure 1, which shows that these keywords appear more frequently in these 368 documents, and also reflect the intelligent characteristics of China's AI-enabled agile Internet of Things. Combined with the relevant keyword data in the two figures, it can be analyzed that China's

AI-enabled agile Internet of Things involves a wide range of fields, focusing on the construction of smart homes and cities, security hardware equipment and so on. In addition, the keyword clustering related to scenario-based and cloud platforms shown in Figure 2 corresponds to the real-time, digital and interconnected characteristics of China's AI-enabled agile Internet of Things.

Secondly, by studying the literature on AI-enabled agile Internet of Things in WOS through CiteSpace and repeating the above operations, we can get the keyword co-occurrence map in Figure 3 and the keyword clustering map in Figure 4 below. In Figure 3, the distribution of keywords is relatively scattered, and the frequency of keywords is relatively average. However, there are other keywords with relatively small font sizes in Figure 3, such as chemistry, open-label and so on, indicating that scholars still pay attention to other topics. From the keyword clustering in Figure 4, it can be found that some clusters are disconnected from the subject——AIoT. This shows that AI-enabled agile Internet of Things technology has been mentioned in biological research and scientific and technological research, but deeper communication and integration need further research and mining, which establish more new "bridges".

In addition, according to the network structure and the clarity of clustering, CiteSpace provides two indicators: Modularity Q and Man Silhouette. When the Q value is greater than 0.3, the clustering structure is significant. When the S value reaches 0.7, clustering can be considered convincing. The data in the upper left corner of Figure 2 shows that Q=0.624, S=0.9135, and the data in the upper left corner of Figure 4 shows that Q=0.7441, S=0.9339. Therefore, the clustering structures of the two clustering maps are very significant, and the results are convincing.

Finally, comparing Figures 1 and 2 with Figures 3 and 4, it can be found that the literature research on CNKI focuses more on the integrated development of the Internet of Things and other technical fields, which is applied to more innovation of intelligent products and services, highlighting the characteristics of China's AI-enabled agile Internet of Things in three aspects: intelligence, real-time and digitization. The literature on the WOS focuses more on the value of AI-enabled agile Internet of Things in the field of medical technology and biological health research. They are biased towards scientific research, so they can not accurately extract and summarize the characteristics of AI-enabled agile Internet of Things. However, the emergence of the "smart city" in Figure 1 is related to the emergence of "quality of life" in Figure 3, which shows that AI-enabled agile Internet of Things has been widely concerned and recognized by scholars in improving people's living standards and helping people form a healthier and smarter lifestyle. The analysis also reflects the frontier of AI-enabled agile Internet of Things in this field.

Figure 1. The keyword co-occurrence map through CNKI
Data source: CNKI

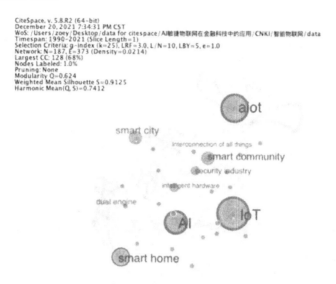

Figure 2. The keyword clustering atlas through CNKI
Data source: CNKI

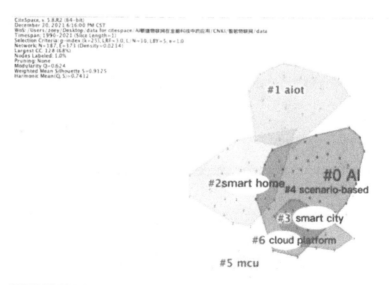

Figure 3. The keyword co-occurrence map through WOS
Data source: Web of Science

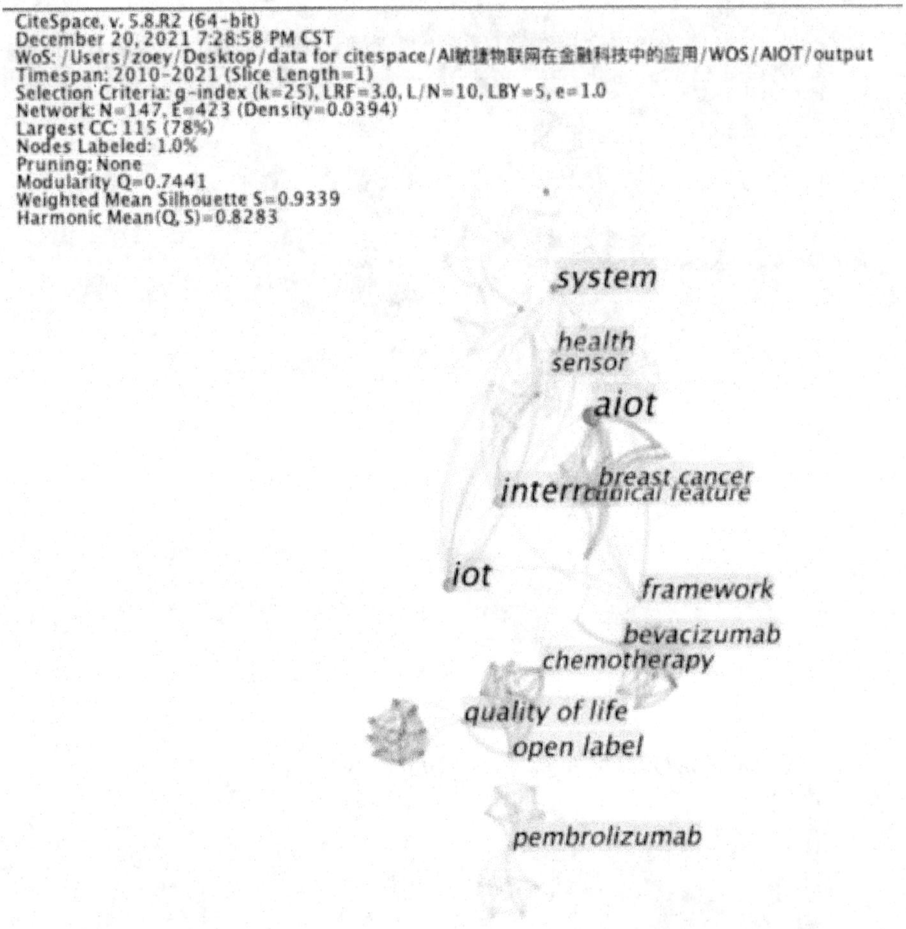

```
CiteSpace, v. 5.8.R2 (64-bit)
December 20, 2021 7:28:58 PM CST
WoS: /Users/zoey/Desktop/data for citespace/AI敏捷物联网在金融科技中的应用/WOS/AIOT/output
Timespan: 2010-2021 (Slice Length=1)
Selection Criteria: g-index (k=25), LRF=3.0, L/N=10, LBY=5, e=1.0
Network: N=147, E=423 (Density=0.0394)
Largest CC: 115 (78%)
Nodes Labeled: 1.0%
Pruning: None
Modularity Q=0.7441
Weighted Mean Silhouette S=0.9339
Harmonic Mean(Q, S)=0.8283
```

system

health
sensor

aiot

breast cancer
interr clinical feature

iot

framework

bevacizumab
chemotherapy

quality of life

open label

pembrolizumab

Figure 4. The keyword clustering atlas through WOS
Data source: Web of Science

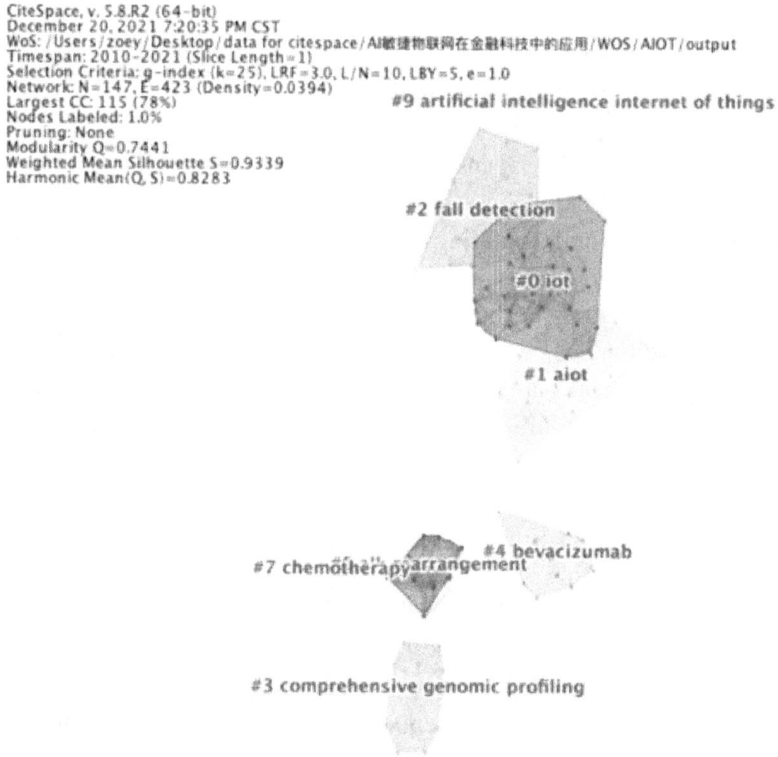

CiteSpace, v. 5.8.R2 (64-bit)
December 20, 2021 7:20:35 PM CST
WoS: /Users/zoey/Desktop/data for citespace/AI赋能物联网在金融科技中的应用/WOS/AIOT/output
Timespan: 2010-2021 (Slice Length=1)
Selection Criteria: g-index (k=25), LRF=3.0, L/N=10, LBY=5, e=1.0
Network: N=147, E=423 (Density=0.0394)
Largest CC: 115 (78%)
Nodes Labeled: 1.0%
Pruning: None
Modularity Q=0.7441
Weighted Mean Silhouette S=0.9339
Harmonic Mean(Q, S)=0.8283

#9 artificial intelligence internet of things

#2 fall detection

#0 iot

#1 aiot

#4 bevacizumab

#7 chemotherapyarrangement

#3 comprehensive genomic profiling

SUSTAINABLE FINTECH ECOSYSTEMS THROUGH INTEGRATED AI-ENABLED AGILE INTERNET OF THINGS INNOVATION MANAGEMENT

With the rapid development of network technology and Internet technology, the innovation of various traditional Chinese industries is booming. In a broad sense of view, FinTech is the application of various advanced technologies in the financial field to support the development of the financial industry (Darolles, 2016). Innovative development of the sustainable FinTech ecosystem includes digital innovation in the financial sector and technology-supported business model innovation, such as new blockchain technologies, P2P lending, mobile payment systems, mobile banking and so on. These innovations can influence the existing business model, change the way that enterprises produce and sell products, promote enterprise internal innovation management, improve business efficiency, promote the effective provision of financial services, and enhance the core competitiveness of the overall economy. This section will study China's FinTech ecosystem innovation management through integrated AI-enabled agile Internet of Things from the perspective of financial institutions and financial technologies.

Transformation of Financial Institutions

From the perspective of financial institutions, the transformation and expansion of traditional commercial banks into the online mobile banking mode is a classic example of the innovation and upgrading of the FinTech ecosystem (Yu et al., 2022). In the era of artificial intelligence, commercial banks' industrial model, management mode and operation form will change greatly. With the rapid development of China's economy and the deep opening of foreign economic and trade, traditional or regional commercial banks are not only limited by their conditions but also face internal competition and pressure from international commercial banks who seek to broaden their economic model in China. Thus, commercial banks must accelerate the application of AI-enabled agile Internet of Things, involving the digitalization, automation and intelligence of different business models. The innovative management improvement of the banking business not only lies in internal operation and management efficiency but also in enabling customers to interact remotely and even open bank accounts from the comfort of home. Only by enhancing the ability of financial service, the core competitiveness of commercial banks can be truly improved. With the theoretical support mentioned above, the innovative management of commercial banks through AI-enabled agile Internet of Things can be discussed from the following three specific measures.

Accurate Marketing and Intelligent Services

Based on the common drive of accurate marketing and intelligent services, realizing the precise delivery of retail business is the primary direction of the innovation and transformation of commercial banks through the AI-enabled agile Internet of Things in the era of artificial intelligence. On the one hand, in the face of the increasingly fierce customer group competition of commercial banks, it needs to spend a lot of manpower, material and financial resources to carry out in-depth investigation and analysis, to accurately lock the targeted customer groups in line with the current situation of banks (Vlačić et al, 2021). Therefore, how to improve the new efficiency of customer groups and reduce the new cost of customer groups has become an important subject and common concern for commercial banks. Through the help of accurate analysis of AI-enabled agile Internet of Things, data locking can be achieved for the target customers of commercial banks, thus laying a solid foundation for efficient and precise marketing.

On the other hand, to solve the current dilemma of insufficient stock services of commercial banks, commercial banks should actively develop intelligent investment consulting, promote the effective supplement of intelligent services to staff services, and constantly improve the service experience of customer groups (Zhang, 2021). For example, commercial banks have expanded the customer service platform of intelligent robots, and let the platform robots provide intelligent and automatic responses to customer questions according to the needs and preferences of customer groups from multiple levels, angles and aspects. Based on simplicity and timeliness, they can provide effective solutions to customer problems and collect customers' feedback and evaluation. It can be seen that the AI-enabled agile Internet of Things has promoted the construction of marketing and service platforms, and realizes the collaborative mutual assistance and mutual empowerment of commercial bank marketing and service, to truly improve the operating environment of commercial banks (Lin et al., 2013).

Standardized Investment Consulting and Customized Scheme

Promoting the continuous integration of standardized investment consulting and customized schemes, and ensuring the efficient coordination of institutional business is the core direction of commercial banks' innovation and transformation through AI-enabled agile Internet of things in the era of artificial intelligence (Kumar & Mehany, 2022). On the one hand, commercial banks actively promote standardized intelligent investment consulting services, with the help of the Internet of Things big data technology with AI as the core, so that the customer service level of commercial banking institutions continues to improve. This not only enhances the satisfaction of customer groups but also is conducive to the expansion of its institutional business, improving the comprehensive income generation of commercial banks and their profitability.

On the other hand, commercial banks can understand customer preferences and quickly match customer needs with the help of intelligent Internet of things technology. Then, they can fully consider and analyze the high threshold, high standards and high requirements of some customers for services, and continuously polish the corresponding service schemes to form a comprehensive and scientific customized institutional business service content, which improves customer stickiness and realize the rapid growth of business income.

Targeted Support and Inclusive Finance

Ensuring the cooperation of targeted support and inclusive finance is an important complementary direction for the innovation and transformation of commercial banks through AI-enabled agile Internet of Things in the era of artificial intelligence. Its goal is to achieve the all-around development of commercial banking enterprise business. In the profit model of commercial banks with the deposit and loan interest spread as the core, the enterprise business occupies a very important position, especially the enterprise credit granting and financing have almost become an important sector to determine the operating level of commercial banks (Xiao, 2020). Therefore, commercial banks should use the technical power of AI-enabled agile Internet of Things to gradually reduce their excessive reliance on enterprise credit business.

Based on the relevant policies and technology finance strategies of the national regulatory authorities, commercial banks can increase investment in inclusive financial technology, broaden the financing channels of Internet investment, innovate characteristic credit products, such as P2P lending, crowd-funding financing and so on, develop and improve loan products such as renewal without repayment of principal and repayment with borrowing, to improve the convenience of loan use and reduce the comprehensive financial cost of financing for SMEs (Yu et at.). This is conducive to promoting the targeted credit to SMEs, optimizing the credit products and services to individual industrial and commercial households, expanding the coverage of inclusive financial services, realizing the common growth of banks and enterprises, and laying a solid foundation for realizing the all-round development of enterprise business.

Innovation in Financial Technology

Policy Support

Since 2019, with the further maturity of blockchain technology and the continuous expansion of industry applications, countries around the world have had a deeper understanding of blockchain technology and its value, realizing that blockchain is an important part of the new generation of the information technology revolution, and have launched policies to encourage and give guidance. China's support for blockchain is also increasing. On April 20, 2020, the National Development and Reform Commission for the first time clarified the scope of "new infrastructure", including three aspects: information infrastructure, integrated infrastructure and innovation infrastructure, and pointed out that blockchain and the Internet of Things belong to information infrastructure. As shown in the figure below, during this period, the blockchain industrial policies ushered in a blowout growth. As of December 31, 2020, the central government and various ministries and commissions have issued 62 blockchain relevant policies in 2020, up nearly four times compared with 2019 (QKLW, 2021).

Figure 5. Number of policies from 2016 to 2020
Data source: Zero One Think Tank Information Technology

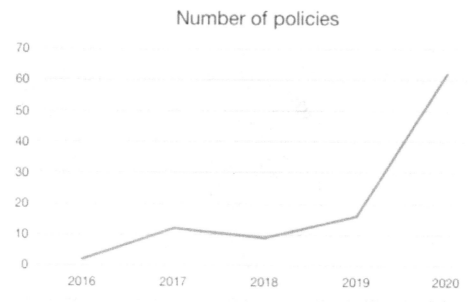

Data source: Zero One Think Tank Information Technology

In 2020, the blockchain policy involve more diversified industries, including economy, finance, supervision, logistics, government affairs, agriculture and other aspects. At the same time, many policies emphasize expanding the interaction between blockchain and the Internet of Things, big data, AI, cloud computing and other front-end technologies. As can be seen from the figure below, among the keywords of blockchain policies issued by local governments, "big data" accounts for 33.3%, "the Internet" accounts for 11.1%, and "the logistics industry" accounted for 8.33%. This indicates that the interaction of blockchain technology and big data has been relatively popular, and the advanced advantages in the logistics industry are also obvious.

Figure 6. Keywords proportion of blockchain policies
Data source: Zero One Think Tank Information Technology

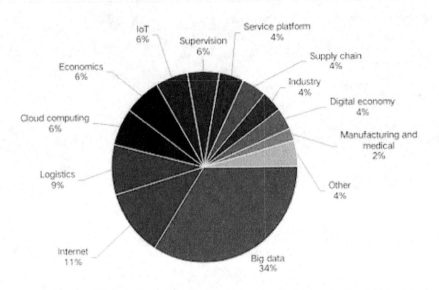

Data source:Zero One Think Tank Information Technology

In addition, the keywords——"economy" "Internet of things" and "cloud computing" are about 6%, it can be seen that after being included in the scope of new infrastructure, blockchain has gradually accelerated the application of new infrastructure and the building of smart city together with other cutting-edge technologies, "blockchain+" gradually become the work points of the district government. The construction of "blockchain+" and other application scenarios can promote the deep integration of all walks of life and promote technological innovation and industrial development. At present, blockchain technology has been widely used in emerging fields such as the Internet of Things, digital economy, intelligent manufacturing, digital assets and so on.

To sum up, the major measure of including blockchain in the scope of new infrastructure marks the gradually enhanced universality of blockchain technology, which also puts forward certain requirements for the richness and universality of blockchain applications. The interaction and linkage of blockchain and other cutting-edge technologies and the integration of various industries have become a future development trend.

"Blockchain+IoT" Enables the Digital Transformation of FinTech

Finance is an industry of business risks. The core of risk assessment, risk pricing and risk monitoring is information processing. The recording, collection and analysis of credible data will allow people or institutions who have not been able to access financial services to enter the scope of financial services (Zou, 2021). In the era of big data, the number of the Internet of Things devices will exceed the number of mobile Internet devices, and the compatibility of the Internet of Things data will also far exceed the Internet data. The Internet of Things data will become an important part of the data factor market. In addition, the blockchain has both the functions of information Internet and value Internet, corresponding to the two application directions of the blockchain, and has many binding points with the Internet of Things. Therefore, the "blockchain+IoT" will be one of the important trends in the new infrastructure, and on this basis, it will play an important role in the FinTech ecosystem.

"Blockchain+IoT" enables the Internet of Things data to ensure security and credibility at a higher level of technology, and can significantly improve the existing FinTech services. At present, the digital RMB has made pilot trials on E-bike charging piles and automatic retail machines (Shen & Hou, 2021). Take automatic charging scenarios of shared E-bike as an example, Internet of Things devices can participate in digital currency transactions and call smart contracts within the blockchain. When the shared E-bike finds the corresponding charging pile and the charging plug is in a state for charging, the data cable on the charging plug will interact between the charging pile and the E-bike (Van et al., 2022). E-bikes reflect their charging needs according to their existing electricity, while the charging pile provides feedback in the form of digital currency transfer transactions, and writes the transaction records into the blockchain. When the charging pile checks the digital currency receipt record, it starts charging the shared E-bike. In this process, the payment data and transaction records between E-bike and charging piles are automatically transmitted into the blockchain, reducing human intervention and helping to ensure the accuracy of the data in the chain link.

In addition, from the example above, it is not difficult to see that the joint interaction between blockchain and Internet of Things devices has created a better payment scenario for digital RMB. Double offline payment or non-contact payment is more suitable for payment scenarios between devices than credit card swiping or QR code scanning (Zou, 2021). Credit card or QR code scanning is paid through bank accounts or third-party payment platforms. When the connected equipment is too much, such payment methods may be inefficient. However, "Blockchain+IoT" has the characteristics of open inclusiveness and data automation, when the Internet of things equipment ID bound the digital wallet address, the data storage and transmission system can quickly produce economic value interaction. The Internet of Things' economic activities related to data can also be calculated through the digital RMB (Shen & Hou, 2021). This improves the operational efficiency between machines or equipment and also promotes the application of digital RMB.

Moreover, the risk management platform built based on the "Blockchain+IoT" technology monitors the asset data through the Internet of Things equipment and uses the blockchain technology to comprehensively record the relevant data, which is conducive to alleviating the problem of information asymmetry and improving the credibility of the assets. To some extent, the risk management platform has improved the difficulty and expensive financing of some enterprises, and also improves the overall security of the FinTech ecosystem.

CASE STUDIES ———CURRENT AI-ENABLED AGILE IOT PRACTICE IN CHINA FINANCIAL SECTORS: AGILE INTERNET OF THINGS PRACTICE AND ITS IMPACT ON THE BUSINESS SECTOR IN THE REGION

Case 1: Business Automation in FinTech using Agile IoT-Digital Commercial Banking

The 2021 World AI Conference was recently held in Shanghai. With the theme of 'Digital New Bank of Communications has more 'AI' ', Bank of Communications focuses on displaying a series of financial products created by itself to enable the digital transformation of cities. The innovation of BCM mainly has two aspects. On the one hand, BCM created a series of financial products serving the society and economy to create better living conditions for people. On the other hand, as one of the pilot operating institutions of digital RMB, BCM also showed to the public the consumption scene of digital RMB used in self-service vending machines, food businesses and small supermarkets and other stores at this conference.

FinTech Helps Improve People's Living Standard

Bank of Communications used big data and agile IoTs together with Shanghai's government services and urban operation system, to launch a series of products and services with the theme of 'Bank of Communications e affairs'. Focusing on the needs of people's livelihood and with the attributes of bank financial services, they effectively assist the government to improve its ability to serve small and micro enterprises and citizens through digital means (Lyons et al., 2021).

For example, the mini-program of 'Huimin medical treatment' is a digital credit product tailored by the Bank of Communications with the promotion and digital transformation of Shanghai medical payment, for the citizens with Shanghai medical insurance. Citizens can realize the fast online application of insurance money through the 'Sui Shen Ban' APP. By reshaping the medical payment process, the product greatly improves the health institutions, reduces the patients' waiting time, and further alleviates the congestion of registration payments during peak times. It is understood that the product has covered more than 400 public medical institutions in Shanghai, and the application approval rate is more than 95% (Yang, 2021).

In addition, based on the consideration of SMEs and the real economy, the Bank of Communications has also launched 'convenient account opening', 'inclusive e-loan', 'cross-border e-finance' and other financial products. Through online credit, the investment and financing channels for SMEs have become much broader. Through mobile banking, people can do credit certification and evaluation quickly and easily participate in financial activities. The agile IoT coordinates big data, carries out risk assessment and analysis on all kinds of financial products, and summarizes and promotes financial hot spots, to escort family financial management to the greatest extent. All of these fully reflect the service concept of the Bank of Communications of 'running more data and allowing customers to run less,' and show the application achievements of new technologies such as big data and artificial intelligence.

Digital RMB Helps with the New Consumption Experience

In recent years, the collection and payment functions of third-party payment platforms such as WeChat and Alipay have become people's daily used tools, which has also laid the foundation for the pilot issuance of digital RMB. As of June 30, 2021, the pilot scenarios of digital RMB have exceeded 1.32 million, covering living payment, catering services, transportation, shopping and consumption, government services and other fields according to the White Paper on China Digital RMB Research and Development Progress on the official website of the central bank. More than 20.87 million personal accounts and more than 3.51 million corporate accounts have been opened, with a total amount of about 34.5 billion yuan and more than 70.75 million transactions.

The rapid development of the e-commerce economy has made it possible for JD Group and Bank of Communications jointly issued 20 million digital RMB gift packages in Shanghai and Suzhou during the 2021 Double 12 shopping festival activities. The activity realized the sharing of digital RMB consumption scenarios between Shanghai and Jiangsu and strengthened the linkage of digital RMB consumption between Shanghai and Jiangsu (Shen & Hou, 2021). During the cooperation between BCM and Jingdong technology company (JDT), JDT gave support to enterprises, merchants, and financial institutions to get access to the digital RMB system and brought users a better digital RMB consumption experience relied on the "supply chain + scene + technology" multiple advantages and its strong technical service output ability and through the bank of communications newly developed "digital wallet" platform.

Digital RMB helps to improve the efficiency and security of the payment system, provides a new universal payment method for the public, and further improves the financial ability to serve the real economy and expand the universality of finance (Aysan & Kayani, 2022).

Case 2: Cloud-Based Intelligent IoT and Wireless Payment Systems Increasing Business Efficiency

With the development of new technologies such as intelligent IoT, big data, blockchain and cloud computing, the combination of intelligent IoT technology based on 'cloud' and other emerging technologies have become an important choice to promote the development of inclusive finance and the structural reform of the supply front. They use information technology methods to empower inclusive product innovation, business process transformation and other aspects, effectively reduce information asymmetry and improve the operational efficiency of the FinTech ecosystem, and promote the development of inclusive finance. The following takes China's small and micro enterprises as an example and elaborates this from two perspectives.

Blockchain Enables the Authenticity of SMEs Information

The Blockchain is a technical system integrating the core and underlying technologies such as data storage, distributed computing, cryptography, point-to-point network, and consensus algorithm. The block in the blockchain represents the information block with data records, and the chain represents the chain-link structure of the information block (Wang, 2021). Since the outbreak of COVID-19, financial institutions have successfully provided financing services for small and micro enterprises in the industrial chain through blockchain technology to help them relieve their liquidity pressure and promote their resumption of work and production.

Blockchain takes the method of centralized bookkeeping and distributed storage, which ensures the security of data storage and improves collaborative efficiency (Kowalski et al., 2021). In addition, the decentralization of blockchain and data traceability can improve the credibility of enterprise data, and effectively solves the problems such as information asymmetry and untimely information update. For example, the bank of Jiangsu launched 'blockchain +' trade services, linked the state administration of foreign exchange cross-border trade chain service platform and Jiangsu international trade single window information through opening banking platform technology, solved the problem of the traditional trade financing process information asymmetry. The trade service also allows the entire online operation, automatic verification declaration, helps small and medium-sized enterprises trade financing time shorten to minutes (Wang, 2021).

The Internet of Things Provides Soft Power for SMEs

When it comes to the IoT, 'the Internet of Things' is its key. From the characteristics of the intelligent IoT mentioned above, it is not difficult to see that the IoT can provide objective and effective information for small and micro-enterprises. It can use direct connection technology with the terminal sensors of financial institutions to realize real-time and objective data collection. In addition, IoT technology can be applied to the daily operation scenarios of small and medium-sized enterprises. Huge network expansion can be used to integrate with the real economy and the enterprise's financial needs and risks will be automatically analyzed combined with big data to realize smart financial services (Yu et al, 2022). For example, FinTech companies can use IoT technology to transform the logistics information in the daily operation process of small and medium-sized enterprises into transaction credit which can be used in enterprise financing risk control.

Cloud Computing Provides Intelligent Analysis for the Financing of SMEs

Cloud computing is a kind of distributed computing that uses the network 'cloud' to decompose huge data computing processing programs into countless small programs, then uses the analysis system distributed around the data, and finally summarizes and feedback the results (Song et al., 2020). Cloud computing promotes financial institutions to deal with massive amounts of financial data more quickly, and to some extent makes financial institutions focus on the financial service innovation of SMEs, and realize large-scale and intensive business development.

Case 3: Contribution of FinTech to the Sustainable Development in the Digital Age: Ant Forest and Land Restoration

Ant Forest, a land restoration method initiated by Alibaba, China's largest FinTech company, has made significant progress in land restoration in degraded China. It represents a new model of transforming the user's environmental intentions and activities into practical environmental benefits by planting trees (Ding et al., 2018).

Ant Forest is an application, but also a carbon savings account and public welfare activity. Green energy points are obtained when the user performs low-carbon activities, which can be accumulated to a degree to program a virtual tree (Rukikaire, 2019). When these "trees" grow up, locals can harvest fruit from some mature "trees" and sell it on Ant Forest shopping platforms. For example, fruit juice made from hawthorn is a popular drink in China. The Ant Forest platform helps locals advertise the product and sell it online through a campaign themed "plant trees together and reap fruit together". For one thing, this helps help solve the restoration of local land desertification. Secondly, this type of activity promotes local social and economic development and the integration of the economy in different regions of China. Except local farmers receive some profit, the remaining funds are donated to the China Foundation to protect the environment in western Chinese provinces and help local families out of poverty.

FinTech can play an important role in combining the individual and private sectors to achieve the public good (Galazetal, 2018). FinTech can manage its customers through agile Internet of things, big data and cloud platform technologies and increase revenue without additional costs. The agile IoTs enable the platform to build personal carbon accounts that connect users to environmental protection, which facilitates a full understanding of people's carbon footprint. Wherever these users are located, they can contribute to carbon reduction and socioeconomic benefits. For example, information technology that connects users and land degraded areas can significantly help achieve land recovery in areas facing desertification risk and other types of environmental problems. This raises individual enthusiasm and inspires the potential for public transformation (Luan & Li, 2018). In addition, the intelligent Internet of Things, big data and other technologies enable FinTech to use online green credit to guide capital flows, broaden the channels for providing loan support for environment-related industries, and provide funds to ecological or environmental protection industries, which promote a virtuous cycle of ecological recovery. Therefore Ant Forest has a great impact on the green financial model, which is conducive to reducing carbon emissions, helping to achieve carbon neutrality, and promoting a low-carbon economy and sustainable development.

The greatest value of Ant Forest is that it changes people's lifestyles and promotes low-carbon awareness and social responsibility, contributing to sustainable sustainability, which is a long-term success.

CONCLUSION AND RECOMMENDATIONS

In the background of global economic development and China's financial opening-up, based on new technologies such as AI-enabled agile Internet of things, cloud computing and blockchain, FinTech with data as the core continues to develop. The AI-enabled agile Internet of Things has improved the business efficiency of China's FinTech ecosystem and effectively promotes financial innovation and the transformation and upgrading of financial institutions. However, development is not achieved overnight. There is still a lot of room for improvement in the new ecosystem of "AI + FinTech". On the one hand, compared with traditional financial services, FinTech uses the powerful functions of new technologies to provide users with more convenient, efficient and cheaper precision services. However, on the other hand, behind the rapid development of FinTech, there may be problems such as financial chaos, moral risks and personal privacy protection and so on, which not only bring greater risks to the majority of investors but also make financial regulators face severe challenges. Therefore, the support of enriching policy systems, the transformation of the traditional financial supervision, the privacy of users' data under cloud payment, and the security development of financial technology are all aspects that we need to focus on and improve.

In this paper, by analyzing the development status of the FinTech ecosystem in China, we focus on the FinTech regulatory issues, which include Business closed-loop, Asset-light and high leverage, excessive consumption view, and privacy problems. Then we give several related solutions such as promoting the regulatory sandbox, implementing separate business management, and using the new regulatory path to the FinTech regulatory problems we analyzed.

Development Status of the FinTech Ecosystem

According to the China FinTech Report (2020), as of 2019, global FinTech financing reached $150 billion. Since 2015, China's FinTech investment and financing development has seized historical opportunities, reaching a high record in 2018, and has slowed down in the last two years. In terms of investment, the total technical investment of Chinese financial institutions reached 177.09 billion yuan, of which the banking industry accounted for at most 68.6%. The proportion of capital investment in insurance, securities and funds has also increased year by year. Due to the COVID-19 epidemic, FinTech investment and financing funds declined in the first half of 2020, but the impact on the scale of investment in FinTech is not large. On the contrary, in the long run, the COVID-19 epidemic has led to the urgent digital transformation of financial institutions, thus promoting the further innovation and application of FinTech. FinTech services are also constantly enriched, including payment, financial credit, investment, insurance, intelligent investment consulting, wealth management, etc. It can be seen that in recent years, the amount of FinTech investment and financing has been continuously rising, and the business scope is constantly expanding, the overall trend shows a step-by-step upward trend.

In addition, in China's FinTech ecosystem, FinTech companies dominated by large companies have the possibility of monopoly (Li et al., 2020). Large platforms have a wide range of business and technology permeates types of financial services. They take advantage of the congenital conditions of abundant capital to gather a large number of user information and data and quickly occupy the market segments such as payment, lending, and finance management. Therefore, the development opportunities of small companies will be small, which presents an industry pattern dominated by large companies and small companies compete fiercely on segment tracks.

FinTech Regulatory Issues

Business Closed-Loop

FinTech companies have developed rapidly, involving a wide range of areas and cross nesting between businesses. There may be co-debt risk between some financial products. FinTech companies firstly take payment as the starting point, accumulate a large number of user information, and then go deep into FinTech and insurance technology platforms, which use technology to conduct an accurate credit evaluation for users, and finally provide small and microloans to users, to promote the expansion of business scope. This forms a closed-loop ecological chain of "industrial chain + finance + technology". Under this ecosystem, financial activities continue to operate, funds are constantly circulating, and business processes are difficult to penetrate, resulting in supervision being unable to effectively monitor risks promptly, and inevitably creating certain regulatory gaps, which may lead to arbitrage activities. The risk caused by a closed loop is hidden, sudden and infectious. Once triggered, it will quickly spread across the market, causing immeasurable losses.

Asset-Light and High Leverage

To accelerate the efficiency of capital operation and make greater use of the original funds, FinTech companies mostly use asset securitization means to realize the company's asset-light and high leverage operation mode, to realize the rapid expansion of capital amount and liquidity. Huang (2020) believes that Ant Group's "Ant Cash Now" platform uses more than 3 billion yuan of principal and passes more than 40 loans through the asset-backed securitization (ABS) cycle, issuing more than 300 billion yuan of loans. There is high leverage more than 100 times in this progress. "Ant Cash Now" makes high profits and shifts the risk to investors who buy financial products. High yield, high risk. The continuous expansion of capital is also accompanied by the expansion of risk. Some investors have a weak ability to resist risks and low financial literacy. Once there are big problems in the process of internal circulation, neither investors nor FinTech companies will be unable to bear them, and it may even cause a chain reaction in the whole financial industry and pose a threat to the country's financial security.

Excessive Consumption View

From the case analysis above, it is not difficult to see that FinTech companies have alleviated the expensive financing problems of SMEs through AI-enabled agile Internet of Things and blockchain to a certain extent. They have played a positive role in reducing information asymmetry, reducing transaction costs and improving operating efficiency, especially the penetration in the consumer finance field providing inclusive financial services for enterprises and individual users, thus gaining a lot of recognition. However, for now, FinTech companies have not achieved real inclusive finance. Taking the actual operation of Ant Group as an example, Alipay has lowered the threshold of investment and expanded the scope of financial services. "Ant Credit Pay" makes more people experience the convenience of using first before paying, but ignores the supervision of personal credit problems. Most of the "Ant Credit Pay" credit line is used for consumption, which promotes the young people's view of advanced consumption and even makes them fall into huge online loans in debt due to excessive consumption (Yu et al., 2022). Overdrawing the future wealth in advance can be easy to form a bad consumption view and abnormal values, which seriously affect the family savings. Such a situation also deviates from the essence of FinTech investment in real businesses, helping SMEs and improving the development of inclusive finance.

Privacy Problem

Convenient and efficient technology is accompanied by network risks such as customer information leakage, hackers, remote electronic fraud and so on (Liu, 2021). Because the FinTech ecosystem is based on emerging science and technologies such as AI-enabled Internet of Things and big data, the security of sensitive customer data and customers' privacy information has become a major challenge in FinTech supervision. Any lack of security on the FinTech side will directly affect the security of the banks' systems as well as the financial accounts it holds (Degerli, 2019). This is not only the security of the financial technology ecosystem, but it also represents people's trust in artificial intelligence or technology intelligence, when people are no longer afraid of the process of collecting and transmitting personal private data through technical information systems, FinTech can play their utility angle and help the development of human society and economy.

Supervisory Measures

Promote the Regulatory Sandbox

In 2015, the Financial Conduct Authority (FCA) first introduced the concept of the "Regulatory Sandbox" and introduced it into financial regulation. The regulatory sandbox program was widely welcomed internationally. In December 2019, the People's Bank of China also first carried out a pilot FinTech supervision program in Beijing, introducing and building a Chinese version of the "regulatory sandbox" in line with China's national conditions. Regulatory sandbox as a supervised safety test area, by setting up restrictive conditions and formulate risk management measures, allowing enterprises to test innovative products, services and business models with real individual users and enterprise users in a real market environment, which is conducive to reducing the time of innovative ideas into the market and regulatory uncertainty (Yu et al., 2022).

By opening up pilot regulatory sandboxes and testing financial innovative products, regulators can effectively explore possible risks, effectively formulate solutions to relevant problems, and keep the bottom line of no systemic risks occurring. Zhang (2018) believes that the regulatory sandbox not only realizes the flexible supervision of the government, promotes the cooperation between the government and the regulatory objects, but also protects the consumers of innovative financial products and prevents financial risks. At present, increasingly innovative financial products also pose a great challenge to China's traditional financial regulation. The emergence of regulatory sandboxes has prompted us to use modern information technology to improve the quality and efficiency of finance, and to create a positive, safe, inclusive and open FinTech innovation and development environment.

Implement Separate Business Management

FinTech companies continue to launch various kinds of financial products. The overlapping and superposition of products make it impossible for regulators to implement precise measures. Based on this, on the one hand, FinTech companies need to cooperate with regulatory departments, carefully divide financial products according to their nature, timely rectify businesses beyond the scope, and reduce the ecological closed loop of payment business development, to eliminate some financial risks. On the other hand, regulatory authorities need to formulate detailed regulatory guidelines, accurately classify FinTech products and services, and formulate different risk regulatory measures for different businesses (Anagnostopoulos, 2018). They can strengthen macro-prudential management, different regulatory authorities implement supervision according to their business scope. For businesses that are difficult to be divided, regulators are supposed to negotiate and cooperate for joint-supervision. Products with homogeneous services for FinTech companies, commercial banks, insurance, securities and other institutions shall be included in a unified regulatory framework and implemented by unified regulatory standards.

New Regulatory Path

Regulators can promote a new regulatory path which is the trinity of regulatory technology, risk control technology and safety technology. Regulatory technology aims to use big data, AI-enabled agile Internet of Things and other technologies to collect, analyze and manage the data, starting from the use of historical data and past regulatory experience, to promote the transformation and upgrading of the regulatory model. Risk control technology aims to complete the risk control model, rely on the real-time update performance of cloud computing, accurately identify and conduct dynamic management of the risks that consumers may face, and promote the improvement of the whole process of risk control including prior prevention, in-process monitoring and post-audit. Security technology is designed to ensure the safe operation of the FinTech ecosystem. Personal data needs to be protected, and data use also needs the corresponding code of conduct and moral standards.

ACKNOWLEDGMENT

The authors extend sincere gratitude to:

• Our colleagues from Soochow University, the Australian Studies Centre of Shanghai University, KCA University and Krirk University as well as the independent research colleagues who provided insight and expertise that greatly assisted the research, although they may not agree with all of the interpretations/conclusions of this chapter.

• China Knowledge for supporting our research.

• The Editor and the International Editorial Advisory Board (IEAB) of this book who initially desk reviewed, arranged a rigorous double/triple blind review process and conducted a thorough, minute and critical final review before accepting the chapter for publication.

All anonymous reviewers who provided very constructive feedbacks for thorough revision, improvement and fine tuning of the chapter.

REFERENCES

Abbasi, K., Alam, A., Brohi, N. A., Brohi, I. A., & Nasim, S. (2021). P2P lending Fintechs and SMEs' access to finance. *Economics Letters*, *204*, 109890. doi:10.1016/j.econlet.2021.109890

Admati, A. R., & Hellwig, M. (2013). *The Bankers' New Clothes*. Princeton University Press.

Anagnostopoulos, I. (2018). Fintech and regtech: Impact on regulators and banks. *Journal of Economics and Business*, *100*, 7–25. doi:10.1016/j.jeconbus.2018.07.003

Aysan, A.F., & Kayani, F.N. (2022). China's transition to a digital currency does it threaten dollarization? *Asia and the Global Economy*, *2*(1).

Bollaert, H., Lopez-de-Silanes, F., & Schwienbacher, A. (2021). Fintech and access to finance. *Journal of Corporate Finance*, *68*, 101941. doi:10.1016/j.jcorpfin.2021.101941

Chen, C. (2017). Science Mapping: A Systematic Review of the Literature. *Journal of Data and Information Science*, *2*(2), 1–40. doi:10.1515/jdis-2017-0006

Chen, X., Teng, L., & Chen, W. (2022). How does FinTech affect the development of the digital economy? evidence from China. *The North American Journal of Economics and Finance*, *61*, 61. doi:10.1016/j.najef.2022.101697

Chen, X., You, X., & Chang, V. (2021). FinTech and commercial banks' performance in China: A leap forward or survival of the fittest? *Technological Forecasting and Social Change*, *166*, 120645. doi:10.1016/j.techfore.2021.120645

China FinTech Report. (2020). https://report.iresearch.cn/wx/report.aspxid=3687.shtml

Darolles, S. (2016). The rise of Fintechs and their regulation. *April Finance. Stability Rev.*, *20*.

Degerli, K. (2019). Regulatory Challenges and Solutions for Fintech in Turkey. *Procedia Computer Science*, *158*, 929–937. doi:10.1016/j.procs.2019.09.133

Ding, D., Chong, G., Lee, K. C., & Cheng, T. L. (2018). From Ant Financial to Alibaba's Rural Taobao Strategy - How Fintech Is Transforming Social Inclusion. In *Handbook of Blockchain, Digital Finance, and Inclusion* (Vol. 1). Academic Press.

Ding, N., Gu, L., & Peng, Y. (2022). Fintech, financial constraints and innovation: Evidence from China. *Journal of Corporate Finance*, *73*, 73. doi:10.1016/j.jcorpfin.2022.102194

Forbeschina. (2021). *How will fintech drive the development of The Times?* http://www.forbeschina.com/entrepreneur/56653

Galaz, V., Crona, B., Dauriach, A., Scholtens, B., & Steffen, W. (2018). Finance and the Earth system – exploring the links between financial actors and non-linear changes in the climate system. *Global Environmental Change*, *53*, 296–302. doi:10.1016/j.gloenvcha.2018.09.008

Gomber, P., Kauffman, R. J., Parker, C., & Weber, B. W. (2018). On the Fintech revolution: Interpreting the forces of innovation, disruption, and transformation in financial services. *Journal of Management Information Systems*, *35*(1), 220–265. doi:10.1080/07421222.2018.1440766

Huang, Q. F. (2020). *Structural reform—problems and Countermeasures of China's economy*. Beijing United Press.

IDC. (2020). *2020-2021 evaluation report on the development of human intelligence computing power in China.* https://baijiahao.baidu.com/s?id=1686138096205100 527&wfr=spider&for=pc

Jagtiani, J., & John, K. (2018). Fintech: The Impact on Consumers and Regulatory Responses. *Journal of Economics and Business*, *100*, 1–6. doi:10.1016/j.jeconbus.2018.11.002

Keegan, B. J., Canhoto, A. I., & Yen, D. A.-W. (2022). Power negotiation on the tango dancefloor: The adoption of AI in B2B marketing. *Industrial Marketing Management*, *100*, 100. doi:10.1016/j.indmarman.2021.11.001

Knieps, G., & Bauer, J. M. (2022). Internet of things and the economics of 5G-based local industrial networks. *Telecommunications Policy*, *46*(4), 102261. doi:10.1016/j.telpol.2021.102261

Kolagar, M., Parida, V., Sjödin, D., & Wincent, J. (2020). An agile co-creation process for digital servitization: A micro-service innovation approach. *Journal of Business Research*, *112*, 478–491. doi:10.1016/j.jbusres.2020.01.009

Kowalski, M., Lee, Z. W. Y., & Chan, T. K. H. (2021). Blockchain technology and trust relationships in trade finance. *Technological Forecasting and Social Change*, *166*, 166. doi:10.1016/j.techfore.2021.120641

Kumar, S., & Mehany, M. S. H. M. (2022). A standardized framework for quantitative assessment of cities' socioeconomic resilience and its improvement measures. *Socio-Economic Planning Sciences*, *79*, 79. doi:10.1016/j.seps.2021.101141

Lee, I., & Shin, Y. J. (2018). Fintech: Ecosystem, business models, investment decisions, and challenges. *Business Horizons*, *61*(1), 35–46. doi:10.1016/j.bushor.2017.09.003

Li, K., Kim, D. J., Lang, K. R., Kauffman, R. J., & Naldi, M. (2020). How should we understand the digital economy in Asia? Critical assessment and research agenda. *Electronic Commerce Research and Applications*, *44*(1), 101004. doi:10.1016/j.elerap.2020.101004 PMID:32922241

Lin, H.-F., & Chen, C.-H. (2013). An Intelligent Embedded Marketing Service System based on TV apps: Design and implementation through product placement in idol dramas. *Expert Systems with Applications*, *40*(10), 4127–4136. doi:10.1016/j.eswa.2013.01.034

Liu, Y.L. (2021). Research on the safe development of FinTech from the perspective of ant group's suspension of listing. *Gansu Finance,* (9), 60-64.

Luan, T., & Li, J. (2018). *Internet+personal Carbon Finance in Land Desertification Control Scheme Design in Xinjiang*. Xinjiang University of Finance and Economics.

Lyons, A. C., Kass-Hanna, J., & Fava, A. (2021). Fintech development and savings, borrowing, and remittances: A comparative study of emerging economies. *Emerging Markets Review*.

Ng, A. W., & Kwok, B. K. (2017). Emergence of Fintech and cybersecurity in a global financial centre. *Journal of Financial Econometrics*, *25*(4), 422–434.

PBOC. (2021). *White paper on research and development progress of China's digital RMB*. http://www.gov.cn/xinwen/2021-07/16/content_5625569.htm

Petralia, K., Philippon, T., Rice, T., & Veron, N. (2019). *Banking disrupted? Financial intermediation in an era of transformational technology*. Technical Report 22, Geneva Reports on the World Economy. ICMB and CEPR.

Philippon, T. (2015). Has us finance industry become less efficient? On the theory and measurement of financial intermediation. *The American Economic Review*, *105*(4), 1408–1438. doi:10.1257/aer.20120578

Philippon, T. (2016). *The Fintech opportunity*. NBER Working Paper.

QKLW. (2021). *China block-chain policy survey and regulatory trend analysis report*. https://www.qklw.com/specialcolumn/20210304/172943.html

Rejeb, A., Suhaiza, Z., Rejeb, K., Seuring, S., & Treiblmaier, H. (2022). The Internet of Things and the circular economy: A systematic literature review and research agenda. *Journal of Cleaner Production, 350*(20), 131439. doi:10.1016/j. jclepro.2022.131439

Rukikaire, K. (2019). *Chinese initiative ant Forest wins UN champions of the earth award.* UNEP - UN Environment Programme. http://www. unenvironment.org/ news-and-stories/press-release/chinese-initiative-ant-forestwins-un-champions-earth-award

Senyo, P. K., & Ellis, L. C. (2020). Unearthing antecedents to financial inclusion through FinTech innovations. *Technovation, 98,* 102155. doi:10.1016/j. technovation.2020.102155

Shen, W., & Hou, L. (2021). China's central bank digital currency and its impacts on monetary policy and payment competition: Game changer or regulatory toolkit? *Computer Law & Security Review, 41,* 41. doi:10.1016/j.clsr.2021.105577

Song, H., Yang, X., & Yu, K. (2020). How do supply chain network and SMEs' operational capabilities enhance working capital financing? An integrative signaling view. *International Journal of Production Economics, 220,* 220. doi:10.1016/j. ijpe.2019.07.020

Van Cauwenberg, J., Schepers, P., Deforche, B., & de Geus, B. (2022). Effects of e-biking on older adults' biking and walking frequencies, health, functionality and life space area: A prospective observational study. *Transportation Research Part A, Policy and Practice, 156,* 156. doi:10.1016/j.tra.2021.12.006

Vlačić, B., Corbo, L., Costa e Silva, S., & Dabić, M. (2021). The evolving role of artificial intelligence in marketing: A review and research agenda. *Journal of Business Research,* 128.

Wall, L. D. (2018). Some financial regulatory implications of artificial intelligence. *Journal of Economics and Business, 100,* 55–63. doi:10.1016/j.jeconbus.2018.05.003

Wang, R., Liu, J., & Luo, H. (2020). Fintech development and bank risk taking in China. *European Journal of Finance, 2020*(13), 1–22.

Wang, Y.F. (2021). How can FinTech fully empower Inclusive Finance? *Academic Research,* 74-80.

Wojcik, D., & Ioannou, S. (2020). COVID-19 and finance: Market developments so far and potential impacts on the financial sector and centres. *Tijdschrift Voor Economischeen Sociale Geografie, 111*(3), 387–400. doi:10.1111/tesg.12434 PMID:32836484

Xiao, Y., Li, S.L., & Liang, B. (2020). Banking FinTech application under COVID-19: theoretical logic, practical characteristics and reform path. *Research on Financial Economics Investigate, 35*(3), 90-103.

Yang, J., Cheng, L., & Luo, X. (2009). A comparative study on e-banking services between China and the USA. *International Journal Electrochemical Finance, 3*(3), 235–252. doi:10.1504/IJEF.2009.027848

Yang, W., Sui, X., & Qi, Z. (2021). Can fintech improve the efficiency of commercial banks?—An analysis based on big data. *Research in International Business and Finance, 55*, 101338. doi:10.1016/j.ribaf.2020.101338

Yang, Y. M. (2021). BCM: Digital new bank of communications has more AI appeared at the world Artificial Intelligence Conference. *Rural Financial Times,* (3).

Yu, P., Hu, Y., Waseem, M., & Rafay, A. (2021). Regulatory Developments in Peer-to-Peer (P2P) Lending to Combat Frauds: The Case of China. In A. Rafay (Ed.), Handbook of Research on Theory and Practice of Financial Crimes (pp. 172-194). IGI Global.

Yu, P., Li, C., Sampat, M., & Chen, Z. (2022). How the Development of FinTech Can Bolster Financial Inclusion Under an Era of Disruptive Innovation? Case Study on China. In M. Anshari, M. Almunawar, & M. Masri (Eds.), *FinTech Development for Financial Inclusiveness* (pp. 135–167). IGI Global. doi:10.4018/978-1-7998-8447-7.ch009

Yu, P., Lu, S., Hanes, E., & Chen, Y. (2022). The Role of Blockchain Technology in Harnessing the Sustainability of Chinese Digital Finance. In P. Swarnalatha & S. Prabu (Eds.), *Blockchain Technologies for Sustainable Development in Smart Cities* (pp. 155–186). IGI Global. doi:10.4018/978-1-7998-9274-8.ch009

Zhang, H. (2018). Regulatory sandbox and compatibility with China's administrative law system. *Zhejiang Journal,* (1).

Zhang, M. (2021). Discussion on the transformation and development direction of commercial banks in the era of AI. *Economics and Management Science,* 107-108.

Zhang, Y. F., Chen, J. Y., Han, Y., Qian, M. X., Guo, X., Chen, R., Xu, D., & Chen, Y. (2021). The contribution of Fintech to sustainable development in the digital age: Ant forest and land restoration in China. *Land Use Policy, 103*, 105306. doi:10.1016/j. landusepol.2021.105306

Zou, C.W., Du, Y., Hao, K., & Jiang, D.F. (2020). Block-chain+IoT enabling the digital transformation of FinTech. *Zhangjiang Science and Technology Review,* 29-31.

ADDITIONAL READING

Aggeri, F. (1999). Environmental policies and innovation: A knowledge-based perspective on cooperative approaches. *Research Policy, 28*(7), 699–717. doi:10.1016/S0048-7333(99)00015-3

Allen, F., Gu, X., & Jagtiani, J. (2022). Fintech, Cryptocurrencies, and CBDC: Financial Structural Transformation in China. *Journal of International Money and Finance, 124*, 102625. doi:10.1016/j.jimonfin.2022.102625

Cho, T. Y., & Chen, Y. S. (2021). The impact of financial technology on China's banking industry: An application of the metafrontier cost Malmquist productivity index. *The North American Journal of Economics and Finance, 57*, 101414. doi:10.1016/j.najef.2021.101414

Fasano, F., & Cappa, F. (2022). How Do Banking Fintech Services Affect SME Debt? *Journal of Economics and Business.* doi:10.1016/j.jeconbus.2022.106070

Gao, J. (2022). Has COVID-19 hindered small business activities? The role of Fintech. *Economic Analysis and Policy, 74*, 297–308. doi:10.1016/j.eap.2022.02.008

Luo, S., Sun, Y., & Zhou, R. (2022). Can fintech innovation promote household consumption? Evidence from China family panel studies. *International Review of Financial Analysis, 82*, 102137. doi:10.1016/j.irfa.2022.102137

Mahalakshmi, V., Kulkarni, N., Kumar, K. P., Kumar, K. S., Sree, D. N., & Durga, S. (2022). The Role of implementing Artificial Intelligence and Machine Learning Technologies in the financial services Industry for creating Competitive Intelligence. *Materials Today: Proceedings, 56*, 2252–2255. doi:10.1016/j.matpr.2021.11.577

Murinde, V., Rizopoulos, E., & Zachariadis, M. (2022). The impact of the FinTech revolution on the future of banking: Opportunities and risks. *International Review of Financial Analysis, 81*, 102103. doi:10.1016/j.irfa.2022.102103

Tao, R., Su, C. W., Naqvi, B., & Rizvi, S. K. A. (2022). Can Fintech development pave the way for a transition towards low-carbon economy: A global perspective. *Technological Forecasting and Social Change, 174*, 121278. doi:10.1016/j.techfore.2021.121278

Yang, L., & Wang, S. (2022). Do fintech applications promote regional innovation efficiency? Empirical evidence from China. *Socio-Economic Planning Sciences*. doi:10.1016/j.seps.2022.101258

KEY TERMS AND DEFINITIONS

Artificial Intelligence (AI): The ability of a computer or a robot controlled by a computer to do tasks that are usually done by humans because they require human intelligence and discernment. Although there are no AIs that can perform the wide variety of tasks an ordinary human can do, some AIs can match humans in specific tasks.

Asset-Backed Security (ABS): A type of financial investment that is collateralized by an underlying pool of assets—usually ones that generate a cash flow from debt, such as loans, leases, credit card balances, or receivables. It takes the form of a bond or note, paying income at a fixed rate for a set amount of time, until maturity. For income-oriented investors, asset-backed securities can be an alternative to other debt instruments, like corporate bonds or bond funds.

Blockchain-Based Service Network (BSN) Blockchain: A cross-cloud, cross-portal, cross-framework global infrastructure network used to deploy and operate all types of blockchain applications.

Central Bank Digital Currency (CBDC): A CBDC is issued and regulated by a nation's monetary authority or central bank. CBDCs promote financial inclusion and simplify the implementation of monetary and fiscal policy.

Crowdfunding: A way to raise money for an individual or organization by collecting "donations" through family, friends, friends of friends, strangers, businesses, and more. By using social media to spread awareness, people can reach more potential donors than traditional forms of fundraising.

FinTech: The term that describes the group of new financial technologies designed to enhance and automate the use and delivery of financial services. It is changing how we save, borrow, and invest money by making digital financial transactions easier and simpler, without the need for a traditional bank.

Internet of Things (IoT): A giant network of connected things and people all of which collect and share data about the way they are used and about the environment around them.

Regulatory Sandbox: A set of rules that allow businesses, usually within a specific industry, to test themselves in the market for a set period of time — generally two to three years — without being subject to any particular set of regulations.

Small and Medium-Sized Enterprises (SMEs): Businesses that maintain revenues, assets or a number of employees below a certain threshold. Each country has its own definition of what constitutes a small and medium-sized enterprise (SME). Certain size criteria must be met and occasionally the industry in which the company operates in is taken into account as well.

Chapter 10
Internet of Things in the Aerospace Industry:
Market Analysis

Prasad G.
Dayananda Sagar University, Bangalore, India

ABSTRACT

The international aviation market was worth USD 4.95 billion in 2020 and is anticipated to increase at a compound annual growth rate (CAGR) of 21.4% between 2021 and 2028. The industry is projected to increase because of the exponential growth in air passenger volume and a significant emphasis on improving customer experience. Continuous advancements in wireless technology, as well as an increasing desire for smart airport construction, are driving market expansion. In recent years, the aviation sector has seen unparalleled growth in passenger volume. The major companies in the aviation sector, in particular, are using data-driven techniques to make business choices. The internet of things (IoT) plays an important role in data collection in the aviation sector by providing statistical summaries to aid airport management. These data summaries may be used by aviation firms to gain meaningful information while eliminating human intervention.

INTRODUCTION

The Internet of Things (IoT) is transforming operations on the ground and in the air in the aircraft industry. Passengers may anticipate a variety of interesting new in-flight experiences as a result of real-time analytics via IoT, which is already driving improvements in quality and productivity. Kevin Ashton, a pioneering MIT

DOI: 10.4018/978-1-6684-4176-3.ch010

technologist, was obsessed in 1999 with optimising supply chain operations using a network of smart devices that used radio-frequency identification tags (RFIDs). And in the end, his efforts were fruitful. He developed a global standard system for RFID and other sensors with his colleagues at MIT's Auto-ID Centre. It remained unclear, however, what to title this brand-new area of study. He came to terms with the phrase "Internet of Things" in the end. Since then, the idea of the Internet of Things (IoT)—which today includes a global ecosystem of sensors, embedded computers, and smart gadgets that connect and share data—has grown tremendously. In the present day and age, there are around 14.2 billion linked gadgets in use worldwide. Cloud computing power, falling hardware costs, and quicker 5G data transfer will speed growth to over 25 billion is attained in 2021, according to Gartner research. They include wearable trackers, as well as smart home gadgets and a wide range of industrial advances to increase manufacturing and operating efficiency in the home and workplace.

Industrial IoT is helping to enhance manufacturing efficiency in the aerospace industry. As a result of enhanced analytics, manufacturers are able to quickly rectify inefficiencies after a flight. Aircraft manufacturers may save a large amount of money if they used IoT-enabled smart metres to track their energy consumption throughout production. A 20 percent reduction in energy consumption is possible thanks to powerful analytics algorithms that analyse usage and recommend ways to save energy (UN General Assembly, 2015; United Nations Environment Programme, 2011).

The Internet of Things (IoT) can also provide real-time visibility into how a whole factory floor is running. A "digital shadow" of the complete assembly line is created in Airbus' Saint Eloi factory using data from machines and conveyors. This makes it possible for users to keep tabs on processes in real time and run very precise simulations to figure out how to make them even more efficient. Meanwhile, quality and productivity can both be enhanced. The Internet of Things, for example, can assist in the monitoring and management of a tool's torque on the assembly line. When the tool senses too much or too little torque, it quickly stops and alerts the user. This strategy has resulted in a 20-30% increase in Airbus' efficiency.

Transportation as a Platform for Internet of Things (IoT) Innovation

For airlines and passengers, the Internet of Things (IoT) is opening up new possibilities for travel because of its integration into the cabin. New applications provide increased interactions with the immediate surroundings of the passengers, such as customised entertainment and food options, and this includes a more personalised atmosphere. Airbus has introduced its Connected Experience solution to help create the new passenger environment. Built in collaboration with numerous industry leaders, this open ecosystem will enable real-time communication between key cabin components including the kitchen, lavatory and meal carts. Digital services will be available to flight attendants. Predictive maintenance, cabin operations, and dependability will all benefit from consolidated, real-time data collected during flight and analysed on Airbus' Skywise platform. Crew members will have immediate access to important information thanks to connected seating, such as whether or not their seatbelts are fastened, their armrests are lowered, and their backrests are upright. The data gathered from post-flight research will help airlines better understand their customers in the future.

Figure 1. Applications of internet of things

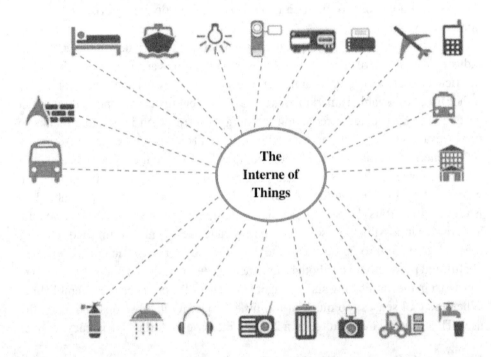

Figure 1 shows the applications of Internet of Things. As the Internet of Things (IoT) grows more prevalent across aeroplanes, it will be necessary to innovate in a wide range of areas. Difficulty and services in Airbus's cabins will be improved with the implementation of dozens of projects. When it comes to IoT adoption in the aerospace industry, Airbus is a pioneer. As part of its Connected Experience initiative, the business introduced a machine and conveyor data collection system that makes use of the Internet of Things (IoT). In order to produce a "digital shadow" – a real-time visualisation of the complete assembly line and its inefficiencies – the data is examined and pooled. When developing and testing production methods, Airbus uses real-life models modelled after the assembly line's visual representation in order to increase operational efficiency even further (National Bureau of Statistics of China, 2016a; Wübbeke et al., 2016)

Figure 2. Overview of internet of things

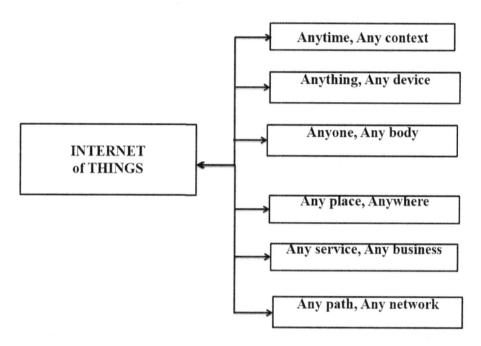

Figure 2 depicts the Overview of Internet of Things. With the use of IoT sensors, Rolls Royce can track the performance of its jet engines, helicopter blades and other items in real-time using analytics. It makes use of the information to anticipate problems with engine performance and maintenance needs. It's important to note, however, that the way data is being used is changing and now includes significant aftermarket services like route optimization for its clients.

ARTIFICIAL INTELLIGIENT (AI) SYSTEM IN AEROSPACE

Commercial aircraft burn billions of gallons of fuel each year all over the world. Global fuel consumption is expected to reach a record high of 97 billion gallons in

2019, according to insights. The aerospace industry as a whole will be concerned going forward with fuel conservation. Various businesses are now using 3D printing to create lightweight components as a result of this. For example, aerospace companies may be able to improve their fuel efficiency with artificial intelligence (AI).

The climb stage is when a plane uses the most fuel. Artificial intelligence models can analyse the amount of fuel used by different aircraft and numerous pilots during the climb period in order to create profiles of the climb stages for each of the pilots. When used during the ascent stage, these profiles can save time and fuel. It is possible for pilots to save fuel during flights by using AI-generated climb stage profiles. Particularly in commercial aviation, customer satisfaction and loyalty are extremely important. Artificial intelligence can help aircraft provide better customer service and enhance the client experience. Artificial intelligence can be used in a variety of ways to improve customer service. AI-based digital devices that can respond to customers' requests in real time and in a human-like manner are an obvious example of this: chatbots. Using online chatbots to automate customer service can save customers both time and effort.

These challenges can be solved more efficiently because of the ease of implementation of IS. Another advantage that IS experts have discovered is the ability to rapidly develop and test complicated ideas. All of this is made possible by the widespread use of computing devices powered by supercomputers from the early part of the twentieth century. The applications have grown in popularity among both the technical and general public for a variety of reasons. Spacecraft autonomy, aeroplane control, modelling, airfoil design, satellite operations, missile design, and vehicle health management are just a few examples of innovative uses for IS. Both as intelligent assistants and as a substitute for human expertise are the roles played by intelligent systems in aircraft engineering. Intelligent assistants can save money, time, and lives by augmenting human skill where it is needed. Humans benefit from intelligent systems' ability to reliably search through a large number of options when confronted with a challenging optimization task.

- Autonomous rovers, on the other hand, use sophisticated systems to save money and lives.
- Intelligent systems have certain uses in aircraft engineering.
- Computer-aided design for model building
- Automated Design Intelligence
- Control systems with advanced intelligence
- Educator-friendly AI Systems
- Adaptive Intelligence for Autonomous Systems

Figure 3. Elements of industry 5.0 in aviation

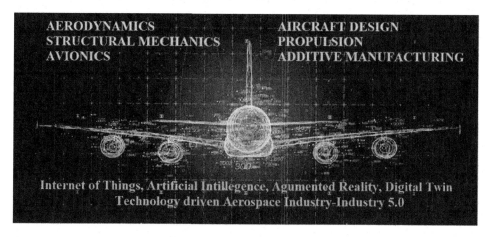

Figure 3 illustrates the elements of Industry 5.0 in Aviation. These are the thrust area where multi-disciplinary research is required. Although it is impossible to estimate the revolutionary influence of IoT in the aerospace industry, the economic implications of IoT use cases are enormous (National Bureau of Statistics of China, 2016b; National Bureau of Statistics of China, 2016c). To begin, any delays in manufacturing reduce the return on investment (ROI). Delays squander precious financial resources that may be used to make money in other areas. Increasing efficiency has the potential to liberate vast sums of money while also improving return on investment. Aerospace firms' efforts now have a better chance of paying off because of the Internet of Things (IoT). The Internet of Things (IoT) simplified Airbus' operations and increased productivity by 20%-30%. Aerospace firms can save money on energy costs by implementing IoT-enabled smart metres. Smart metres that are connected to the Internet of Things (IoT) can cut energy use by up to 20%, according to Airbus. Return on investment (ROI) comes more quickly and easily the more you save. The service provider benefits as well from assisting customers with appropriate maintenance plans. Aircraft on the ground are very expensive, and they can't generate enough revenue to offset their high maintenance expenses. For instance, the daily cost of a stranded Airbus A380 is over $1.2 million. Maintenance service companies can reduce downtime and increase uptime by using Internet of Things (IoT) sensors.

AUGMENTED REALITY IN AEROSPACE INDUSTRY

A look at how augmented reality has been applied in real-world aerospace applications like as engineering, navigation, training, and simulation. Further development and application opportunities for AR were also discussed. In particular, they are concerned with IFEC, airport operations, and crew assistance (Ma et al., 2017; National Bureau of Statistics of China, 2014). However, despite the fact that each of these uses calls for a different approach to application development, they are all united by the common goal of better human-machine interactions while simultaneously improving work quality, time, and effort. Existing hardware and software advances have made it possible for cellular phones to support augmented reality features. Researchers and developers all across the world can now use technologies like Magic Leap and Google Glass. Thus, AR has gained popularity as a tool in a wide range of industries, including automotive, video-game production, and the arts and entertainment industries. With so many people becoming interested in augmented reality, hardware and software have exploded in popularity. In contrast to aerospace, which is one of the first industries to introduce and employ augmented reality (AR) products, the automobile and entertainment industries continue to advance AR technology for their own use. To keep the aerospace sector interested in AR, more AR development and research focused on the industry is required. The aerospace industry continues to complain about AR's disadvantages, despite recent advances and achievements in other industries. In order to enhance AR's use in aircraft, the aerospace sector needs to work with others to develop new hardware and software solutions. It is obvious that time and effort must be put towards the future of technology, which will be found in augmented reality by helping with operational and daily duties.

Because of this, both ground and air operations in the aircraft industry are being transformed by IoT adoption. Manufacturing firms like Aerospace use the Internet of Things to develop and deploy operational efficiency-improving analytic techniques. IoT's extensive connectivity makes it possible for devices to work together and for humans and machines to coordinate, cooperate, communicate, and interoperate effectively. The aircraft industry relies heavily on these factors, and you risk falling behind your competitors if you don't make the necessary expenditures (Ministry of Environmental Protection the People's Republic of China, 2017; World Health Organization Regional Office for Europe, 2016).

Persistent problems have plagued the aerospace sector for years, undermining the profitability of aircraft makers. Manufacturing delays are the industry's most pressing problem. Due to manufacturing and operational inefficiencies, most aeroplane production programmes are three years or more behind schedule. Complications in production have led to costly delays, missed revenues, and cancelled orders for many years. Aside from straining customer relations, these delays damage the reputation of aircraft manufacturers. Particularly in the aerospace industry, one's reputation is priceless.

The most expensive part of an aircraft is the energy it need to fly. Unsustainable operations can lead to increased energy consumption and associated expenditures, which can have a significant impact on the company's bottom line. The expense of maintenance and repairs is also a persistent issue. As the number of planes flying grows, it becomes increasingly difficult to sustain the costs of maintaining airlines in the air.

Solution is that, In order to improve sustainability and keep aircraft in the air, data collected by IoT devices is utilised. There are numerous ways in which Internet of Things (IoT) is demonstrating its benefits in the aerospace industry. As a result of the Industrial Internet of Things (IIoT), enterprises now have the ability to integrate and synchronise all aspects of their processes. For starters, supply chain miscalculations can be addressed with enhanced IoT analytics. They provide a great deal of transparency and can reveal inefficiencies in the engineering process. The Internet of Things (IoT) is reducing the complexity of production while also reducing delays.

To provide accurate and real-time information on energy usage across the whole production process, aerospace companies are implementing IoT-enabled smart metres in aircraft manufacturing. By utilising cutting-edge analytics algorithms, these smart metres evaluate energy usage and make recommendations for ways to save money on utility bills.

Keeping an aeroplane in the air for the shortest possible period of time is vital to its performance. The use of IoT sensors in aerospace was a logical next step. Aerospace businesses can keep planes in the air and minimise costs by resolving problems as soon as they land thanks to robust IoT sensors that collect performance data from thousands of angles. Regular maintenance can be cut in cost, labour, and time by using data collected from IoT devices.

IOT IN AEROSPACE AND DEFENCE MARKET

Market Size, Trends, and Analysis for the Global IoT in Aerospace and Defense Sector – Projections to 2026 Component-by-component (Hardware, Software, Services), It's possible to segment the data by connectivity (such as cellular or Wi-Fi), application (such real-time fleet management), health monitoring (such as wearables or fitness trackers), and end-user (such as mobile devices) (Space Systems, Ground Vehicles, Others), Competitive Landscape Company Market Share Analysis and Competitor Analysis by Region (North America, Asia Pacific, Central & South America, Europe, and the Middle East and Africa)

The global aerospace and defence IoT market is expected to develop at a CAGR of 11.5 percent from 2021 to 2026, from USD 40.94 billion in 2021 to USD 70.55 billion in 2026. Internet of Things (IoT) technologies and services help the aerospace and defence industries work more smoothly in today's modern environment. There are several uses for the Internet of Things (IoT). Many factors are supporting the growth of the market, including the increasing need to implement Industry 5.0 and the transformation of aerospace industry mobility, production and sales, as well as the growing need for data privacy and storage. The benefits of IoT, such as increased connectivity, enhanced security, and the ability to make quick decisions, are driving the market. Additionally, the aerospace and defence IoT market is being propelled by the growing demand for cutting-edge and dependable aerospace services.

Figure 4. Aerospace engineering in industry 5.0

Figure 4 shows the technology behind the aerospace engineering in Industry 5.0. Military and commercial airlines generate gigabytes of data every day as more manufacturers integrate sensor technology into their equipment. As a result of the increasing requirement to store massive amounts of data, the aerospace and defence IoT industry will grow significantly. When IoT integration is implemented, aeroplane manufacturers can expect to see improvements in engine fuel efficiency, as well as noise and emission reductions. As a result, these Internet of Things (IoT) technologies offer new revenue streams to OEMs, engine manufacturers, and airline operators. Military situational awareness may be improved with the use of satellite communication, ISR, and GPS. With better reporting, medical personnel can be notified of a soldier's health status without having to manually contact them. Another advantage is that sensors are used to anticipate how long a piece of equipment will last and whether or not it needs to be replaced or repaired. IoT in aerospace and defence was significantly affected by the COVID-19 outbreak. Many sectors were compelled to stop operations as a result of the lockout, which reduced demand for IoT in Aerospace and Defense and limited market growth. It also disrupted the supply chain, lowering market demand. Technology is a large expense to consider, but it's also a significant problem that will hamper the expansion of the market. In addition, the move to digitally connected systems has boosted the demand for highly skilled workers, which could unintentionally lower the demand for low-skill workers.

Aerospace and Defense Industry IoT Components and Applications

The market is divided into hardware, software, and services based on the IoT aerospace and defence component. Over the projection period, services are expected to dominate the market. Some of these offerings include consultation as well as development as well as data analytics as well as app maintenance with the goal of improving and automating the operations of the firm. This benefit is anticipated to enhance the segment's expansion between 2021 and 2026..

Technology for Connectivity in the Aerospace and Defense Markets: IoT

The market is divided into cellular, Wi-Fi, satellite communication, and radio frequency identification based on IoT aerospace and defence connection technologies. With more consistent bandwidth correspondence for a variety of audio / data real-time applications, cellular connectivity technology of IoT in aerospace and defence market is predicted to hold the greatest share during the projection period.

The Aerospace and Defense Industry's Use of Internet of Things

IoT in aerospace and defence has led to market segments including real-time fleet management and training & simulation as well as health monitoring and equipment maintenance and inventory management. During the forecast period, the real-time fleet management is predicted to hold the greatest share of the market. It takes time and effort to keep track of a fleet, and it becomes increasingly difficult with time. A great degree of precision, accuracy, and attention are also required for the monitoring. By integrating the appropriate IoT solutions, fleet operators may equip themselves with cutting-edge capabilities and boost operational efficiency. With IoT-enabled fleet management solutions, performance might be improved by increasing visibility of assets and vehicle utilisation, which would cut down on waiting times while also saving money on preventive maintenance.

End-User IoT in Aerospace and Defense

The aerospace and defence IoT market is divided into space systems, ground vehicles, and others based on the numerous end-users who have adopted it. The market for ground vehicles is projected to be dominated by this sector. To update algorithms on the basis of user data, interact with infrastructure to acquire environmental information, and connect other cars on the road, grounded vehicles use Internet technology. IoT in space is only a theoretical concept due to the numerous obstacles that must be overcome. Aging, lack of power, physical destruction, or an external attack can all cause satellite IoT devices to fail. To launch new Internet of Things satellites into space, organisations that want to replace old ones will need funds and launchers.

Internet of Things in the Aerospace and Defense Industry: A Geographical Analysis

The market is divided geographically into areas such as North America, Europe, Central and South America, the Middle East and Africa, and the Asia-Pacific region. As a result of its well-equipped technological infrastructure, high adoption of the Internet of Things (IoT), and increasing demand for IoT-enabled aerospace and defence products, North America is expected to hold the largest market share in the next years.

ICT Infrastructure is Developed as a Result of Technological Advancements.

The aerospace and defence industry's growing demand for Internet of Things (IoT) will help Asia-Pacific expand at the fastest rate. The increasing number of government initiatives in various developing countries to upgrade their defence and aerospace sectors would provide an opportunity for APAC IoT to grow in the aerospace and defence market.

Market Share and Competitor Analysis for IoT in Aerospace and Defense

Key participants in the aerospace and defence IoT market include AT&T Environment, Freewave Technologies, Elbit Systems, Honeywell International, Inc., General Atomics Aeronautical Systems, Prox Dynamics, Northrup Grunman, Textron Systems, and Radisys.

CONCLUSION

Innovation in Industry 5.0 technology to decrease costs, shorten the design cycle, improve maintenance and update products will be critical in the aerospace industry during the next 15 years. Simulation, prototyping, optimization, maintenance and production will all be driven by technology. Advances in artificial intelligence (AI) could benefit aerospace manufacturers by helping them streamline their production processes. A lack of access to high-quality data, growing reliance on basic models rather than sophisticated models, as well as a shortage of trained workers and partners to properly deploy machine learning techniques are all reasons for the industry's limited adoption of these approaches. AI, on the other hand, has the potential to be a game-changing technology for aerospace companies, impacting efficiency, productivity, as well as speed and innovation. Smart Concessions Management is today's aerospace industry innovation.

- Repairs Management using Smarts.
- Automatic Part Geo Location
- To identify parts on a DMU or a production line.
- Device for storing NC documentation.
- KBE (Knowledge-Based Engineering).
- Choosing an alternative fastener.
- Predictive Aircraft Component Maintenance

- Aeronautical component size and weight calculations
- Reverse Engineering.
- Aircraft damage prediction based on region of operation.
- Any repetitious non-engineering activities

ACKNOWLEDGMENT

We acknowledge all the staff members of Aerospace Engineering, Dayananda Sagar University, Bangalore, India for the constant support and encouragement to carry out the research. I also thank Dr. K.N.B. Murthy (Vice Chancellor), Dr. A. Srinivas (Dean), Dr. BVN Ramakumar (Head of the Department), Dayananda Sagar University, Bangalore, India. I also thank my family members for the understanding and encouragement to preserve the research work. This research received no specific grant from any funding agency in the public, commercial, or not-for-profit sectors.

REFERENCES

Ma, Q., Cai, S., Wang, S., Zhao, B., Martin, R. V., Brauer, M., Cohen, A., Jiang, J., Zhou, W., Hao, J., Frostad, J., Forouzanfar, M. H., & Burnett, R. T. (2017). Impacts of coal burning on ambient PM2.5 pollution in China. *Atmospheric Chemistry and Physics*, *17*(7), 4477–4491. doi:10.5194/acp-17-4477-2017

Ministry of Environmental Protection the People's Republic of China. (2017). *Pollution Curbs Set to Make Skies Clearer*. Ministry of Environmental Protection the People's Republic of China.

National Bureau of Statistics of China. (2014). *China Statistical Yearbook 2015: 8-19 Ambient Air Quality in Key Cities of Environmental Protection*. Available online: http://www.stats.gov.cn/tjsj/ndsj/2015/ indexeh.htm

National Bureau of Statistics of China. (2016a). *China Statistical Yearbook: 3-6 Value-added by Sector*. Available online: http://www.stats.gov.cn/tjsj/ndsj/2016/ indexeh.htm

National Bureau of Statistics of China. (2016b). *China Statistical Yearbook: 9-3 Overall Energy Balance Sheet*. Available online: http://www.stats.gov.cn/tjsj/ ndsj/2016/indexeh.htm

National Bureau of Statistics of China. (2016c). *China Statistical Yearbook: 9-2 Total Consumption of Energy and Its Composition.* Available online: http://www. stats.gov.cn/tjsj/ndsj/2016/indexeh.htm

UN General Assembly. (2015). *Transforming our World: The 2030 Agenda for Sustainable Development.* UN General Assembly. https://sustainabledevelopment. un.org/post2015/transformingourworld

United Nations Environment Programme. (2011). *Towards a Green Economy: Pathways to Sustainable Development and Poverty Eradication.* UNEP.

World Health Organization Regional Office for Europe. (2016). *WHO Expert Consultation: Available Evidence for the Future Update of the WHO Global Air Quality Guidelines (AQGs).* WHO.

Wübbeke, J., Meissner, M., Zenglein, M. J., Ives, J., & Conrad, B. (2016). *Made in China 2025. The Making of a High-Tech Superpower and Consequences for Industrial Countries.* Mercator Institute for China Studies. https://www.merics.org/ sites/default/files/2017-09/MPOC_No.2_ MadeinChina2025.pdf

Compilation of References

Ministry of Environmental Protection the People's Republic of China. (2017). *Pollution Curbs Set to Make Skies Clearer*. Ministry of Environmental Protection the People's Republic of China.

United Nations Environment Programme. (2011). *Towards a Green Economy: Pathways to Sustainable Development and Poverty Eradication*. UNEP.

UN General Assembly. (2015). *Transforming our World: The 2030 Agenda for Sustainable Development*. UN General Assembly. https://sustainabledevelopment.un.org/post2015/transformingourworld

National Bureau of Statistics of China. (2016a). *China Statistical Yearbook: 3-6 Value-added by Sector*. Available online: http://www.stats.gov.cn/tjsj/ndsj/2016/indexeh.htm

Wübbeke, J., Meissner, M., Zenglein, M. J., Ives, J., & Conrad, B. (2016). *Made in China 2025. The Making of a High-Tech Superpower and Consequences for Industrial Countries*. Mercator Institute for China Studies. https://www.merics.org/sites/default/files/2017-09/MPOC_No.2_MadeinChina2025.pdf

National Bureau of Statistics of China. (2016b). *China Statistical Yearbook: 9-3 Overall Energy Balance Sheet*. Available online: http://www.stats.gov.cn/tjsj/ndsj/2016/indexeh.htm

National Bureau of Statistics of China. (2016c). *China Statistical Yearbook: 9-2 Total Consumption of Energy and Its Composition*. Available online: http://www.stats.gov.cn/tjsj/ndsj/2016/indexeh.htm

Ma, Q., Cai, S., Wang, S., Zhao, B., Martin, R. V., Brauer, M., Cohen, A., Jiang, J., Zhou, W., Hao, J., Frostad, J., Forouzanfar, M. H., & Burnett, R. T. (2017). Impacts of coal burning on ambient PM2.5 pollution in China. *Atmospheric Chemistry and Physics*, 17(7), 4477–4491. doi:10.5194/acp-17-4477-2017

National Bureau of Statistics of China. (2014). *China Statistical Yearbook 2015: 8-19 Ambient Air Quality in Key Cities of Environmental Protection*. Available online: http://www.stats.gov.cn/tjsj/ndsj/2015/ indexeh.htm

World Health Organization Regional Office for Europe. (2016). *WHO Expert Consultation: Available Evidence for the Future Update of the WHO Global Air Quality Guidelines (AQGs).* WHO.

Abbasi, K., Alam, A., Brohi, N. A., Brohi, I. A., & Nasim, S. (2021). P2P lending Fintechs and SMEs' access to finance. *Economics Letters, 204*, 109890. doi:10.1016/j.econlet.2021.109890

Admati, A. R., & Hellwig, M. (2013). *The Bankers' New Clothes.* Princeton University Press.

Afroze, D., & Aulad, A. (2020). Perception of professional accountants about the application of artificial intelligence (AI) in auditing industry of Bangladesh. *Journal of Social Economics Research, 7*(2), 51–61. doi:10.18488/journal.35.2020.72.51.61

Ahmad, S. (2020). Reimagining sustainable financing through Fintech. *Business Line.* Available at: https://www.thehindubusinessline.com/opinion/reimagining-sustainable-financing-through-Fintech/article30878735.ece

Ahmad, S. N., & Whig, P. (2011). *On the Performance of ISFET-based Device for Water Quality Monitoring.* Academic Press.

Ajay Rupani, P. (2019). The development of big data science to the world. *Engineering Reports, 2*(2), 1–7.

Ajibade, P. (2018). Technology acceptance model limitations and criticisms: Exploring the practical applications and use in technology-related studies, mixed-method, and qualitative researches. *LibraryPhilosophy & Practice, 1941.* https://digitalcommons.unl.edu/libphilprac/1941

Ajzen, I. (1991). The theory of planned behavior. *Organizational Behavior and Human Decision Processes, 50*(2), 179–211. doi:10.1016/0749-5978(91)90020-T

Ajzen, I., & Fishbein, M. (1975). A Bayesian analysis of attribution processes. *Psychological Bulletin, 82*(2), 261–277. doi:10.1037/h0076477

Ajzen, I., & Fishbein, M. (1980). *Understanding attitudes and predicting social behaviour.* Prentice-Hall.

Akhtar, S. I., & Morrison, W. M. (2017). *Digital trade and U.S. trade policy.* Report R44565, Congressional Research Service, U.S. Government.

Akturan, U., & Tezcan, N. (2012). Mobile banking adoption of the youth market: Perceptions and intentions. *Marketing Intelligence & Planning, 30*(4), 444–459. doi:10.1108/02634501211231928

Albashrawi, M., & Motiwalla, L. (2017). Privacy and Personalization in Continued Usage Intention of Mobile Banking: An Integrative Perspective. *Information Systems Frontiers, 21*(5), 1031–1043. doi:10.100710796-017-9814-7

Albawwat, I., & Frijat, Y. (2021). An analysis of auditors' perceptions towards artificial intelligence and its contribution to audit quality. *Accounting, 7*(4), 755–762. doi:10.5267/j.ac.2021.2.009

Alfadda, H. A., & Mahdi, H. S. (2021). Measuring students' use of zoom application in language course based on the technology acceptance model (tam). *Journal of Psycholinguistic Research*, *50*(4), 883–900. doi:10.100710936-020-09752-1 PMID:33398606

Al-Fuqaha, Guizani, Mohammadi, Aledhari, & Ayyash. (n.d.). Internet of Things: A Survey on Enabling Technologies, Protocols, and Applications. *IEEE Communications Surveys and Tutorials*. . doi:10.1109/COMST.2015.2444095

Ali, J. M., &Gopalan, L. V. (2018). E-Wallet Payment: Swot Analysis from Customer Perception. *International Journal of Recent Research Aspects,* 155-158.

AlkaliY.RoutrayI.WhigP. (2022). Study of various methods for reliable, efficient and Secured IoT using Artificial Intelligence. Available at SSRN 4020364. doi:10.2139/ssrn.4020364

Alliance for Financial Inclusion. (2020). *Digital financial services supervision in Bangladesh.* Alliance for Financial Inclusion.

Almadhoun, R., Kadadha, M., Alhemeiri, M., Alshehhi, M., & Salah, K. (2019). A User Authentication Scheme of IoT Devices using Blockchain-Enabled Fog Nodes. *Proceedings of IEEE/ACS International Conference on Computer Systems and Applications, AICCSA*. 10.1109/AICCSA.2018.8612856

Almuhammadi, A. (2020). An overview of mobile payments, fintech, and digital wallet in Saudi Arabia.In *2020 7th International Conference on Computing for Sustainable Global Development (INDIACom)* (pp. 271-278).IEEE.

Al-Sayyed, S., Al-Aroud, S., & Zayed, L. (2021). The effect of artificial intelligence technologies on audit evidence. *Accounting*, *7*(2), 281–288. doi:10.5267/j.ac.2020.12.003

Alshehhi, A., Nobanee, H., & Khare, N. (2018). The impact of sustainability practices on corporate financial performance: Literature trends and future research potential. *Sustainability*, *10*(2), 494. doi:10.3390u10020494

Althunibat, S., Antonopoulos, A., Kartsakli, E., Granelli, F., & Verikoukis, C. (2016). Countering Intelligent-Dependent Malicious Nodes in Target Detection Wireless Sensor Networks. *IEEE Sensors Journal*, *16*(23), 8627–8639. doi:10.1109/JSEN.2016.2606759

Anagnostopoulos, I. (2018). Fintech and regtech: Impact on regulators and banks. *Journal of Economics and Business*, *100*, 7–25. doi:10.1016/j.jeconbus.2018.07.003

Ananda, S., Kumar, R. P., & Singh, D. (2022). A mediation analysis of perceived service quality, customer satisfaction and customer engagement in the banking sector. *Journal of Financial Services Marketing*, 1–15.

Anand, M., Velu, A., & Whig, P. (2022). Prediction of Loan Behaviour with Machine Learning Models for Secure Banking. *Journal of Computing Science and Engineering: JCSE*, *3*(1), 1–13.

Anjali, R., & Suresh, A. (2019). A Study on Customer Satisfaction of Bharat Interface for Money (BHIM). *International Journal of Innovative Technology and Exploring Engineering*.

Anu, P., & Vimala, S. (2019). Reputation based Malicious Node Detection and Elimination in Open Shortest Path First. *Journal of Advanced Research in Dynamic and Control Systems, 11*, 855–860. doi:10.5373/JARDCS/V11SP11/20193107

Aremu, A. M., & Adeyemi, L. S. (2011). Small and medium scale enterprises as a survival strategy for employment generation in Nigeria. *CiteSeerX, 4*(1), 200–206. doi:10.5539/jsd.v4n1p200

Arena, M., Bengo, I., Calderini, M., & Chiodo, V. (2018). Unlocking Finance for social tech start-ups: Is there a new opportunity space? *Technological Forecasting and Social Change, 127*, 154–165. doi:10.1016/j.techfore.2017.05.035

ArnerD. W.BuckleyR. P.CharambaK.SergeevA.ZetzscheD. A. (2021). BigTech and Platform Finance: Governing Fintech 4.0 for Sustainable Development. Available at SSRN doi:10.2139/ssrn.3915275

Ashta, A., & Herrmann, H. (2021). Artificial intelligence and fintech: An overview of opportunities and risks for banking, investments, and microfinance. *Strategic Change, 30*(3), 211–222. doi:10.1002/jsc.2404

Aysan, A.F., & Kayani, F.N. (2022). China's transition to a digital currency does it threaten dollarization? *Asia and the Global Economy, 2*(1).

Azad, M. A. K. (2016). Predicting mobile banking adoption in Bangladesh: A neural network approach. *Transnational Corporations Review, 8*(3), 207–214. doi:10.1080/19186444.2016.12 33726

Bao, Z., Shi, W., He, D., & Chood, K.-K. R. (2018). *IoTChain: A Three-Tier Blockchain-based IoT Security Architecture*. https://arxiv.org/abs/1806.02008v2

Beerbaum, D. (2021). *Applying Agile Methodology to Regulatory Compliance Projects in the Financial Industry: A Case Study Research*. Academic Press.

Bhargav, R., & Whig, P. (2021). More Insight on Data Analysis of Titanic Data Set. *International Journal of Sustainable Development in Computing Science, 3*(4), 1–10.

Bhattacherjee, A. (2001). Understanding Information Systems Continuance: An Expectation-Confirmation Model. *Management Information Systems Quarterly, 25*(3), 351. doi:10.2307/3250921

Biswas, S., Carson, B., Chung, V., Singh, S., & Thomas, R. (2020). *AI-Bank of the future: Can Banks meet the AI Challenges*. McKinsey & Company. Available at:https://www.mckinsey.com/industries/financial-services/our-insights/ai-bank-of-the-future-can-banks-meet-the-ai-challenge

Biswas, S., Sharif, K., Li, F., Nour, B., & Wang, Y. (2019). A scalable blockchain framework for secure transactions in IoT. *IEEE Internet of Things Journal, 6*(3), 4650–4659. doi:10.1109/JIOT.2018.2874095

Bofondi, M., & Gobbi, G. (2017). The big promise of FinTech. *European Economy, 1*(2), 107-119.

Bollaert, H., Lopez-de-Silanes, F., & Schwienbacher, A. (2021). Fintech and access to finance. *Journal of Corporate Finance, 68*, 101941. doi:10.1016/j.jcorpfin.2021.101941

Boşcoianu, M., Ceocea, C., Vladareanu, V., & Vladareanu, L. (2020). Special purpose vehicles for sustainable finance of innovation in Romania-the case of intelligent robotic systems. *Periodicals of Engineering and Natural Sciences, 8*(3), 1418–1424.

Brue, M. (2021). *Keeping An "AI" On Fintech: AI-Based Use Cases Poised To Take Financial Services To The Next Level.* Available at: https://www.forbes.com/sites/moorinsights/2021/10/26/keeping-an-ai-on-Fintech-ai-based-use-cases-poised-to-take-financial-services-to-the-next-level/?sh=690d13a34b9f

Brynjolfsson, E., & Collis, A. (2019). How should we measure the digital economy? *Harvard Business Review Home, 97*(6), 140–146.

Buttle, F. (1996). *SERVQUAL Model: Review, critique and research agenda.* Available at: https://pdfs.semanticscholar.org/2311/5dc190a4d045bc0e6ec08bb0e 80485 e2c872.pdf

CaoL. (2020). *AI in finance: A review.* Available at SSRN 3647625.

Cashless India. (n.d.). *Digital Payment Methods, Mobile Wallets.* Ministry of Electronics and Information Technology, Government of India. http://cashlessindia.gov.in/mobile_wallets.html

Chanda, P. K., & Rupani, A. (n.d.). *A Review of Technology Paradigm for Near-Field Communication Sensors and Cloud-Based Smart Campus Management System.* Academic Press.

Chaudhary, N., & Anand, S. (2022). Effectiveness of Online Payment System during COVID-19. *Education, 109*, 54–50.

Chen, H., Qian, W., & Wen, Q. (2020). *The impact of the COVID-19 pandemic on consumption: Learning from high frequency transaction data. SSRN* preprint no. 3568574.

Chen, M., Xu, S., Husain, L., & Galea, G. (2021). Digital health interventions for COVID-19 in China: a retrospective analysis. *Intelligent Medicine, 1*(1), 29-36. doi:10.1016/j.imed.2021.03.001

Chen, Y. (2020). Improving market performance in the digital economy. *China Economic Review, 62*.

Chen, Z., Zhang, R., Ju, L., & Wang, W. (2013). Multivalued trust routing based on topology level for wireless sensor networks. *Proceedings - 12th IEEE International Conference on Trust, Security and Privacy in Computing and Communications, TrustCom 2013*, 1516–1521. 10.1109/TrustCom.2013.185

Chen, C. (2017). Science Mapping: A Systematic Review of the Literature. *Journal of Data and Information Science, 2*(2), 1–40. doi:10.1515/jdis-2017-0006

Chen, X. (2018). The development of China's digital economy shows obvious provincial differences. *International Finance, 2018*(4), 80.

Chen, X., Teng, L., & Chen, W. (2022). How does FinTech affect the development of the digital economy? evidence from China. *The North American Journal of Economics and Finance, 61,* 61. doi:10.1016/j.najef.2022.101697

Chen, X., You, X., & Chang, V. (2021). FinTech and commercial banks' performance in China: A leap forward or survival of the fittest? *Technological Forecasting and Social Change, 166,* 120645. doi:10.1016/j.techfore.2021.120645

China FinTech Report. (2020). https://report.iresearch.cn/wx/report.aspxid=3687.shtml

China's digital economy development white paper. (2021). *China Academy of Information and Communications Technology.* Retrieved from http://cnnic.cn/gywm/xwzx/rdxw/20172017_7084/202102/t20210203 _71364.htm

Chin, W. W. (2010). How to write up and report PLS analyses. In *Handbook of partial least squares* (pp. 655–690). Springer. doi:10.1007/978-3-540-32827-8_29

Chopra, G., & Whig, P. (2022a). A clustering approach based on support vectors. *International Journal of Machine Learning for Sustainable Development, 4*(1), 21–30.

Chopra, G., & Whig, P. (2022b). Using machine learning algorithms classified depressed patients and normal people. *International Journal of Machine Learning for Sustainable Development, 4*(1), 31–40.

Chopra, G., & Whig, P. (2022). Energy Efficient Scheduling for Internet of Vehicles. *International Journal of Sustainable Development in Computing Science, 4*(1).

Chouhan, S. (2019). Using an Arduino and a temperature, humidity sensor, Automate the fan speed. *International Journal of Sustainable Development in Computing Science, 1*(2).

Chow, T., & Cao, D. B. (2008). A survey study of critical success factors in agile software projects. *Journal of Systems and Software, 81*(6), 961–971. doi:10.1016/j.jss.2007.08.020

Christidis, K., & Devetsikiotis, M. (2016). Blockchains and Smart Contracts for the Internet of Things. *IEEE Access: Practical Innovations, Open Solutions, 4,* 2292–2303. doi:10.1109/ACCESS.2016.2566339

Cooper, D. R., Schindler, P. S., & Sun, J. (2006). *Business research methods* (Vol. 9). McGraw-Hill.

Cory, S. N., & Pruske, K. A. (2012). A factor analysis of the skills necessary in accounting graduates. *Journal of Business and Accounting, 5*(1), 121–128.

Cui, Z., Xue, F., Cai, X., Cao, Y., Wang, G. G., & Chen, J. (2018). Detection of Malicious Code Variants Based on Deep Learning. *IEEE Transactions on Industrial Informatics, 14*(7), 3187–3196. doi:10.1109/TII.2018.2822680

Curran, D. (2018). Risk, innovation, and democracy in the digital economy. *European Journal of Social Theory, 21*(2), 207–226. doi:10.1177/1368431017710907

Damerji, H., & Salimi, A. (2021). Mediating effect of user perceptions on technology readiness and adoption of artificial intelligence in accounting. *Accounting Education, 30*(2), 107–130. doi:10.1080/09639284.2021.1872035

Daniel & Berinyuy. (2010). *Using the SERVQUAL Model to assess Service Quality and Customer Satisfaction. An Empirical study of grocery stores in Umea.* http://www.diva-portal.org/smash/get/diva2:327600/fulltext01

Darolles, S. (2016). The rise of Fintechs and their regulation. *April Finance. Stability Rev., 20.*

Das, S., & Das, A. (2015). An algorithm to detect malicious nodes in wireless sensor network using enhanced LEACH protocol. *Conference Proceeding - 2015 International Conference on Advances in Computer Engineering and Applications, ICACEA 2015*, 875–881. 10.1109/ICACEA.2015.7164828

Davis, F. D. (1986). *A technology acceptance model for empirically testing new end-user information systems: Theory and results* (Doctoral dissertation). ProQuest Dissertations and Theses database. (UMI No. 0374529)

Davis, F. D. (1989). Perceived Usefulness, Perceived Ease of Use, and User Acceptance of Information Technology. *Management Information Systems Quarterly, 13*(3), 319–340. doi:10.2307/249008

Degerli, K. (2019). Regulatory Challenges and Solutions for Fintech in Turkey. *Procedia Computer Science, 158*, 929–937. doi:10.1016/j.procs.2019.09.133

Delaporte, A., & Naghavi, N. (2019). *The promise of mobile money for further advancing women's financial inclusion* [Blog]. Retrieved February 5 2022, from https://www.gsma.com/mobilefordevelopment/blog/the-promise-of-mobile-money-for-further-advancing-womens-financial-inclusion/

DeLone, W. H., & McLean, E. R. (1992). Information Systems Success: The Quest for the Dependent Variable. *Information Systems Research, 3*(1), 60–95. doi:10.1287/isre.3.1.60

Demir, A., Pesqué-Cela, V., Altunbas, Y., & Murinde, V. (2020). Fintech, financial inclusion and income inequality: a quantile regression approach. *The European Journal of Finance*, 1-22. doi:10.1080/1351847X.2020.1772335

Demirguç-Kunt, A., Klapper, L., Singer, D., Ansar, S., & Hess, J. (2018). *Measuring financial inclusion and the fintech revolution.* The Global Findex Database, World Bank Group. doi:10.1596/978-1-4648-1259-0

Dewantari, D., Raharjo, T., Hardian, B., Wahbi, A., & Alaydrus, F. (2021, November). Challenges of Agile Adoption in Banking Industry: A Systematic Literature Review. In *2021 25th International Computer Science and Engineering Conference (ICSEC)* (pp. 357-362). IEEE. 10.1109/ICSEC53205.2021.9684622

Ding, D., Chong, G., Lee, K. C., & Cheng, T. L. (2018). From Ant Financial to Alibaba's Rural Taobao Strategy - How Fintech Is Transforming Social Inclusion. In Handbook of Blockchain, Digital Finance, and Inclusion (Vol. 1). Academic Press.

Ding, N., Gu, L., & Peng, Y. (2022). Fintech, financial constraints and innovation: Evidence from China. *Journal of Corporate Finance*, *73*, 73. doi:10.1016/j.jcorpfin.2022.102194

DMR. (2022). *PayTm Statistics and Facts*. Available at https://expandedramblings.com/index. php /PayTm-statistics-facts/

DQIndia Online. (2017). *Paytm crosses milestone of 200 Mn Wallet users Dataquest*. Available at: https://www.dqindia.com/paytm-crosses-milestone-of-200-mn-wallet-users/

Elder-Vass, D. (2016). *Profit and Gift in the Digital Economy*. Cambridge Univ. doi:10.1017/CBO9781316536421

Ellul, J., & Pace, G. J. (2018). AlkylVM: A Virtual Machine for Smart Contract Blockchain Connected Internet of Things. *2018 9th IFIP International Conference on New Technologies, Mobility and Security, NTMS 2018 - Proceedings*, 1–4. 10.1109/NTMS.2018.8328732

ePaisa Content Team. (2016). *Payment Trends in India 2017*. https://www.epaisa.com/payment-trends-india-2017/

Esoimeme, E. E. (2018). A comparative analysis of the prepaid card laws/regulations in Nigeria, the UK, the USA and India. *Journal of Money Laundering Control*.

EY. (n.d.). *Case for mobile payments in India*. http://www.ey.com/Publication /vwLUAssets/EY-the-case-for-mobile-payments-in-india/%24FILE/EY-the-case-for-mobile-payments-in-india.PDF

Faccia, A., Al Naqbi, M. Y. K., & Lootah, S. A. (2019, August). Integrated cloud financial accounting cycle: how artificial intelligence, blockchain, and XBRL will change the accounting, fiscal and auditing practices. In *Proceedings of the 2019 3rd International Conference on Cloud and Big Data Computing* (pp. 31-37). 10.1145/3358505.3358507

Fainusa, A. F., Nurcahyo, R., & Dachyar, M. (2019, December). Conceptual Framework for Digital Wallet User Satisfaction. In *2019 IEEE 6th International Conference on Engineering Technologies and Applied Sciences (ICETAS)* (pp. 1-4). IEEE.

Fernandes, N. (2020). *Economic effects of coronavirus outbreak (COVID-19) on the world economy. SSRN* Preprint no. 3557504.

Financial Institutions Division. (2019). *National Financial Inclusion Strategy-Bangladesh*. Retrieved from https://fid.portal.gov.bd/sites/default/files/files/fid.portal.gov.bd/notices/43182ae2_205c_4 17f_919f_172c5cb60566/Final-Submitted%20to%20FID_NFIS-B-v2.doc#:~:text=National%20 Financial%20Inclusion%20Strategy%20(NFIS)%20is%20a%20roadmap%20of%20actions,to%20 achieve%20financial%20inclusion%20objectives.&text=Ingraining%20Financial%20 Inclusion%20in%20National,3

Fishbein, M., & Ajzen, I. (1975). *Belief, attitude, intention and behaviour: An introduction to theory and research.* Academic Press.

Forbeschina. (2021). *How will fintech drive the development of The Times?* http://www.forbeschina.com/entrepreneur/56653

Fukas, P., Rebstadt, J., Remark, F., & Thomas, O. (2021). Developing an Artificial Intelligence Maturity Model for Auditing. *29th European Conference on Information Systems Research Papers.* https://aisel.aisnet.org/ecis2021_rp/133

Galaz, V., Crona, B., Dauriach, A., Scholtens, B., & Steffen, W. (2018). Finance and the Earth system – exploring the links between financial actors and non-linear changes in the climate system. *Global Environmental Change, 53,* 296–302. doi:10.1016/j.gloenvcha.2018.09.008

George, N., Muiz, K., Whig, P., & Velu, A. (2021). Framework of Perceptive Artificial Intelligence using Natural Language Processing (PAIN). *Artificial & Computational Intelligence.*

Ghazvini, M. A. F., Faria, P., Ramos, S., Morais, H., & Vale, Z. (2015). Incentive-based demand response programs designed by asset-light retail electricity providers for the day-ahead market. *Science Direct, 2015*(82), 786–799.

Global Partnership for Financial Inclusion. (2016). *G20 high level principles for digital financial inclusion.* Global Partneship for Financial Inclusion. Retrieved from https://www.gpfi.org/publications/g20-high-level-principles-digital-financial-inclusion

Golić, Z. (2019). Finance and artificial intelligence: The fifth industrial revolution and its impact on the financial sector. *Zbornik radova Ekonomskog fakulteta u Istočnom Sarajevu,* (19), 67-81.

Gomber, P., Kauffman, R. J., Parker, C., & Weber, B. W. (2018). On the fintech revolution: Interpreting the forces of innovation, disruption and transformation in financial services. *Journal of Management Information Systems, 35*(1), 220–265. doi:10.1080/07421222.2018.1440766

Gomber, P., Koch, A., & Siering, M. (2017). Digital finance and research: Current research and future research directions. *Business Economics (Cleveland, Ohio), 87,* 537–580.

Goodhue, D. L., & Thompson, R. L. (1995). Task-Technology Fit and Individual Performance. *Management Information Systems Quarterly, 19*(2), 213–236. doi:10.2307/249689

Gopal, R. D., Ramesh, R., & Whinston, A. B. (2003). Microproducts in a digital economy: Trading small, gaining large. *International Journal of Electronic Commerce, 8*(2), 9–30. doi:10.1080/10864415.2003.11044292

Gozmann, D., Libenau, J., & Mangan, J. (2018). The Innovation Mechanisms of Fintech Start-Ups: Insights from SWIFT's Innotribe Competition. *Management Information Systems, 35*(1), 145–179. doi:10.1080/07421222.2018.1440768

GSMA Connected Women. (2021). *The Mobile Gender Gap Report 2021.* GSMA.

Guo, H., & Polak, P. (2021). Artificial intelligence and financial technology Fintech: How AI is being used under the pandemic in 2020. The Fourth Industrial Revolution: Implementation of Artificial Intelligence for Growing Business Success, 169-186.

Gusai, O. P. (2019). Robot human interaction: Role of artificial intelligence in accounting and auditing. *Indian Journal of Accounting*, *51*(1), 59–62.

Haddad, C., & Hornuf, L. (2019). The emergence of the global Fintech market: Economic and technological determinants. *Small Business Economics*, *53*(1), 81–105. doi:10.100711187-018-9991-x

Hair, J. F., Hult, G. T. M., Ringle, C. M., Sarstedt, M., & Thiele, K. O. (2017). Mirror, mirror on the wall: A comparative evaluation of composite-based structural equation modeling methods. *Journal of the Academy of Marketing Science*, *45*(5), 616–632. doi:10.100711747-017-0517-x

Hair, J. F., Risher, J. J., Sarstedt, M., & Ringle, C. M. (2019). When to use and how to report the results of PLS-SEM. *European Business Review*, *31*(1), 2–24. doi:10.1108/EBR-11-2018-0203

Halvadia, N. B., Halvadia, S., & Purohit, R. (2022). *Using Text Mining to Identify Key Dimensions of Service Quality for the Indian Public Sector Banks' Mobile Banking Apps*. Academic Press.

Hammi, M. T., Hammi, B., Bellot, P., & Serhrouchni, A. (2018). Bubbles of Trust: A decentralized blockchain-based authentication system for IoT. *Computers & Security*, *78*, 126–142. doi:10.1016/j.cose.2018.06.004

Hamza, A., & Shah, A. (2014). Gender and mobile payment system adoption among students of tertiary institutions in Nigeria. *International Journal of Computer and Information Technology*, *3*(1), 13–20. www.ijcit.com/archives/volume3/issue1/Paper030103.pdf

Hanafizadeh, P., Behboudi, M., Koshksaray, A. A., & Tabar, M. J. S. (2012). Mobile-banking adoption by Iranian bank clients. *Telematics and Informatics*, *31*(1), 62–78. doi:10.1016/j.tele.2012.11.001

Hazra, U., & Priyo, A. K. K. (2021). Mobile financial services in Bangladesh: Understanding the affordances. *The Electronic Journal on Information Systems in Developing Countries*, *87*(3), e12166. doi:10.1002/isd2.12166

Herrero, A. G., & Xu, J. (2018). *How Big IS China's Digital Economy?* www.jstor.org/stable/resrep28511

Hew, T. S., Leong, L. Y., Ooi, K. B., & Chong, A. Y. L. (2016). Predicting drivers of mobile entertainment adoption: A two-stage SEM-artificial-neural-network analysis. *Journal of Computer Information Systems*, *56*(4), 352–370. doi:10.1080/08874417.2016.1164497

Himel, M. T. A., Ashraf, S., Bappy, T. A., Abir, M. T., Morshed, M. K., & Hossain, M. N. (2021). Users' attitude and intention to use mobile financial services in Bangladesh: An empirical study. *South Asian Journal of Marketing*, *2*(1), 72–96. Advance online publication. doi:10.1108/SAJM-02-2021-0015

Hindman, M. (2018). *The Internet Trap: How the Digital Economy Builds Monopolies and Undermines Democracy*. Princeton University Press.

Hsu, C. L., Wang, C. F., & Lin, J. C. C. (2011). Investigating customer adoption behaviours in Mobile Financial Services. *International Journal of Mobile Communications*, *9*(5), 477. doi:10.1504/IJMC.2011.042455

Hu, Y. (2020). The Nature and Function of State-Owned Enterprises from the COVID-19 Prevention and Control. China State-Owned Enterprise Management.

Huang, Q. F. (2020). *Structural reform—problems and Countermeasures of China's economy*. Beijing United Press.

Humbani, M., & Wiese, M. (2019). An integrated framework for the adoption and continuance intention to use mobile payment apps. *International Journal of Bank Marketing*, *37*(2), 646–664. doi:10.1108/IJBM-03-2018-0072

IDC. (2020). *2020-2021 evaluation report on the development of human intelligence computing power in China*. https://baijiahao.baidu.com/s?id=1686138096205100527&wfr=spider&for=pc

Islam, M. N., & Kundu, S. (2018). Poster abstract: Preserving IoT privacy in sharing economy via smart contract. *Proceedings - ACM/IEEE International Conference on Internet of Things Design and Implementation, IoTDI 2018*, 296–297. 10.1109/IoTDI.2018.00047

Jagtiani, J., & John, K. (2018). Fintech: The Impact on Consumers and Regulatory Responses. *Journal of Economics and Business*, *100*, 1–6. doi:10.1016/j.jeconbus.2018.11.002

Jaint, B., Indu, S., Pandey, N., & Pahwa, K. (2019). Malicious Node Detection in Wireless Sensor Networks Using Support Vector Machine. *2019 3rd International Conference on Recent Developments in Control, Automation and Power Engineering, RDCAPE 2019*, 247–252. 10.1109/RDCAPE47089.2019.8979125

Jiang, X., & Jin, J. (2021). Review and prospect of China's digital economy. *Journal of the Party School of the CPC Central Committee (National School of Governance)*, 1-15. . doi:10.14119/j.cnki.zgxb.20211204.001

Jin, X., Zhang, M., Sun, G., & Cui, L. (2021). The impact of COVID-19 on firm innovation: Evidence from Chinese listed companies. *Finance Research Letters*.

Jiwani, N., Gupta, K., & Whig, P. (2021). Novel HealthCare Framework for Cardiac Arrest With the Application of AI Using ANN. *2021 5th International Conference on Information Systems and Computer Networks (ISCON)*, 1–5.

Kang, E. S., Pee, S. J., Song, J. G., & Jang, J. W. (2018). A Blockchain-Based Energy Trading Platform for Smart Homes in a Microgrid. *2018 3rd International Conference on Computer and Communication Systems, ICCCS 2018*, 291–296. 10.1109/CCOMS.2018.8463317

Kapadia, S. (2020). *New frontiers for financial inclusion: Gender impact & fintechs align*. Roots of Impact & SDC. Retrieved from https://www.roots-of-impact.org/

Kaushik, S., Chouhan, Y. S., Sharma, N., Singh, S., & Suganya, P. (2018). Automatic fan speed control using temperature and humidity sensor and Arduino. *International Journal of Advanced Research*, *4*(2), 453–467.

Kautish, S., Reyana, A., & Vidyarthi, A. (2022). SDMTA: Attack Detection and Mitigation Mechanism for DDoS Vulnerabilities in Hybrid Cloud Environment. *IEEE Transactions on Industrial Informatics*.

Keegan, B. J., Canhoto, A. I., & Yen, D. A.-W. (2022). Power negotiation on the tango dancefloor: The adoption of AI in B2B marketing. *Industrial Marketing Management*, *100*, 100. doi:10.1016/j.indmarman.2021.11.001

Khan, T. (2015). Snapdeal stands to gain big from Freecharge acquisition. *Business Today.IN*. Retrieved from https://www.businesstoday.in/current/corporate/snapdeal-stands-to-gain-big-from-freecharge-acquisition/story/216909.html

Khera, Y., Whig, P., & Velu, A. (2021). efficient effective and secured electronic billing system using AI. *Vivekananda Journal of Research*, *10*, 53–60.

Kim, B., Choi, M., & Han, I. (2009). User behaviors toward mobile data services: The role of perceived fee and prior experience. *Expert Systems with Applications*, *36*(4), 8528–8536. doi:10.1016/j.eswa.2008.10.063

Knieps, G., & Bauer, J. M. (2022). Internet of things and the economics of 5G-based local industrial networks. *Telecommunications Policy*, *46*(4), 102261. doi:10.1016/j.telpol.2021.102261

Koay, K. Y., Cheah, C. W., & Chang, Y. X. (2022). A model of online food delivery service quality, customer satisfaction and customer loyalty: A combination of PLS-SEM and NCA approaches. *British Food Journal*.

Koenig-Lewis, N., Palmer, A., & Moll, A. (2010). Predicting young consumers' take up of mobile banking services. *International Journal of Bank Marketing*, *28*(5), 410–432. doi:10.1108/02652321011064917

Kokina, J., & Davenport, T. H. (2017). The Emergence of Artificial Intelligence: How Automation is Changing Auditing. *Journal of Emerging Technologies in Accounting*, *14*(1), 115–122. doi:10.2308/jeta-51730

Kolagar, M., Parida, V., Sjödin, D., & Wincent, J. (2020). An agile co-creation process for digital servitization: A micro-service innovation approach. *Journal of Business Research*, *112*, 478–491. doi:10.1016/j.jbusres.2020.01.009

Kowalski, M., Lee, Z. W. Y., & Chan, T. K. H. (2021). Blockchain technology and trust relationships in trade finance. *Technological Forecasting and Social Change*, *166*, 166. doi:10.1016/j.techfore.2021.120641

Kulašin & Fortuny-Santos. (2005). *Review of the Servqual Concept*. Available at: http://www.quality.unze.ba/zbornici/QUALITY%202005/021-Q05-005.pdf

Kumar, R., Kishore, S., Lu, H., & Prakash, A. (2020).Security analysis of unified payments interface and payment apps in India. In *29th USENIX Security Symposium (USENIX Security 20)* (pp. 1499-1516). USENIX.

Kumar, S., & Mehany, M. S. H. M. (2022). A standardized framework for quantitative assessment of cities' socioeconomic resilience and its improvement measures. *Socio-Economic Planning Sciences*, *79*, 79. doi:10.1016/j.seps.2021.101141

Ladhari, R. (2009). *A review of twenty years of SERVQUAL research*. Available at: http://www.emeraldinsight.com/doi/abs/10.1108/17566690910971445?src=recsys&journalCode=ijqss

Lamberton, C., & Stephen, A. T. (2016). A thematic exploration of digital, social media, and mobile marketing: Research evolution from 2000 to 2015 and an agenda for future inquiry. *Journal of Marketing*, *80*(6), 146–172. doi:10.1509/jm.15.0415

Lee, I., & Shin, Y. J. (2018). Fintech: Ecosystem, business models, investment decisions, and challenges. *Business Horizons*, *61*(1), 35–46. doi:10.1016/j.bushor.2017.09.003

Legris, P., Ingham, J., & Collerette, P. (2003). Why do people use information technology? A critical review of the technology acceptance model. *Information & Management*, *40*(3), 191–204. doi:10.1016/S0378-7206(01)00143-4

Le, M. T. (2021). Examining factors that boost intention and loyalty to use Fintech post-COVID-19 lockdown as a new normal behavior. *Heliyon*, *7*(8), e07821. doi:10.1016/j.heliyon.2021.e07821 PMID:34458639

Lentner, C., Szegedi, K., & Tatay, T. (2015). Corporate social responsibility in the banking sector. *PénzügyiSzemle. Public Finance Quarterly*, *60*(1), 95–103.

Leong, K., & Sung, A. (2018). Fintech (FinancialTechnology): What is it and how to use technologies to create business value in Fintech way? *International Journal of Innovation, Management and Technology*, *9*(2), 74–78. doi:10.18178/ijimt.2018.9.2.791

Li, K., Kim, J. D., Lang, R. K., Kauffman, J. R., & Naldi, M. (2020). How should we understand the digital economy in Asia? Critical assessment and research agenda. *Electronic Commerce Research and Applications*, *44*. doi:10.1016/j.elerap.2020.101004

Lim, W. M., Gupta, G., Biswas, B., & Gupta, R. (2021). Collaborative consumption continuance: A mixed-methods analysis of the service quality-loyalty relationship in ride-sharing services. *Electronic Markets*, 1–22.

Lin, H.-F., & Chen, C.-H. (2013). An Intelligent Embedded Marketing Service System based on TV apps: Design and implementation through product placement in idol dramas. *Expert Systems with Applications*, *40*(10), 4127–4136. doi:10.1016/j.eswa.2013.01.034

Liu, C., Yin, X., & Wang, L. (2020). Regional differences and distribution of China's digital economy development dynamic evolution. *China Science and Technology Forum*, *2020*(3), 97-109.

Liu, X. (2020). Various efforts were made to consolidate the foundation for the development of the digital economy. *Economic Daily.*

Liu, Y.L. (2021). Research on the safe development of FinTech from the perspective of ant group's suspension of listing. *Gansu Finance, (9)*, 60-64.

Luan, Q. (2021). *The Trinity: Create new competitive advantages in the digital economy.* China Public Research Network. Retrieved from http://www.zgzcinfo.cn/expertsbbs/show-32267.html

Luan, T., & Li, J. (2018). *Internet+personal Carbon Finance in Land Desertification Control Scheme Design in Xinjiang.* Xinjiang University of Finance and Economics.

Luarn, P., & Lin, H.-H. (2005). Toward an understanding of the behavioral intention to use mobile banking. *Computers in Human Behavior, 21*(6), 873–891. doi:10.1016/j.chb.2004.03.003

Luo, X., Zhang, W., Li, H., Bose, R., & Chung, Q. B. (2018). Cloud computing capability: Its technological root and business impact. *Journal of Organizational Computing and Electronic Commerce, 28*(3), 193–213. doi:10.1080/10919392.2018.1480926

Lv, M., & Ma, L. (2021). Promoting the upgrading of traditional industries by digitization. *Economic Daily.*

Lwoga, E. T., & Lwoga, N. B. (2017). User acceptance of mobile payment: The effects of user-centric security, system characteristics and gender. *The Electronic Journal on Information Systems in Developing Countries, 81*(1), 1–24. doi:10.1002/j.1681-4835.2017.tb00595.x

Lyons, A. C., Kass-Hanna, J., & Fava, A. (2021). Fintech development and savings, borrowing, and remittances: A comparative study of emerging economies. *Emerging Markets Review.*

Macchiavello & Siri. (2020). *Sustainable Finance and Fintech: Can Technology Contribute to Achieving Environmental Goals? A Preliminary Assessment of 'Green Fintech'.* European Banking Institute Working Paper Series 2020 – no. 71. Available at *SSRN*: https://ssrn.com/abstract=3672989 doi:10.2139/ssrn.3672989

Macchiavello, E., & Siri, M. (2020). Sustainable Finance and Fintech: Can Technology Contribute to Achieving Environmental Goals? A Preliminary Assessment of 'Green FinTech'. *Technological Forecasting and Social Change, 1*(174), 121–172.

Madhu, G., Govardhan, A., & Ravi, V. (2022). DSCN-net: A deep Siamese capsule neural network model for automatic diagnosis of malaria parasites detection. *Multimed Tools Appl.* doi:10.1007/s11042-022-13008-6

Madhu, M., & Whig, P. (2022). A survey of machine learning and its applications. *International Journal of Machine Learning for Sustainable Development, 4*(1), 11–20.

Majcherczyk, M., & Shuqiang, B. (2019). Digital Silk Road - The Role of Cross-Border E-commerce in Facilitating Trade. *Journal of WTO and China, 9*(2), 106–128. https://heinonline.org/HOL/Page?handle=hein.journals/jwtoch9&id=234&div=&collection=

Mamza, E. S. (2021). Use of AIOT in Health System. *International Journal of Sustainable Development in Computing Science, 3*(4), 21–30.

Mante, E. A., & Piris, D. (2002). SMS use by young people in the Netherlands. *Revista de Estudios de Juventud, 52,* 47-58. Retrieved from https://www.itu.int/osg/spu/ni/ubiquitous/Papers/Youth_and_mobile_2002.pdf#page=45

Markovic, S., Koporcic, N., Arslanagic-Kalajdzic, M., Kadic-Maglajlic, S., Bagherzadeh, M., & Islam, N. (2021). Business-to-business open innovation: COVID-19 lessons for small and medium-sized enterprises from emerging markets. *Technological Forecasting and Social Change, 170.*

Maurya, S., Lakhera, S., Srivastava, K. A., & Kumar, M. (2021). Cost analysis of amazon web services–From an eye of architect and developer. *Materials Today: Proceedings, 46*(20), 10757-10760.

McDonald, L. M., & Korabik, K. (1991). Sources of stress and ways of coping among male and female managers. *Journal of Social Behavior and Personality, 6*(7), 185–198.

Mello, M. (2018). *US Fintech Sector: short-run and long-run performance of initial public offerings* (Doctoral dissertation).

Mir, R. A., Rameez, R., & Tahir, N. (2022). Measuring Internet banking service quality: An empirical evidence. *The TQM Journal.*

Mishra, L. (2016). *E-wallet customer base surges.* Available at http://www.thehindu.com/business/E-wallet-firms'-customer-base-surges/article16695644.ece

Moon, J. W., & Kim, Y. G. (2001). Extending the TAM for a World-Wide-Web context. *Information & Management, 38*(4), 217–230. doi:10.1016/S0378-7206(00)00061-6

Moorthy, T. V. K., Budati, A. K., Kautish, S., Goyal, S. B., & Prasad, K. L. (2022). Reduction of satellite images size in 5G networks using Machinelearning algorithms. *IET Communications, 16,* 584–591. https://doi.org/10.1049/cmu2.12354

Musleh Al-Sartawi, A. M., Razzaque, A., & Kamal, M. M. (Eds.). (2021). *Artificial Intelligence Systems and the Internet of Things in the Digital Era. EAMMIS 2021* (Vol. 239). Lecture Notes in Networks and Systems.

Nadikattu, R. R., Mohammad, S. M., & Whig, P. (2020b). *Novel economical social distancing smart Device for COVID-19* (SSRN Scholarly Paper ID 3640230). Social Science Research Network. Https://Papers. Ssrn. Com/Abstract

Nadikattu, R. R., Mohammad, S. M., & Whig, P. (2020a). *Novel economical social distancing smart device for covid-19. International Journal of Electrical Engineering and Technology.*

Nambisan, S., Lyytinen, K., Majchrzak, A., & Song, M. (2017). Digital innovation management: Reinventing innovation management research in a digital world. *Management Information Systems Quarterly, 41*(1), 223–238. doi:10.25300/MISQ/2017/41:1.03

Nassiry, D. (2018). *The role of Fintech in unlocking green finance: Policy insights for developing countries* (No. 883). ADBI Working Paper.

National Development and Reform Commission. (2021). *China E-commerce Report 2020 was released in Ningbo.* National Development and Reform Commission. Retrieved from https://www.ndrc.gov.cn/fggz/qykf/xxjc/202107/t20210701_1285221.html

Ng, A. W., & Kwok, B. K. (2017). Emergence of Fintech and cybersecurity in a global financial centre. *Journal of Financial Econometrics, 25*(4), 422–434.

Nguyen, V. H. (2021, December). An Agile Approach for Managing Microservices-Based Software Development: Case Study in FinTech. In *European, Mediterranean, and Middle Eastern Conference on Information Systems* (pp. 723-736). Springer.

Niu, B., Mu, Z., Cao, B., & Gao, J. (2021). Should multinational firms implement blockchain to provide quality verification? *Transportation Research Part E, Logistics and Transportation Review, 145*, 102121.

Noor, N. R. A. M., & Mansor, N. (2019). Exploring the adaptation of artificial intelligence in whistleblowing practice of the internal auditors in Malaysia. *Procedia Computer Science, 163*, 434–439. doi:10.1016/j.procs.2019.12.126

Nurlaily, F., Aini, E. K., & Asmoro, P. S. (2021). Understanding the FinTech continuance intention of Indonesian users: The moderating effect of gender. *Business: Theory and Practice, 22*(2), 290–298. doi:10.3846/btp.2021.13880

OECD. (2017a). *The Next Production Revolution: Implications for Governments and Business.* doi:10.1787/9789264271036-en

OECD. (2020). *Coronavirus (COVID-19). SME policy responses.* Retrieved from https://read.oecd-ilibrary.org/view/?ref=119_119680-di6h3qgi4x&title=Covid-19_SME_Policy_Responses

Oliveira, T., Faria, M., Thomas, M. A., & Popovič, A. (2014). Extending the understanding of mobile banking adoption: When UTAUT meets TTF and ITM. *International Journal of Information Management, 34*(5), 689–703. doi:10.1016/j.ijinfomgt.2014.06.004

Oliver, R. L. (1980). A Cognitive Model of the Antecedents and Consequences of Satisfaction Decisions. *JMR, Journal of Marketing Research, 17*(4), 460–469. doi:10.1177/002224378001700405

Ong, J. W., Poong, Y. S., & Ng, T. H. (2008). 3G services adoption among university students: Diffusion of innovation theory. *Communications of the IBIMA, 3*(16), 114–121.

Pan, W., Xie, T., Wang, Z., & Ma, M. (2021). Digital economy: An innovation driver for total factor productivity. *Journal of Business Research, 139*, 303-311. doi:10.1016/j.jbusres.2021.09.061

Pan, J., Wang, J., Hester, A., Alqerm, I., Liu, Y., & Zhao, Y. (2019). EdgeChain: An edge-IoT framework and prototype based on blockchain and smart contracts. *IEEE Internet of Things Journal, 6*(3), 4719–4732. doi:10.1109/JIOT.2018.2878154

Papadopoulos, T., Baltas, N. K., & Balta, E. M. (2020). The use of digital technologies by small and medium enterprises during COVID-19: Implications for theory and practice. *International Journal of Information Management, 55*. doi:10.1016/j.ijinfomgt.2020.102192

Paradise, J. F. (2019). China's Quest for Global Economic Governance Reform Journal of Chinese Political Science. *Springer Link, 24*(3), 471–493.

Parasuraman, A. (2000). Technology Readiness Index (TRI) a multiple-item scale to measure readiness to embrace new technologies. *Journal of Service Research, 2*(4), 307–320. doi:10.1177/109467050024001

Parasuraman, A., & Colby, C. L. (2015). An updated and streamlined technology readiness index: TRI 2.0. *Journal of Service Research, 18*(1), 59–74. doi:10.1177/1094670514539730

Parasuraman, A., Zeithaml, V. A., & Berry, L. L. (1985). A conceptual model of service quality and its implications for future research. *Journal of Marketing, 49*(4), 41–50. doi:10.1177/002224298504900403

Parihar, V., & Yadav, S. (n.d.). *Comparison estimation of effective consumer future preferences with the application of AI*. Academic Press.

Pawar, V. S. (2021). IoT architecture with embedded AI. *International Journal of Sustainable Development in Computing Science, 3*(4), 11–20.

PBOC. (2021). *White paper on research and development progress of China's digital RMB*. http://www.gov.cn/xinwen/2021-07/16/content_5625569.htm

People's Daily Overseas Edition. (2020). *Digital trade will be the accelerator of a "double cycle"*. Available at: http://www.gov.cn/xinwen/2020-09/08/content_5541389.htm

Petralia, K., Philippon, T., Rice, T., & Veron, N. (2019). *Banking disrupted? Financial intermediation in an era of transformational technology*. Technical Report 22, Geneva Reports on the World Economy. ICMB and CEPR.

Philippon, T. (2016). *The Fintech opportunity*. NBER Working Paper.

Philippon, T. (2015). Has us finance industry become less efficient? On the theory and measurement of financial intermediation. *The American Economic Review, 105*(4), 1408–1438. doi:10.1257/aer.20120578

Pinto, E. M. D. L., Lachowski, R., Pellenz, M. E., Penna, M. C., & Souza, R. D. (2018). A machine learning approach for detecting spoofing attacks in wireless sensor networks. *Proceedings - International Conference on Advanced Information Networking and Applications, AINA*, 752–758. 10.1109/AINA.2018.00113

Popy, N. N., & Bappy, T. A. (2020). Attitude toward social media reviews and restaurant visit intention: a Bangladeshi perspective. *South Asian Journal of Business Studies*. doi:10.1108/SAJBS-03-2020-0077

Poulton, C., Gibbon, P., Hanyani-Mlambo, B., Kydd, J., Maro, W., Larsen, M. N., Osorio, A., Tschirley, D., & Zulu, B. (2004). Competition and coordination in liberalized African cotton market systems. *World Development*, *32*(3), 519–536. doi:10.1016/j.worlddev.2003.10.003

Pramani, R., & Iyer, S. V. (2022). Adoption of payments banks: A grounded theory approach. *Journal of Financial Services Marketing*, 1–15. doi:10.105741264-021-00133-w

Punschmann, T. (2017). Fintech. *Business & Information Systems Engineering*, *59*(1), 69–76. doi:10.100712599-017-0464-6

Pustokhina, I. V., Pustokhin, D. A., Mohanty, S. N., García, P. A. G., & García-Díaz, V. (2021). Artificial intelligence assisted Internet of Things based financial crisis prediction in Fintech environment. *Annals of Operations Research*, 1–21.

Qasim, A., & Kharbat, F. F. (2020). Blockchain technology, business data analytics, and artificial intelligence: Use in the accounting profession and ideas for inclusion into the accounting curriculum. *Journal of Emerging Technologies in Accounting*, *17*(1), 107–117. doi:10.2308/jeta-52649

Qi, L., Zhang, X., Dou, W., Hu, C., Yang, C., & Chen, J. (2018). A two-stage locality-sensitive hashing based approach for privacy-preserving mobile service recommendation in cross-platform edge environment. *Future Generation Computer Systems*, *88*, 636–643. doi:10.1016/j.future.2018.02.050

Qiu, T., Liu, X., Li, K., Hu, Q., Sangaiah, A. K., & Chen, N. (2018). Community-Aware Data Propagation with Small World Feature for Internet of Vehicles. *IEEE Communications Magazine*, *56*(1), 86–91. doi:10.1109/MCOM.2018.1700511

QKLW. (2021). *China block-chain policy survey and regulatory trend analysis report*. https://www.qklw.com/specialcolumn/20210304/172943.html

Räisänen, J., & Tuovinen, T. (2018). Digital innovations in rural micro-enterprises. *Science Direct*, *73*, 56–67. doi:10.1016/j.jrurstud.2019.09.010

Raj, R. (2016). *Are mobile wallets still to stay, or is cash still the king*. Available at https://inc42.com/resources/mobile-wallet-scenario-india/

Rajawat, A. S., Bedi, P., Goyal, S. B., Kautish, S., Xihua, Z., Aljuaid, H., & Mohamed, A. W. (2022). Dark Web Data Classification Using Neural Network. *Computational Intelligence and Neuroscience*.

Ram Prabha, V., & Latha, P. (2017). Fuzzy Trust Protocol for Malicious Node Detection in Wireless Sensor Networks. *Wireless Personal Communications: An International Journal*, *94*(4), 2549–2559. doi:10.100711277-016-3666-1

Ranchber, S. (2018). *Stimulating Green Fintech Innovation for Sustainable Development: An Analysis of the Innovation Process*. Academic Press.

Ray, N., & Ghosh, D. (2017). Online Banking Service: A Boon or Bane? *Asian Journal of Research in Banking and Finance*, *7*(5), 179–194.

RBI. (2014). *Report of the Committee on Comprehensive Financial Services for Small Business and Low Income Households*. The Reserve Bank of India. https://rbi.org.in/scripts/BS_PressReleaseDisplay.aspx?prid=30353

Reddy, R. (n.d.). Role of information science during COVID-19. *COVID-19, 149*.

Reddy, S. (2018). Announcement of payment banks and stock performance of commercial banks in India. *Journal of Internet Banking and Commerce, 23*(1), 1–12.

Reddy, R. (2019). Purification of indoor air using a novel pseudo PMOS ultraviolet photocatalytic oxidation (PP-UVPCO) sensor. *International Journal of Sustainable Development in Computing Science, 1*(3).

Rejeb, A., Suhaiza, Z., Rejeb, K., Seuring, S., & Treiblmaier, H. (2022). The Internet of Things and the circular economy: A systematic literature review and research agenda. *Journal of Cleaner Production, 350*(20), 131439. doi:10.1016/j.jclepro.2022.131439

Reji Kumar, G., & Ravindran, D. S. (2012). An Empirical Study on Service Quality Perceptions and Continuance Intention in Mobile Banking Context in India. *Journal of Internet Banking and Commerce, 17*(1), 1–22.

Research Group of Digital Economy Situation Analysis of CCID Think Tank. (2021). Digital economy: The enabling effect on the real economy will be further released. *Network Security and Informatization, 4*(3), 4-6.

Rogers, E. (1995). *Diffusion of innovations*. Free Press.

Rogers, E. M. (1976). New product adoption and diffusion. *The Journal of Consumer Research, 2*(4), 290–301. doi:10.1086/208642

Rogers, E. M. (2004). A prospective and retrospective look at the Diffusion Model. *Journal of Health Communication, 9*(sup1), 13–19. doi:10.1080/10810730490271449 PMID:14960401

Rogers, M. (2018). *Country overview: Bangladesh Mobile industry driving growth and enabling digital inclusion*. GSM Association. Retrieved from https://data.gsmaintelligence.com/api-web/v2/research-file-download?id=30933394&file=Country%20overview%20Bangladesh.pdf

Roy, P. M. (2021). Anatomy of the Digital Payment Ecosystem in India. *Bimaquest, 21*(3), 40–61.

Ruchin, C. M., & Whig, P. (2015). Design and Simulation of Dynamic UART Using Scan Path Technique (USPT). *International Journal of Electrical, Electronics & Computing in Science & Engineering*.

Ruiz-Real, J. L., Uribe-Toril, J., Torres, J. A., & De Pablo, J. (2021). Artificial intelligence in business and economics research: Trends and future. *Journal of Business Economics and Management, 22*(1), 98–117. doi:10.3846/jbem.2020.13641

Rukikaire, K. (2019). *Chinese initiative ant Forest wins UN champions of the earth award.* UNEP - UN Environment Programme. http://www. unenvironment.org/news-and-stories/press-release/chinese-initiative-ant-forestwins-un-champions-earth-award

Rupani, A., & Sujediya, G. (2016). A Review of FPGA implementation of Internet of Things. *International Journal of Innovative Research in Computer and Communication Engineering, 4*(9).

Saad, G., & Gill, T. (2000). Applications of evolutionary psychology in marketing. *Psychology and Marketing, 17*(12), 1005–1034. doi:10.1002/1520-6793(200012)17:12<1005::AID-MAR1>3.0.CO;2-H

Sagib, G. K., & Zapan, B. (2014). Bangladeshi mobile banking service quality and customer satisfaction and loyalty. *Management & Marketing, 9*(3).

Saima, F. N., Rahman, M. H. A., & Ghosh, R. (2022). MFS usage intention during COVID-19 and beyond: an integration of health belief and expectation confirmation model. *Journal of Economic and Administrative Sciences.* doi:10.1108/JEAS-07-2021-0133

Saini, D., Rupani, A., Sujediya, G., & Sharma, T. (2017). An ISFET automated output calibration system implementation on reconfigurable FPGA device with MATLAB artificial intelligence interfacing. *2017 3rd International Conference on Applied and Theoretical Computing and Communication Technology (ICATccT),* 354–358.

Salloum, S. A., Alhamad, A. Q. M., Al-Emran, M., Monem, A. A., & Shaalan, K. (2019). Exploring students' acceptance of e-learning through developing a comprehensive technology acceptance model. *IEEE Access: Practical Innovations, Open Solutions, 7,* 128445–128462. doi:10.1109/ACCESS.2019.2939467

Sekaran, U., & Bougie, R. (2016). *Research methods for business: A skill building approach.* john Wiley & Sons.

Senyo, P. K., & Ellis, L. C. (2020). Unearthing antecedents to financial inclusion through FinTech innovations. *Technovation, 98,* 102155. doi:10.1016/j.technovation.2020.102155

Shamraev, A. (2019). Legal and regulatory framework of the payment and e-money services in the BRiCS countries. *BRiCS Law Journal, 6*(2), 60–81.

Sharma, M., Luthra, S., Joshi, S., & Joshi, H. (2022). Challenges to agile project management during COVID-19 pandemic: an emerging economy perspective. *Operations Management Research,* 1-14.

Sharma, C., Sharma, S., Kautish, S., Alsallami, S. A., Khalil, E. M., & Mohamed, A. W. (2022). A new median-average round Robin scheduling algorithm: An optimal approach for reducing turnaround and waiting time. *Alexandria Engineering Journal, 61*(12), 10527–10538.

Sharma, S. K., Govindaluri, S. M., & Al Balushi, S. M. (2015). Predicting determinants of Internet banking adoption: A two-staged regression-neural network approach. *Management Research Review, 38*(7), 750–766. doi:10.1108/MRR-06-2014-0139

Shen, W., & Hou, L. (2021). China's central bank digital currency and its impacts on monetary policy and payment competition: Game changer or regulatory toolkit? *Computer Law & Security Review, 41*, 41. doi:10.1016/j.clsr.2021.105577

Shihadeh, F. (2020). Online Payment Services and Individuals' Behaviour: New Evidence from the MENAP. *International Journal of Electronic Banking, 2*(4), 275–282. doi:10.1504/IJEBANK.2020.114763

Shing, A., & Serret, A. (2021). *Sustainable Finance and FinTech: A necessary marriage.* Retrieved 12 May 2022, from https://www.pwc.com/mu/en/about-us/press-room/sustainable-finance.html

Singh, S., & Srivastava, R. K. (2018). Predicting the intention to use mobile banking in India. *International Journal of Bank Marketing, 36*(2), 357–378. doi:10.1108/IJBM-12-2016-0186

Sinha, R., & Ranjan, A. (2015). Effect of Variable Damping Ratio on design of PID Controller. *2015 4th International Conference on Reliability, Infocom Technologies and Optimization (ICRITO)(Trends and Future Directions)*, 1–4.

Song, H., Yang, X., & Yu, K. (2020). How do supply chain network and SMEs' operational capabilities enhance working capital financing? An integrative signaling view. *International Journal of Production Economics, 220*, 220. doi:10.1016/j.ijpe.2019.07.020

Spence, M. (2021). Government and economics in the digital economy. *Journal of Government and Economics, 3.* doi:10.1016/j.jge.2021.100020

Srivastava, J., Bhagat, R., & Kumar, P. (2020). Analog inverse filters using OTAs. *2020 6th International Conference on Control, Automation and Robotics (ICCAR)*, 627–631.

State Bank Buddy-Mobility. (n.d.). Retrieved from: https://mobility.onlinesbi.com/sbf_buddy.html

Stockholm Green Digital Finance. (2017). *Unlocking the potential of green Fintech.* Author.

Stoner, G. (2009). Accounting students' IT application skills over a 10-year period. *Accounting Education, 18*(1), 7–31. doi:10.1080/09639280802532224

Sun, Y., Zeng, X., Cui, X., Zhang, G., & Bie, R. (2019). An active and dynamic credit reporting system for SMEs in China. *Personal and Ubiquitous Computing.* Advance online publication. doi:10.100700779-019-01275-4

Su, X., Gao, X. F., & Lu, Y. (2018). Credibility based WSN trust model. *Electron. Opt. Control, 25*(3), 32–36.

Talky, S. (n.d.). *Indian Startup success story: MobiKwik.* http://www.startuptalky.com/startup/mobikwik/

Talwar, S., Dhir, A., Khalil, A., Mohan, G., & Islam, A. N. (2020). Point of adoption and beyond. Initial trust and mobile-payment continuation intention. *Journal of Retailing and Consumer Services, 55*, 102086. doi:10.1016/j.jretconser.2020.102086

Tapscott, D. (2014). *The Digital Economy Anniversary Edition: Rethinking Promise and Peril in the Age of Networked Intelligence* (2nd ed.). Amazon.

Tariq, B., Najam, H., Han, H., Sadaa, A. M., Abbasi, A. A., Christopher, N., & Abbasi, G. A. (2021). Examining mobile financial services in Pakistan: Rural and urban perspective with gender as a moderator. In *Recent advances in technology acceptance models and theories* (pp. 225–245). Springer. doi:10.1007/978-3-030-64987-6_14

The Business Standard. (2020). *Bangladesh gets 3.9m new mobile, internet subscribers in September*. Retrieved from https://www.tbsnews.net/bangladesh/telecom/bangladesh-gets-39m-new-mobile-internet-subscribers-september-153343

The World Bank. (2018, October 2). *Financial Inclusion Overview.* Author.

Tougaard, W. E. (2020). *Greening China - How Fintech drives Green Finance in China*. Available at: https://www.china-experience.com/china-experience-insights/how-Fintech-accelerates-chinas-sustainable-finance-ambitions

Turluev, R., & Hadjieva, L. (2021). Artificial Intelligence in Corporate Governance Systems. In *SHS Web of Conferences* (Vol. 93, p. 03015). EDP Sciences. 10.1051hsconf/20219303015

Twum, K. K., Kosiba, J. P. B., Hinson, R. E., Gabrah, A. Y. B., & Assabil, E. N. (2022). Determining mobile money service customer satisfaction and continuance usage through service quality. *Journal of Financial Services Marketing*, 1–13.

Ucoglu, D. (2020). Current Machine Learning Applications in Accounting and Auditing. *PressAcademia Procedia*, *12*(1), 1–7. doi:10.17261/Pressacademia.2020.1337

Uddin, B., Imran, A., & Rahman, M. A. (2017). Detection and locating the point of fault in distribution side of power system using WSN technology. *4th International Conference on Advances in Electrical Engineering, ICAEE 2017,* 570–574. 10.1109/ICAEE.2017.8255421

UNFCCC. (2015). *Paris Agreement. FCCC/CP/2015/10/Add.1.* Available at: https://unfccc.int/files/essential_background/convention/application/pdf/english_paris_agreement.pdf

United Nations. (2015a). *Transforming our world: the 2030 Agenda for Sustainable Development.* Available at: http://www.un.org/ga/search/view_doc.asp?symbol=A/RES/70/1&Lang=E

Van Cauwenberg, J., Schepers, P., Deforche, B., & de Geus, B. (2022). Effects of e-biking on older adults' biking and walking frequencies, health, functionality and life space area: A prospective observational study. *Transportation Research Part A, Policy and Practice*, *156*, 156. doi:10.1016/j.tra.2021.12.006

Vasudeva, S., & Chawla, S. (2019). Does Gender, Age and Income Moderate the Relationship Between Mobile Banking Usage and Loyalty? *International Journal of Online Marketing*, *9*(4), 1–18. doi:10.4018/IJOM.2019100101

Velu, A., & Whig, P. (n.d.). *Studying the Impact of the COVID Vaccination on the World Using Data Analytics*. Academic Press.

Velu, A., & Whig, P. (2021). Protect Personal Privacy And Wasting Time Using Nlp: A Comparative Approach Using Ai. *Vivekananda Journal of Research*, *10*, 42–52.

Veluvali, P. (2019). Legal Framework and Governing Design for IPOs in India. In *Retail Investor in Focus* (pp. 33–58). Springer. doi:10.1007/978-3-030-12756-5_3

Venkatesh, V., & Davis, F. D. (2000). A Theoretical Extension of the Technology Acceptance Model: Four Longitudinal Field Studies. *Management Science*, *46*(2), 186–204. doi:10.1287/mnsc.46.2.186.11926

Venkatesh, V., Morris, M. G., Davis, G. B., & Davis, F. D. (2003). User Acceptance of Information Technology: Toward a Unified View. *Management Information Systems Quarterly*, *27*(3), 425–478. doi:10.2307/30036540

Verhoef, C. P., Broekhuizen, T., Bart, Y., Bhattacharya, A., Dong, Q. J., Fabian, N., & Haenlein, M. (2021). Digital transformation: A multidisciplinary reflection and research agenda. *Journal of Business Research*, *122*, 889–901. doi:10.1016/j.jbusres.2019.09.022

Verhoef, P. C., Kannan, P. K., & Inman, J. (2015). From multi-channel retailing to omni-channel retailing: Introduction to the special issue on multi-channel retailing. *Journal of Retailing*, *91*(2), 174–181. doi:10.1016/j.jretai.2015.02.005

Verma, T. (2019). A comparison of different R2R D/A converters. *International Journal of Sustainable Development in Computing Science, 1*(2).

Vijai, C. (2019). Mobile wallet and its future in India. *Journal of Emerging Technologies and Innovative Research*, *6*(5), 574–580.

Vlačić, B., Corbo, L., Costa e Silva, S., & Dabić, M. (2021). The evolving role of artificial intelligence in marketing: A review and research agenda. *Journal of Business Research*, 128.

Wall, L. D. (2018). Some financial regulatory implications of artificial intelligence. *Journal of Economics and Business*, *100*, 55–63. doi:10.1016/j.jeconbus.2018.05.003

Wang, Y.F. (2021). How can FinTech fully empower Inclusive Finance? *Academic Research*, 74-80.

Wang, R., Liu, J., & Luo, H. (2020). Fintech development and bank risk taking in China. *European Journal of Finance*, *2020*(13), 1–22.

Wang, Y. S., Wang, Y. M., Lin, H. H., & Tang, T. I. (2003). Determinants of user acceptance of Internet banking: An empirical study. *International Journal of Service Industry Management*, *14*(5), 501–519. doi:10.1108/09564230310500192

Whig, P. (2022). More on Convolution Neural Network CNN. *International Journal of Sustainable Development in Computing Science*, *1*(1).

Whig, P., Nadikattu, R. R., & Velu, A. (2022). COVID-19 pandemic analysis using application of AI. *Healthcare Monitoring and Data Analysis Using IoT: Technologies and Applications*, 1.

Whig, Priyam, & Ahmad. (2018). Simulation & performance analysis of various R2R D/A converter using various topologies. *International Robotics & Automation Journal, 4*(2), 128–131.

Whig, P. (2017). Temperature and Frequency Independent Readout Circuit for PCS System. *SF J Material Res Let, 1*(3), 8–12.

Whig, P. (2019a). A Novel Multi-Center and Threshold Ternary Pattern. *International Journal of Machine Learning for Sustainable Development, 1*(2), 1–10.

Whig, P. (2019b). Exploration of Viral Diseases mortality risk using machine learning. *International Journal of Machine Learning for Sustainable Development, 1*(1), 11–20.

Whig, P., & Ahmad, S. N. (2018). Comparison analysis of various R2R D/A converter. *Int J Biosen Bioelectron, 4*(6), 275–279.

Wilson, T. A. (2012). Supporting social enterprises to support vulnerable consumers: The example of community development finance institutions and financial exclusion. *Journal of Consumer Policy, 35*(2), 197–213. doi:10.100710603-011-9182-5

Wojcik, D., & Ioannou, S. (2020). COVID-19 and finance: Market developments so far and potential impacts on the financial sector and centres. *Tijdschrift Voor Economischeen Sociale Geografie, 111*(3), 387–400. doi:10.1111/tesg.12434 PMID:32836484

Wong. (2020). *Constructing a Survey Questionnaire to Collect Data on Service Quality of Business Academics.* http://eprints.utar.edu.my/860/1/6343.pdf

Xiao, Y., Li, S.L., & Liang, B. (2020). Banking FinTech application under COVID-19: theoretical logic, practical characteristics and reform path. *Research on Financial Economics Investigate, 35*(3), 90-103.

Yadav, N. (2017). *PayTm launches e-commerce platform PayTm Mall.* https://www.bgr.in/news/PayTm-launches-new-e-commerce-platform-PayTm-mall/

Yang, A. S. (2009). Exploring adoption difficulties in mobile banking services. *Canadian Journal of Administrative Sciences/Revue Canadienne des Sciences de l'Administration, 26*(2), 136-149. doi:10.1002/cjas.102

Yang, D. (2020). Civil Code Opens a New Era of Building Digital Economy Legal System. *Procuratorial Daily.*

Yang, X. (2020). Fintech in Promoting the Development of Green Finance in China against the Background of Big Data and Artificial Intelligence. In *2020 4th International Seminar on Education Innovation and Economic Management (SEIEM).* Francis Academic Press.

Yang, Y. (2019, Mar. 4). Report: China becoming digital trade leader. *China Daily.*

Yang, Y. M. (2021). BCM: Digital new bank of communications has more AI appeared at the world Artificial Intelligence Conference. *Rural Financial Times,* (3).

Yang, J., Cheng, L., & Luo, X. (2009). A comparative study on e-banking services between China and the USA. *International Journal Electrochemical Finance*, *3*(3), 235–252. doi:10.1504/IJEF.2009.027848

Yang, W., Sui, X., & Qi, Z. (2021). Can fintech improve the efficiency of commercial banks?—An analysis based on big data. *Research in International Business and Finance*, *55*, 101338. doi:10.1016/j.ribaf.2020.101338

Yawalkar, M. V. V. (2019). A Study of Artificial Intelligence and its role in Human Resource Management. *International Journal of Research and Analytical Reviews*, *6*(1), 20–24.

Yen, Y. S., & Wu, F. S. (2016). Predicting the adoption of mobile financial services: The impacts of perceived mobility and personal habit. *Computers in Human Behavior*, *65*, 31–42. doi:10.1016/j.chb.2016.08.017

Yin, Z., Gong, X., Guo, P., & Wu, T. (2019). What Drives Entrepreneurship in Digital Economy? Evidence from China. *Economic Modelling, 82*, 66-73.

You, C. (2020). Law and policy of platform economy in China. *Computer Law & Security Review, 39*. doi:10.1016/j.clsr.2020.105493

Yu, P., Hu, Y., Waseem, M., & Rafay, A. (2021). Regulatory Developments in Peer-to-Peer (P2P) Lending to Combat Frauds: The Case of China. In A. Rafay (Ed.), Handbook of Research on Theory and Practice of Financial Crimes (pp. 172-194). IGI Global.

Yuan, G. X., & Wang, H. (2019). The general dynamic risk assessment for the enterprise by the hologram approach in financial technology. *International Journal of Financial Engineering*, *06*(01), 1950001. doi:10.1142/S2424786319500014

Yu, P., Li, C., Sampat, M., & Chen, Z. (2022). How the Development of FinTech Can Bolster Financial Inclusion Under an Era of Disruptive Innovation? Case Study on China. In M. Anshari, M. Almunawar, & M. Masri (Eds.), *FinTech Development for Financial Inclusiveness* (pp. 135–167). IGI Global. doi:10.4018/978-1-7998-8447-7.ch009

Yu, P., Lu, S., Hanes, E., & Chen, Y. (2022). The Role of Blockchain Technology in Harnessing the Sustainability of Chinese Digital Finance. In P. Swarnalatha & S. Prabu (Eds.), *Blockchain Technologies for Sustainable Development in Smart Cities* (pp. 155–186). IGI Global. doi:10.4018/978-1-7998-9274-8.ch009

Zavolokina, L., Dolata, M. & Schwabe, G. (2016). The Fintech phenomenon: antecedents of financial innovation perceived by the popular press. *Financial Innovation, 2*(16).

Zawaideh, F., Salamah, M., & Al-Bahadili, H. (2018). A fair trust-based malicious node detection and isolation scheme for WSNs. *Proceedings of 2nd International Conference on the Applications of Information Technology in Developing Renewable Energy Processes and Systems, IT-DREPS 2017*, 1–6. 10.1109/IT-DREPS.2017.8277813

Zemankova, A. (2019, December). Artificial Intelligence in Audit and Accounting: Development, Current Trends, Opportunities and Threats-Literature Review. In *2019 International Conference on Control, Artificial Intelligence, Robotics & Optimization (ICCAIRO)* (pp. 148-154). IEEE. 10.1109/ICCAIRO47923.2019.00031

Zeng, L. G., Yuan, Y., & Wang, H. (2018). Detecting WSN node misbehavior based on the trust mechanism. *J. Zhejiang Normal Univ. Nature and Science, 41*(1), 39–43.

Zhang, H. (2018). Regulatory sandbox and compatibility with China's administrative law system. *Zhejiang Journal,* (1).

Zhang, M. (2021). Discussion on the transformation and development direction of commercial banks in the era of AI. *Economics and Management Science,* 107-108.

Zhang, W., Zhu, S., Tang, J., & Xiong, N. (2017). A novel trust management scheme based on Dempster–Shafer evidence theory for malicious nodes detection in wireless sensor networks. *The Journal of Supercomputing, 74*(4), 1779–1801. doi:10.1007/s11227-017-2150-3

Zhang, Y. F., Chen, J. Y., Han, Y., Qian, M. X., Guo, X., Chen, R., Xu, D., & Chen, Y. (2021). The contribution of Fintech to sustainable development in the digital age: Ant forest and land restoration in China. *Land Use Policy, 103,* 105306. doi:10.1016/j.landusepol.2021.105306

Zhang, Y., Kasahara, S., Shen, Y., Jiang, X., & Wan, J. (2019). Smart contract-based access control for the internet of things. *IEEE Internet of Things Journal, 6*(2), 1594–1605. doi:10.1109/JIOT.2018.2847705

Zilgalvis, P. (2014). The Need for an Innovation Principle in Regulatory Impact Assessment: The Case of Finance and Innovation in Europe. *Policy and Internet, 6*(4), 377–392. doi:10.1002/1944-2866.POI374

Zou, C.W., Du, Y., Hao, K., & Jiang, D.F. (2020). Block-chain+IoT enabling the digital transformation of FinTech. *Zhangjiang Science and Technology Review,* 29-31.

About the Contributors

Guneet Kaur is a certified commercial banking and credit analyst (CBCA), Capital markets and securities analyst (CMSA), and Certified AML FinTech Compliance Associate (CAFCA). She is an MSc Fintech graduate (with distinction) from the University of Stirling, Scotland, United Kingdom. Prior to MSC, she has also done MBA from GNDU (gold medal) and has worked as a global client and partner business manager with Singapore-based MNC. Currently, she is working as an Editor (Cryptopedia) at Cointelegraph. She has written various conference papers and has authored a book titled 'The Magic Of Compounding'. She was the Finalist of the Women in STEM-Lovelace Colloquium that was held in 2019 at the University of Salford, UK, and Royal Bank of Scotland's Hackathon in 2019. Her expertise includes blockchain & fintech research, quantitative analysis, financial modeling, business valuation, business analysis, data visualization, and financial fraud, and anti-money laundering analysis.

* * *

Aashrika Ahuja is an experienced corporate and intellectual property rights lawyer, advisor, researcher, writer and author. With an experience of 8 years in the field of law, she is now well conversant with various aspects of the profession. She has handled legal matters in diverse fields including Civil, Criminal, Intellectual Property Rights, Sexual Harassment against Women and Children, Cyber laws, is a licensed Attorney and is eligible to appear and practice before various courts in India. She is well versed with corporate governance and with strong entrepreneurship skills, has successfully advised as well as worked with various corporates, organizations and institutions. She has an experience of working and handling clients all across the globe. She has a keen interest in research and writing and has authored research paper in the prestigious International Journal for Scientific and Engineering Research. While handling drafting, review of various kinds of legal Agreements, Contracts and other legal documents, she also provides legal opinion on diverse matters relating to Intellectual Property Rights. She is passionate about realizing and working towards United Nations 2030 Agenda for Sustainable Development Goals and with her strong advocacy skills has been actively working in the development field to leave no one behind.

Usha Badhera is an Assistant Professor at Jaipuria Institute of Management, Jaipur. She has 20 years of teaching, research, and administrative experience. She is passionate about extracting business value out of technology. She has organized & conducted several workshops on how technology can effectively be used to work smarter and in an engaging way. She has several publications to her credit and has presented research papers at national and international conferences and journals. Her area of interest in Research, Training, and Consultancy include IoT, Analytics, Data Visualization, and Real-Time Systems.

Pradeep Bedi received the B.Tech. degree in computer science and engineering from Uttar Pradesh Technical University (UPTU), Lucknow, India, in 2005 and M.Tech. in computer science and engineering from Guru Gobind Singh Indraprastha University (GGSIPU), Delhi, India, in 2009. He is GATE, UGC-NET qualified and currently pursuing Ph.D from Indira Gandhi National Tribal University, Amarkantak (Regional Campus Manipur). He started his academic career from Mahatma Gandhi Mission's College of Engineering and Technology in 2005 and served various reputed colleges and universities in India and abroad. Currently, he holds the position of assistant professor in the department of computer science and engineering, Galgotias University, Greater Noida, Uttar Pradesh, India. He has authored or co-authored over 40 technical papers published in national and international journals and conferences and also published 15 patents in India and abroad. He is a member of reputed professional bodies such as CSI, ACM etc. His research interests include applications of artificial intelligence, machine learning, deep learning and IoT in healthcare, automation, etc.

Duo Chen is an independent researcher. Her research interests include FinTech, Chinese economy and business analytics.

Prasad G. is Assistant Professor (Sr.Gr.), Aerospace Engineering, Dayananda Sagar University, Bangalore, India. Prof. Prasad G, received his Masters degree and Bachelors degree PhD in Aeronautical Engineering from Anna University. He has 7 years of teaching experience. Prior to joining Dayananda Sagar University, he worked at Anna University. He has published 40 articles in reputed Scopus Indexed International Journals with good Impact Factor. 25 Journals related to Unmanned Aerial Vehicle and Industry 5.0. He has completed two funded project sponsored by The Institution of Engineers (India) and Tamilnadu State Council for Science and

Technology. Awarded Indian National Science Academy (INSA) Visiting Scientist Programme 2019 and Awarded Science Academies' Summer Research Fellowship Programme (SRPF) 2019. He is a Professional Membership of American Institute of Aeronautics and Astronautics, Institution of Engineers, Life Member in Indian Cryogenic Council and Life Member in Shock Wave Society. Reviewer in Aircraft Engineering and Aerospace Technology, International Journal of Engine Research and Journal of The Institution of Engineers (India): Series C.

Ratan Ghosh has attended in Master of Business Administration in Accounting and Information Systems from the University of Dhaka in 2016. Currently, Mr. Ghosh is serving as an Assistant Professor of Accounting at the Bangladesh University of Professionals (BUP). Before joining BUP, he worked as a Lecturer at Daffodil International University, Bangladesh. His current research interest includes corporate governance, financial reporting, earnings quality, sustainability reporting and accounting information systems. He has publications in different peer-reviewed and indexed international journals.

S. B. Goyal had completed PhD in the Computer Science & Engineering in 2012 from India and served many institutions in many different academic and administrative positions. He is holding 19+ years experience at national and international level. He has peerless inquisitiveness and enthusiasm to get abreast with the latest development in the IT field. He has good command over Industry Revolution (IR) 4.0 technologies like Big-Data, Data Science, Artificial Intelligence & Blockchain, computer networking, deep learning etc. He is the first one to introduce IR 4.0 including Blockchain technology in the academic curriculum in Malaysian Universities. He had participated in many panel discussions on IR 4.0 technologies at academia as well as industry platforms. He is holding 19+ years' experience in academia at National & International level. He is serving as a reviewer or guest editors in many Journals published by Inderscience, IGI Global, Springer. He is contributing as a Co-Editor in many Scopus books. He had contributed in many Scopus/ SCI Journal/ conferences. Currently, Dr Goyal is associated as a Director, Faculty of Information Technology, City University, Malaysia.

Asia Khatun has completed her post-graduation from the department of accounting & information systems, University of Dhaka, Bangladesh in 2016. At present, she has been entrusted to work as a Lecturer in the Department of Accounting & Information Systems, University of Dhaka. Prior to joining there, she has worked as an Assistant Professor of Accounting at the Bangladesh University of Professionals. She fosters a research interest in corporate governance, financial reporting, accounting information systems and integrated reporting.

Ruixuan Li is an independent researcher. Her research interests include FinTech, Chinese economy and business analytics.

Shengyuan Lu is an independent researcher. His research interests include RegTech, FinTech and Cryptocurrencies.

Md. H Asibur Rahman is a young scholar. He is now serving as a lecturer at Bangladesh University of Professionals (BUP) in the Department of Business Administration-General and formerly worked as a faculty member at Gono Bishwabidyalay, a private university in Bangladesh. He earned his MBA in Human Resource Management and his BBA in Management Studies from Jahangirnagar University, Bangladesh. His research interests include tourism and economic growth, HRIS, organizational justice, training and development, work engagement, and citizenship behavior. He has published more than a dozen articles in various international journals as a young academic.

Anand Singh Rajawat is an Assistant Professor in the Computer science and Engineering department, the Shri Vaishnav Institute of Information Technology (SVIIT), SVVV, Indore. He has published 60 research publications in various reputed peer-reviewed international journals, book chapters, and conferences. He has been associated with various technical and training institutes as a faculty. He has a Coordinator Software Development Cell(SDC) at the institute level. He has associated several research journals and also reviewer committee members. His area of interest for Research is Big data, Cyber security analytics, Machine Learning, Deep Learning. He has successfully passed online certification examinations EMC Academic Associate, Cloud Infrastructure and Services and EMC Academic Associate, Information Storage, and Management.

Farjana Nur Saima is currently serving as a Lecturer in the Department of Business Administration, the Faculty of Business & Social Science (FBSS), Bangladesh University of Professionals, Bangladesh. Ms. Saima completed her Bachelor's and Master of Accounting and Information Systems from the University of Dhaka. She is an emerging researcher, and her subjects of interest are corporate governance, financial distress, corporate risk reporting, tourism, and mobile financial systems. She has published several articles in different peer-reviewed national and international journals so far.

Michael Sampat is an independent researcher working in several interdisciplinary capacities. Current projects include books on business geography and mass media psychological conditioning.

Pranav Saraswat is working as Associate Professor at Institute of Commerce, Nirma University Ahmedabad. He holds PhD in Finance from MDS University Ajmer. He has 17 years of teaching experience of UG and PG level in reputed institutions of India. His authored case studies are published with international publishers of repute. He has three books in his credentials. His good numbers of papers are published with Scopus and ABDC indexed journals. He has also written some articles for management magazines of repute. He has attended more than ten Faculty Development workshops for enhancing his teaching and research skills including Faculty Development Program at IIM Ahmedabad. He is also honored by the prestigious BOLT award, given by Air India and Research excellence award from Nirma University Ahmedabad. He is planning to widen his research in Sustainability Accounting Reporting and behavioral finance. In his leisure time he loves to play badminton and play synthesizer.

Divya Prakash Shrivastava is working as an Associate Professor in the domain of Computer Information Science in Dubai Women's College, Higher Colleges of Technology, University, Dubai, UAE. Shrivastava posses more than 25 years teaching Computer Science/Engineering/I.T and Information Science courses . He worked in North West South Africa, North Africa and North East African countries as well as reputed Technical Universities of India. He has a vast experience in the research and academia. Dr Shrivastava carried out educational innovation, development and raising the educational standard of the Organizations. He earned B.Sc (Electronics Instrumentation), Master of Computer Application (MCA), M.Tech (IT) and Ph.D. in Computer Science from reputed Indian Universities. He is having good number of publications in international journals and conferences. He has published a book and many chapters. Presently his research and project development domains are big data, Machine Learning, Digital Marketing and Artificial Intelligence.

Poshan (Sam) Yu is a Lecturer in Accounting and Finance in the International Cooperative Education Program of Soochow University (China). He is also an External Professor of FinTech and Finance at SKEMA Business School (China), a Visiting Professor at Krirk University (Thailand) and a Visiting Researcher at the Australian Studies Centre of Shanghai University (China). Sam leads FasterCapital (Dubai, UAE) as a Regional Partner (China) and serves as a Startup Mentor for AIC RAISE (Coimbatore, India). His research interests include financial technology, regulatory technology, public-private partnerships, mergers and acquisitions, private equity, venture capital, start-ups, intellectual property, art finance, and China's "One Belt One Road" policy.

Index

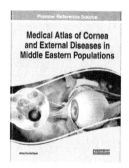
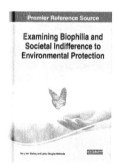
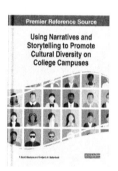

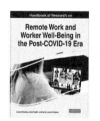